STAGE-HYPNOSIS MADE EASY

HOW TO BECOME A COMEDY HYPNOTIST

Based on an original format entitled:

"The Professional Art of Stage Hypnosis and Hypnotherapy"

Researched, Written and Devised by:

Jonathan Royle (Previously Alex LeRoy)
(D.Hyp) (D.NLP) (D.CMT) (D.SM) (D.CV) (D.SH) (D.Psy)

Special thanks to:

DELAVAR

As ex-President of The British Council of Professional Stage Hypnotists and tutor of some of the worlds leading stage performers and therapists including the author Jonathan Royle, Delavars help, advice and instruction has been invaluable in ensuring this course is the most comprehensive training course of its kind available anywhere.

Entire Course Copyright 2017 Jonathan Royle.

This course was first written in 1994 by Jonathan Royle.

ALL CORRESPONDENCE TO:

www.MagicalGuru.com & www.magicalguru.co.uk

www.HypnosisWeek.com & www.HtgLive.com

<u>**IMPORTANT LEGAL NOTICE:**</u>

This training course is sold on the agreement and understanding that the purchaser and/or reader are responsible for their own actions at all times. Neither the author nor publisher can be held in anyway responsible for misuse of these techniques. It is advised that you obtain suitable insurance cover prior to hypnotising your subjects.

<u>Introduction</u>

Welcome to the mysterious world of Stage Hypnosis. Allow me to introduce myself. My name is Jonathan Royle. I was born on the 13/08/75 into a show business family and made my stage debut aged three as Flap the Clown on Gandeys Circus (voted UK's no.1 circus show).

Since then I have gone from strength to strength, having been a full time professional performer for almost twenty years.

During this time I've performed in many areas of show business from clowning and stand-up comedy, to fire-eating and illusions. Not to mention my other talents of comedy pick pocketing, five object juggling, tarot card reading, paper tearing, balloon modelling, mind reading and Pseudo clairvoyance shows and of course more recently adding Stage Hypnotism and Mind Therapies to my varied repertoire.

A MASTER OF ALL TRADES AND JACK OF NONE.

Since learning Hypnotherapy in 1989 and becoming a member of The Association of Professional Hypnotherapists and Psychotherapists, I have spent a large proportion of my time helping people with their fears, phobias and other emotional problems.

I've stopped hundreds of people from smoking, helped people to lose weight, gain confidence and to achieve numerous other things with great ease all of which has proven to me beyond doubt just how powerful Hypnosis is and can be as a Therapeutic tool.

Always having been a professional performer, I had a desire within to put my Hypnotic skills to use in the entertainment industry, so I searched for any literature I could find on the subject of Stage Hypnosis. And I found that the little which was available was either not worth the paper it was printed on or the author just told you to stage the whole affair with stooges and confederates.

Well, I knew as a qualified hypnotherapist that there was far more to it than this, so I went out and watched as many Hypnotic shows as possible. Being in show business I went back stage after many of the shows and took this most valuable opportunity to get the SECRETS of the art, direct from the horse's mouth so to speak.

Over the period of a few months I had received advice and help from some of the top names in the Hypnotism industry. Little did they know, but within 18 months I was to become their professional rival and in actual fact move further up the "career ladder" than many of them were now at.

To all those that advised me along the way, I thank you from the bottom of my heart, for now I have a recession proof business that has given me the chance of European travel along with an income and lifestyle that others only ever dream of.

I started using Stage Hypnosis just before my sixteenth birthday by way of demonstrating my skills at the Psychic Fairs I attended all over the North West. My first all Hypnotism show was on the 13th of January 1993 (aged 17 years), at Heywood United Services Club. I hired the function room myself and promoted the show so I had a lot to lose if it all backfired. This show attracted much local TV, Radio and Press publicity and on the night in question attendance was very good indeed.

I had learnt my Stage Hypnotism skills and techniques correctly (or so I thought) and I was reasonably confident in the show being a huge success. Well how wrong I was, the show was an absolute failure, only two people's hands ended up locked together and no one went under when I did the Hypnotic inductions. In the end there was no show and I had to refund all the ticket money, I took a great loss in profits, pride and confidence and vowed never to do another Hypnotic show again.

However a few weeks later, by chance I met a gentleman called Peter J. Fox. It turned out he was a stage hypnotist and although born in England had just returned from working in America for the past few years. He was himself taught by top American Stage Hypnotist, Andarmo Polson. We became great friends, but that's another story entirely. The important thing was he entrusted me with the "real" secrets of Stage Hypnosis, suddenly I realised that the only problem I'd ever had was a lack of confidence in my methods and a negative attitude.

He also gave me a huge book called "The Hypnotists Bible" written by Delavar the then President of The British Council of Professional Stage Hypnotists. In this book was Delavar's number and so I telephoned him and arranged for some personal one to one training. This was all happening in a very short space of time and on Friday the 29th of January 1993, (just a few weeks after the failed show) I was engaged to appear on Channel Four's Cult TV show "THE WORD".

Their researchers had seen footage of my local TV interviews and called me about the show. I explained what I did and they told me to come to London the following day for an audition, on the agreement that if the audition went all right I'd get a contract there and then to appear on that Friday's show. I arrived for the audition and after using Self Hypnosis upon myself to programme my mind for success I started my impromptu demonstration.

Although there were only 20 members of the production team and staff in the room, I was able to lock 16 people's hands together. From those 16 people I was able to get 10 of them into a deep Hypnotic Trance, which, as any hypnotist will tell you, is not bad at all!

The thing that won me the audition was when I made the Producers secretary "fall in love" with me and when awoken, she immediately started to nibble my ear, kiss my neck and in general tried to get her tongue down my throat. The producer told me she was normally so quiet and shy and that her behaviour was completely out of character and, as such, he was now convinced that I was good enough to appear on the show that week.

This meant at 17 years of age, I became the youngest Stage Hypnotist ever on British TV and in fact one of only a handful of hypnotists to ever perform on Live TV let alone TV at all. Two days later I returned to London for the show, We went out live on air at 11-05pm precisely and I had the time of my life…suddenly I was a star!

Although my rival Peter Powers won the "Battle of the Hypnotists" competition in which I was competing he did say to the Manchester Evening News and several national newspapers the next day:

"I was absolutely stunned when Mark's Co-presenter Katie Putrick said I had won!".(Peter Powers, Jan 1993). And this, from a master of his craft with many years experience, I was obviously better than I thought and now my confidence was greater than it had ever been.

To cut a long story short since that time in January 1993, at the time of this course being released (August 1998) my Hypnotic career and television career in general has risen to unbelievable heights. During the period of January 1994 to December 1994 I appeared on more TV & Radio shows than any other British Stage Hypnotist including Paul McKenna. I've also had numerous feature Radio appearances, have been featured in most all National, International Daily and Sunday Newspapers and Glossy Magazines.

And most significantly I've progressed from working pubs and clubs for around £150 to £200 per night in 1993 to now earning many times that amount for shows which are now usually held in the type of large capacity venues which are usually reserved for rock concerts. Along the way I've also lectured for Psychology courses, run Stress Management classes for major household name Blue Chip companies and also run self-improvement seminars for the general public.

Now, over seven years since I started to use Stage-Hypnosis I've performed literally 100's if not thousands of shows. I've continued to expand my knowledge in every way possible, by going on courses, reading, and watching videos and through advice and tuition from respected industry experts.

I also feel very proud being able to honestly say that at this time (August 1998), every major Stage Hypnotism society including F.E.S.H., E.G.P.S.H., P.O.S.H. and B.C.P.S.H. amongst others contain at the very least one member who was taught by me!

One man who was a great influence on my act during 1993 was Peter Powers and to him I say thank you for the advice you passed my way in 93! It was also a pleasure during 1993 to be employed by Peter Powers to take his place at a corporate show for Leeds Weekly News, at The Metropole Hotel in you guessed it Leeds!

And thanks also to three more people Payl-Nyles, Andrew Newton and Paul McKenna respectively. In 1989, I met a Stage Hypnotist called Payl Nyles at a Magic Convention in Blackpool. He was the first Hypnotist I ever saw perform on stage, we became great friends and he started me on my road to Hypnotic stardom by both personally teaching me the art and also lending me books, tapes and videos on the subject.

A few months after meeting Payl I became his sound technician and for about a year I assisted Payl in his live shows all over England during which time I learnt an awful lot about Stage Hypnosis. Incidentally Payl was at the time a member of F.E.S.H, The Federation of Ethical Stage Hypnotists.

As for Paul McKenna & Andrew Newton, well I'd like to thank them both for putting Hypnotism back on the map so to speak with their successful UK TV series. I am proud to have worked with these two Hypnotic legends. Paul McKenna worked with me on an edition of ITV's GMTV breakfast show and Andrew Newton and myself briefly worked together on a business project.

So why tell you all this about myself? To show off? To be big headed? Well in truth my real motive is far from either of these. I have told you all this not to show off, but so that you KNOW as a reader of this course that the information contained within is first class and not only is it worth a fortune it can also earn you one.

Having been taught by some of the leading experts in the business and having had the luck to get my break so early into my Hypnotism career, I have amassed a wealth of hands on performing and therapeutic experience from tutors who, in some cases have taken over 50 years to gather.

I would hope now that you have confidence in me as your head tutor, as to benefit fully from what you will learn. You need to have faith in the skills that you learn and you can only have complete faith in these skills by first having faith in your teacher.

Nothing will be held back. This course will contain everything which is of value to a potential Stage Hypnotist who wishes to enter a profession which has mystified people for decades. There follows, hundreds of pages, which explain in clear step by step detail all of the secrets, ploys and techniques that are used to become a safe and competent Stage Hypnotist.

These skills will enable you to enter this lucrative profession which can open new doors in your attitude and lifestyle that you never dreamed possible. I will introduce you to the professional art of Stage Hypnosis and by so doing, initiate you into a profession which will fascinate and astound people including yourself.

To finish this introductory chapter, allow me to explain that this course has been purposely written in a simple to understand manner with plain language and complicated words and phrases removed. As closely to the way the majority of us speak. This has been established as the best possible way to learn, absorb and understand information which may be new and alien to us. Grammar and syntax will be thrown away in the interests of passing on the knowledge easily, quickly, enjoyably and effectively to you.

Hypnosis is a much deeper subject than most realize. The majority of the population is of the opinion that all you do is snap your fingers or swing a shiny watch in front of their eyes and then they will just instantly drop off to sleep. Well I can tell you here and now it is a great deal more complicated than that, yet at the same time if you are prepared to believe what I teach you it is also far easier to learn than you might at first imagine.

Read, study and absorb the contents of this course, it will without doubt place you on the road to ultimate success in Stage Hypnosis. I wish you luck in your future career, although if you absorb the contents of this course which is filled with liquid gold knowledge then your success is almost guaranteed. For this chapter I'll leave you with a piece of advice given to me in a letter from Mr. Hypnotism himself - Paul McKenna.

"GOOD LUCK AND KEEP IT CLEAN!"
Paul McKenna, March 1994.

A BRIEF BIOGRAPHY OF YOUR AUTHOR:

AGED 3
He made his Performance debut as Flap the Clown at Corporate Christmas shows.

AGED 4.
He was warm up artist for the Paul Daniels Magical Exhibition Show on The Golden Mile Blackpool for the entire summer season.

AGED 5.
Whilst on tour and performing with Gandey's Circus, JR (Jonathan Royle) was almost killed when attacked by a Puma but was saved in the nick of time!

AGED 6.
National press debut in The Daily Mirror on October 10th 1981.

AGED 8.
Local Television and Radio debuts on Granada TV & GMR Radio respectively.

AGED 14.
International media debut in Psychic News. He also becomes the youngest ever member of The Association of Professional Hypnotherapists and Psychotherapists. He also works as a Stage Hypnotist's sound technician all over UK. He starts treating people with his Hypnotherapy skills.

AGED 15.
He starts to perform Stage Hypnotism routines as his demonstration pieces at the Psychic Fairs he performs at all over Northwest.

AGED 16.
He releases his first magic book "Original Magic", the first copy of which

is purchased by Paul Daniels.

AGED 17.

JR made his National TV debut on C4's cult TV show "The Word". He also makes his Alternative comedy debut at Manchester's Buzz club. He starts performing his own full one man Hypnotism shows. Also JR's 1993 Training seminar "Hypnosis Fact or Fiction" is a huge success.

AGED 18.

JR makes his National Radio, Tabloid/Broadsheet press, Glossy Magazine and International TV debuts. He also enjoys his own One hour Television Hypnotism special on German RTL Cable TV.

AGED 19.

Gained International TV, Radio & Media Notoriety when he claimed to have slept with 100's of consenting females whilst under his trance to increase the enjoyment they both experienced.

AGED 20

Placed home viewers of GMTV into a Hypnotic Trance causing much fuss and confusion at the television station. Also has his book "Hypnotism & Sex" placed onto International sale. Also makes his debut on primetime Irish TV as the major guest on an edition of "The Kelly Show"

AGED 21

Made his Television Co-Presenting debut on C5's afternoon show "FIVES COMPANY". The training seminar, "Confessions of a Hypnotist" occurs and is a great success.

AGED 22

Regular guest on Nickelodeon Children's TV and also Co-Presenter of a special edition of Manchester LIVE TV's "MAD 4 IT" show whilst also enjoying a week long stint on Derby F.M. amongst many others. Then moving on to Ceefax & Teletext feature interview debuts whilst also making his debut on the Worldwide web followed by recorded pilot talk shows for BBC Scotland.

AGED 23

Develops further the Therapy aspects of Hypnosis and completes the 4 year program of C. M. T (see the therapy course for more details).

ROYLES RESUME UP TO 2017

Born Plain Alex William Smith on the 13th August 1975 into a showbiz family, Royle made his stage debut aged 3 as Flap the Clown, later as Alex-Le-Roy he became Known as a Magician & Illusionist, Mind-Reader and Psychic Entertainer before becoming Internationally known as Jonathan Royle World Famous Hypnotist.

He started treating people Professionally with Hypnotherapy & NLP back in 1989 aged just 14.

His Hypnotic Stage Shows started Professionally in 1990 aged just 15.

His British National Television Debut as a Comedy Stage Hypnotist occurred in Jan 1993 aged 17.

His first Training Seminar teaching other Hypnotists was in September 1993 aged 18.

As Dr. Jonathan Royle Ph.D aka Lord Alex William Smith he has dozens of books available on Amazon and from all major book sellers covering all areas of NLP, Hypnotherapy. Stage-Hypnosis, Street Hypnotism, Magic, Mentalism, Self-Help and Marketing.

To date he is arguably responsible for the original training and/or ongoing mentoring and coaching of more people who are now Successful Professional Comedy Stage Hypnotists and/or Hypnotherapy Practitioners all around the World than any other living Hypnosis trainer today.

His Home Study Training DVDS have been shipped to every Country in the World and he has also acted as a Hypnotic Consultant and Adviser to other Famous Name Stage-Hypnotists, Television Life Coaches, Celebrity Hypnotherapists and even Famous Name Masters of Mentalism Style Mind Control.

He has been featured using his "Mind Skills" on major name celebrities on TV & Radio Shows around the World as well as regualrly being featured in National & International Newspapers and Magazines.

The story about the Lady whose fear of traffic wardens he cured appeared on the Full Front Page along with a double page feature inside "The Sun" which was Britain's biggest read newspaper when the story appeared in the mid 90's.

He was the only British Hypnotherapist to be chosen for and then featured in a therapeutic interaction with Robert De Niro and Billy Crystal to help promote their 2002 Film "Analyse That" - This feature first appeared in Amercias largest Circulated newspaper "USA Today" and was then syndicated to publications all over the World.

Royle is the President of The Association of Complete Mind Therapists (ACMT) which incorporates The Association of Professional Hypnotherapists & Psychotherapists (APHP)

He is also the President of The Professional Organisation of Stage Hypnotists (POSH) which incorporates The Association of Professional Stage Hypnotists (APSH)

Years ago he created his own unique one session treatment approach of "Complete Mind Therapy" - (CMT) which is now used by therapists across the globe to help people overcome their Habits, Addictions, Fears, Phobias and most other things you can possibly think of from A through to Z in a single 45 to 90 minute treatment session.

Whilst in more recent years he has devised "Mind Emotion Liberation Techniques" - (M.E.L.T) which helps you to M.E.L.T. your clients problems away in a matter of minutes...

And most recently of all he has just started training others in "Complete Unconscious Reprogramming of Emotional Disease & Distress (C.U.R.E.D) which enables you to give your clients the C.U.R.E (Complete Unconscious Reprogramming of Emotions) for their issues.

His work and innovations in the field of Hypnosis has led to him becoming only the Fourth Hypnotist in History to date (August 2017) to have ever been inducted into the South African Academy of Hypnotists "HYPNOTISTS HALL OF FAME" as per this info:

Back when Paul McKenna ran a Company with Michael Breen called McKenna Breen Ltd in London, Paul advised the majority of his staff and also seminar supervisors to study Royle's "MindCare Organisation" Home Study Course on Hypnotherapy & Stage-Hypnosis and indeed many of them did exactly that.

When organising The International Hypnosis Conference in London, Valerie Austin invited Royle along as a Guest and his inclusion on the discussion panel was indeed a major talking point amongst those who attended.

When John Cerbone & Richard Nongard came to Manchester England to run one of their "Speed Trance" events, Royle was invited along to act as an Adviser and Consultant on British Stage Hypnosis & Street Hypnotism Laws.

Amercian Hypnotist & Internet Entrepreneur Tellman Knudson engaged Royle to speak on what was at the time (and may well still be) the Worlds Biggest Ever Online Hypnotherapy Training Event "The Hypnosis Event" and also engaged him to take part in what was at the time the World's Biggest Ever Online NLP Training Event "The NLP Event"

British NLP & Hypnotic Marketing Expert James Lavers aka "The Lazy Coach" sought to interview Royle and this was one of the most positively raved about sections of his "NLP Masters of Passive Income" Study Package.

Leading UK NLP Expert, Authour of "The Rainbow Machine" and founder of Integrral Eye Movement Therapy booked Royle to speak for his NLP Meet up group and afterwards he said:

"Undoubtedly one of the funniest, most intelligent and hugely entertaining presentations on hypnosis, NLP and therapy I have experienced. Go and see Jonathan – he will rock your beliefs, make you laugh out loud and

probably outrage you. The hypnosis and NLP world needs more people like him. Jonathan Royle – APPROVED!"
ANDREW T. AUSTIN – CHICHESTER – Nov. 2005

He was also invited by "The Incredible Hypnotist" Richard Barker to be the First Ever Headline Speaker on the First Ever "Hypnotist Entertainment Cruise" and for this he received rave reviews from all who attended.

His Hypnosis training Seminars have SOLD OUT in Las Vegas (organised by Jay Noblezada) - California (Organised by Brian Stracner) and in many other locations around the World.

His October 2017 "The Royle Event" one day training as organised and promoted by Television "Fat Families" Presenter and Clinical Hypnotherapist Steve Miller SOLD OUT in less than a week of the tickets being placed onto sale.

His Home Study Courses, Training Books and Live Events have received rave reviews from experts all over the world as can be seen in the numerous video testimonials at this link:

https://klearthoughtsmentalismhypnosis.wordpress.com/2015/01/09/what-the-experts-say-about-jonathan-royles-hypnotherapy-nlp-stage-and-street-hypnosis-and-mentalism-and-marketing-training-courses/

Recently he was made an Honorary Life member of The United Kingdom Board of Clinical Hypnotherapy - (UKBCH) who have also approved and endorsed his various training courses and materials.

Indeed his training courses and materials are also Approved, Endorsed and/or Accredited by:

*The MindCare Organisation Ltd - UK

*Personal Development Associates - USA

*The Neuro Linguistic Programming Practitioners Association - (NLPPA) - UK

*The Royle Institute of Hypnotherapy & Psychotherapy - (RIHP)

He is considered by many to be the Most Controversial, Outspoken & Daringly Honest Hypnotist of all time and this has led to rumours galore and defamatory lies circulating all over the internet.

The REAL TRUTH behind the negative stuff you may have seen posted can be seen (with evidence) at this link:

http://www.drjonathanroyle-awarning-exposed.com/

And the REAL TRUTH (with evidence) behind how he was also once Britain's Biggest Ever Media Prankster and back in 1998 attempted to expose the dishonest & criminal actions of the now Jailed & Disgraced Rupert Murdoch Journalist The "Fake Sheikh" Mazher Mahmood can be seen at this link:

https://klearthoughtsmentalismhypnosis.wordpress.com/2013/10/19/the-naked-truth-about-dr-jonathan-royle-aka-alex-william-smith-aka-alex-leroy-hypnotist-magician-and-psychic-entertainer/

His Official Website is at **http://www.magicalguru.com/** and his online store is at **http://www.magicalguru.co.uk/**

For those who like the Comedy Stage Hypnosis side of things there are tons of clips from Royle's Hypnotist Shows taken from events around the World over the past 25+ years on his Youtube Channel "CelebrityHypnotist" at these links:

https://www.youtube.com/playlist?list=PLK4pimF35bjhUcUfdlgKSMk6SK_I2u2f8

And also at this link there are even more clips…

https://www.youtube.com/playlist?list=PLDhI8Pk4O_4DXXiDg53V6UzOSJrF1avxf

SUMMING-UP:

His past employers for corporate shows include Debenhams, Littlewoods, Boots, SEI, Kendal's, Rathbones Bread, Madame Tussauds, The London Planetarium and numerous other household name companies.

He has been a support on the alternative circuit for the likes of Lee Evan's & Logan Murray whilst on the mainstream circuit he's supported the likes of Jimmy Cricket.

As a past magical adviser to Simon Drake of C4's "Secret Cabaret" fame, this led to being a magical adviser for IRON MAIDENS "Raising Hell" farewell tour and Internationally networked TV concert.

He's a full Equity Member, appeared in the film "Raining Stones" and is trained in Dance, Drama and Music.

PAST TELEVISION CLIENTS INCLUDE:

Top TV shows that have employed JR's unique talents include, This Morning with Anne & Nick, GMTV, The Big Breakfast, The Word, Funky Bunker, Live at 3, The Zest (Health & Beauty show), Right to Reply, Central Weekend Live, Thursday Night Live, Late & Loud, Up-Front, Kilroy, Here & Now, Tuesday Special Documentary, Sex-Wars, Nickelodeon's Breakfast Show, F.O.T, Taxi, The Time…The Place, The Warehouse, Live-wire, The Kelly Show and literally hundreds of other Local, Regional, National & International Entertainment, Variety and Talk/debate shows.

PAST RADIO SHOW CLIENTS:

Talk Radio UK, 210 FM, GMR, Beacon, Radio One, BBC Scotland, Dublin FM, Mercury, BBC Shropshire and a week long stint on Derby FM's Breakfast show.

PART 1

"BACK TO FRONT"

"Scientists say that we only use 10% of our brain power, well in that case what do we do with the other 47%?"

Seriously though, the potential of the human mind is literally unlimited and far greater than the average person could ever imagine. As you will discover in this chapter the key secret to hypnosis is the belief and expectancy within your subjects mind, may the general public remain ignorant to the way their minds work otherwise we hypnotists will be out of business!

In this part I will reveal all the key secrets of Hypnosis. In other words, within the next few pages you will find everything you require to become a professional Stage Hypnotists like myself or Paul McKenna.   However as you will have, I presume, no previous knowledge of the subjects in hand you may think that the next few pages over simplify the art. The idea of this however is to show you the key points and then to explain to you why these are the key points. As such when you have read the last part of this course you will then realise and more importantly understand just how easy and simple it really is to hypnotise someone. So this is if you like what most people would have made the last chapter of this course, but for reasons you will understand later, it has been presented "Back to front!" The main advantage of doing it this way is that you will learn both the cause of what you are doing and also the effect it has upon people. This will mean that you will automatically know more than a great number of Stage Hypnotists who just know the outcome of what they do and not what has caused it to happen. So always remember <u>EVERY CAUSE HAS AN EFFECT</u> and <u>EVERY EFFECT HAS A UNDERLYING CAUSE.</u>

STAGE HYPNOTISM

Boiled down to the basics Stage Hypnosis is IDENTICAL to all other forms of Hypnosis. The only difference being the way in which it is PRESENTED and the speed at which the volunteers are placed into a DEEP hypnotic trance state. There are seven key points to follow for the use of Hypnotism on stage.

SEVEN STEPS TO STAGE-HYPNOSIS

1. Obtain rapport (done through one liner jokes at start of act).
2. Induction of Hypnotic trance. (Any fast method after handclasp).
3. Deepening of trance (giving suggestion that each time they are   told to return to sleep they will go deeper.)
4. Ego strengthening Therapy (butter them up/compliments etc).
5. Do the Therapy (in this case the comedy routines of your act).
6. Implant the major post Hypnotic suggestion. (This is done at stage two when they are told that when you tell them to return to sleep they will go deeper and is done so that all suggestions given to them are cancelled before they leave the stage).
7. Awaken them from trance (awaken them and ensure they feel ok).

The best piece of advice I could ever give you is to go and see a Stage Hypnotist performing when they are in your area. This will be a most valuable learning experience as you can learn an awful lot by emulating (not copying) the style and manner of established experienced Stage Hypnotists. Basically speaking if you did what they did word for word and with similar actions on someone whom had been made to believe in your abilities then they would go into a trance state and react to your various suggestions.

THE KEYS TO HYPNOTIC INDUCTIONS

When wishing to place someone into a Hypnotic trance there is also a set procedure to follow which is:

A) BELIEF and EXPECTANCY
B) DISORIENTATION and CONFUSION
C) SUGGESTION and REPETITION
D) RELAXATION and SLEEP

Step A means that if you instill into them a belief in your powers as a Hypnotist and as such they believe that you are able to place them under trance, and they also expect to go under if you were to try it upon them, then they are in the correct state of mind to be very successfully and rapidly placed into a Hypnotic trance state.

Step B means that once they are in the correct state of mind to be Hypnotised you then use methods of disorientation and confusion to convince them they are starting to go into trance, and that's why they are feeling these strange effects. As such if they believe this to be the case then they will expect to go under deeper and as such they will, as in the end it's all down to their personal state of mind.

Step C means that once these things are starting to convince them they are beginning to slip into trance then you use methods of suggestion and repetition to confuse and disorientate them even further and also to convince them that they are going under more. If they believe this is the case and expect what you are doing to have an effect upon them, then indeed, in turn it most certainly will.

Step D is the end result of carrying out steps A, B & C and should be that if they believe what you have done to be Hypnosis and expect it to work then this will have the result of relaxation and sleep. And as all Hypnosis really is, is deep relaxation they will then be in the Hypnotic trance state.

So you see the secret to all induction's of any kind whether Stage or Therapy and whether slow, rapid or instantaneous is that if the subject sincerely believes that what you are doing does work and they also sincerely believe and expect it to work on them, then the end result will always be that it works on them. Basically, the key secret to all induction's is to have instilled into the prospective subjects mind, the belief in your powers and the 100% expectancy that should you as the worlds greatest of great Stage Hypnotists picks upon them to be Hypnotised then it will work and as such they will enter a trance.

BELIEF AND EXPECTANCY EQUALS HYPNOSIS.

THE SPEED PROBLEM

Generally speaking if you place a person into trance via a long induction then they will remain in trance longer and go into a deeper state of relaxation. By the same token if you place someone into trance via a rapid or instantaneous induction then they will slip out of the trance state very quickly.

The general rule of thumb in the Hypnotism industry seems to be that:

"QUICKLY IN EQUALS QUICKLY OUT" & "SLOWLY IN EQUALS SLOWLY OUT"

However, from experience I have found a solution so that instant induction's can be used to place them into a trance with the end result of them going into a deep state of relaxation and not slipping out of Hypnosis as might occur otherwise when you don't want them to! The solution is simply:

1) Use your instant inductions and place everyone into the trance.
2) Then use the group deepening method as detailed later to deepen the trance to such a level whereby they will not slip out of it.

So remember that if left to their own devices and a group deepening method is not used, then the subjects of an instant induction would probably slip out of the hypnotic state in a very short space of time indeed.

THE SECRET OF SPEED

The secret of speed inductions is just to make sure that you have an enormous amount of confidence. This confidence must be in your abilities. You must also carry out the instantaneous inductions with no doubt in your mind that they WILL work! This is so that this personal belief is transmitted to the subjects and they are then in no doubt in their minds that it will work. You must do instant style inductions with conviction, also a very commanding tone of voice and attitude and you must transmit to the subject that you expect to be obeyed by them. An element of shock is also used with instant induction's in order to catch them off guard and as such "shock" them into deep hypnosis so to speak.

THE THREE STEPS TO HYPNOSIS

An even simpler way to explain how Hypnosis works to place someone into a trance state is like this:

A. They must know that you are a Professional Hypnotist and can

therefore do as you claim.
B. Ask them to close their eyes and to breathe deeply and regularly.
C. Suggest ideas of heaviness, sleep, tiredness and relaxation to them for a few minutes and then THEY WILL BE IN A HYPNOTIC TRANCE.

Once again I'm sure you can see how it all relates back to those two key words/secrets which of course are belief and expectancy.

PEER GROUP PRESSURE

A small percentage of people will react to your suggestions due to peer group pressure and the fear that if they don't then they will be tormented and subjected to ridicule by their friends as they are unable to at that time be a good Hypnotic subject.

THE I.I.C. SYNDROME

A phrase which I always use in my opening patter is this: "If you've got good powers of intelligence, imagination and concentration then you will be a good Hypnotic subject!" The psychological effect of this is that if they come up to try and be hypnotised and did not react, then they think it will make them look an even bigger fool by not reacting than by taking part and being a "good" subject in the show. As if they were to return to the audience their friends and family would ridicule them for not having good powers of intelligence, imagination and concentration to be a good Hypnotic subject. So again in a way, this relates back to peer group pressure.

THE KARAOKE SYNDROME

The life of an average person is the set 9 to 5 routine, they lack attention and appreciation in their lives and would love to have the chance to be the centre of attention and to be given some appreciation by lots of other people. In fact the secret dream of many people is to perform on stage even if they do make a fool of themselves. It's the Karaoke syndrome and is exactly the reason why Karaoke nights are so successful. Those people that get up know they are awful singers and are making a complete fool of themselves and yet to them, it's an escape from everyday life, a step into the world of fantasy and the chance to be a star! The fact other people are also prepared to make fools of themselves brings the sheep effect into play, so it then doesn't bother them either to make a fool of themselves. In just the same way a high percentage of people who volunteer for your act will have the Karaoke syndrome at work on their mind and as such you have got several more good subjects to partake in your act.

THE SHEEP EFFECT

The sheep effect is such that if one person is prepared to do something or make a fool of themselves, then others will "follow the leader" and they become one of the sheep following the crowd and doing what all the others upon the stage or in life are doing. (Never allow yourself to become a sheep!)

THE EXHIBITIONIST

These come in two forms, the first is the positive one who likes to have a laugh, be the star of the show etc and as such although not actually under Hypnosis, plays along and hams it up so to speak. As entertainment is the key word on stage, if they look convincing you would of course allow them to remain on the stage. Then of course there is also the negative form which manifests itself as the person who has a need to show off to his friends/family just how great they are and what an idiot you are. These people of course should be dismissed from the stage at the earliest opportunity. It is a wise idea to have a friend stood in the wings (side area of the stage) who can keep an eye on the subjects whilst you are facing the audience and have your back turned to the on stage volunteers. This friend can then, if they spot anyone, give you a hand signal which you would of course have prearranged between you to indicate which person is and in which chair they are sitting. You then return them to the audience and by so doing, are now in almost the same position as having eyes in the back of your head. By the way if this observant friend is trained in hypnosis also, they can then also give you hand signals to indicate which of the on stage volunteers will be good to place into trance, which ones not to bother with and those which are under deepest when hypnotised.

PEOPLE HYPNOTISE THEMSELVES

The Hypnotist only tells them that they can do it! Until he told them, they never knew that they could do it. In effect we are "directors" of the film and the subjects become the "actors" doing as we say. We just guide them into what is really just a deep state of relaxation and should really be classed as "Self Hypnosis". So much for the 1952 hypnotism act, 1989 guidelines and 1996 government review then! These are covered later.

GOLDEN RULES TO FOLLOW

<u>RULE ONE</u>: Have total confidence in yourself and your skilful abilities.

<u>RULE TWO</u>: Exude that confidence so that others will then have total confidence in you and your abilities.

<u>RULE THREE</u>: Monotony and repetition is the trade of the Hypnotist so repeat, repeat and then repeat it again.

<u>RULE FOUR</u>: Learn to use your voice so that it can sound demanding and also commanding.

<u>RULE FIVE</u>: Follow the steps and instructions detailed within this course to the letter and your success is guaranteed.

YOUR HYPNOTIC TOOLKIT

As a Hypnotist, the only tools of use to you are self-confidence (which you must have in abundance), suggestion, commanding and demanding tone of voice, rhythm of speech (cadence), monotony, repetition, professional appearance, knowledge and experience. These are the only tools available to you. However, if you learn to use them all effectively then it will become a most powerful tool kit and will make your job far easier. So learn to handle these tools with finesse for they are the start, middle and end of all that you must do and know.

SOME OTHER MOST IMPORTANT POINTS

1. Hypnotists are not Hypnotists, they are merely actors playing the part of the image of a Hypnotist which people expect to see and as such react to.

2. All Hypnosis whether Stage or Therapeutic is really just self hypnosis.

3. Hypnosis occurs due to co-operation and not confrontation or challenge.

4. As Hypnosis is just a state of mind and compliance based on the subjects levels of belief and expectancy, there is no such thing as a "Hypnotised" feeling and this is because each person experiences everything that happens during the course of their life differently.

5. Belief and expectancy are the most powerful keys of all to success.

6. Suggestion correctly expressed is Hypnosis.

7. The correct way to express suggestion is in a commanding and demanding voice, and to keep on repeating it to the subject.

8. One willing co-operative volunteer is worth more than a hundred pressed men.

9. To make life easy for you, use the suggestibility test of hands locking together to find those subjects who will be the easiest to Hypnotise and who are obviously in the correct co-operative state of mind.

10. A Hypnotist is perceived as being a person of authority and people in general expect to be ordered by and to obey as a person of authority says. Just remember your school days and you'll realise both what I mean and also the fact most all people are conditioned in this way.

11. For suggestions of sleep, slow deep tones of voice with words suggesting a downward motion are used.

12. For awakening suggestions, a faster, higher tone of voice with words suggesting an upward motion would be used.

13. The salesmen's techniques of mirroring and matching are used to put people to ease, make them relax and to establish rapport easily.

14. Hypnosis is a state of heightened awareness and as such subjects can

taste, smell, see, feel and hear things better than they usually would be able and are more, rather than less aware of their surroundings.

15. If the mind is focused on one thing, or at least one thing at a time and is not allowed to wander, then as the normal worries of the day are not considered your subject will automatically relax completely. When people relax they tend to lose a lot of their inhibitions and this could also explain why they are then prepared to do daft things.

16. Confidence begets confidence and as a man thinketh so he becomes, which proves that positive thinking is a most positive force.

17. It has to be in the mind first before it becomes an action (in every day life) and it has to be in the subconscious mind first to become an action during Hypnosis.

18. When the imagination (subconscious mind) and the will (conscious mind) are in conflict, the imagination always wins. So if you can get a person to focus their mind on something to the exclusion of everything else, you are then able to bypass the critical area of their minds and firmly embed a suggestion into their imagination without any conscious conflict! Then afterwards even if the conscious mind were to try and oppose the suggestion the far stronger force of the imagination would always win and the suggestion would be acted upon.

19. Hypnosis merely shuts down the analytical (critical) area of the mind that is located between the conscious and subconscious. It acts as a kind of "gate-keeper" and processes all incoming information from the conscious mind before it is allowed to enter the subconscious mind where it is permanently kept on file.

20. As we've already stated if the suggestion can be given directly to the subconscious mind (the imagination) then it will be acted upon immediately and as I've stated already all Hypnosis does is shut down that analytical (critical) area of the mind which in turn makes this action possible.

21. Talk success, think success, act success and dream success and then

successful things will occur.

22. Remember positive thoughts breed positive actions, they are contagious and positive actions breed positive results.

23. Relaxation is the key, which opens the door to the subconscious mind. In this state, get the subjects to visualise your suggestions with implicit faith that it is so and so and it will be.

24. Co-operations with a highly developed imagination are the best qualities your subject can have for successful acceptance of your Hypnotic suggestions.

25. You want your subjects to have confidence, belief and faith with expectation of success, but it is no use just telling them this. They must be "sold" on Hypnosis and its effects to possess these real qualities.

26. Rapport, observation, recognition and leadership. These are the four stages of inducing a Hypnotic trance. All are lead by the subject and merely followed by the Hypnotist as will be explained later. Rapport should establish three things, trust, comfort and of course belief.

27. Hypnosis is merely a form of communication. Tone of voice is essential in all communication and indeed in Hypnosis also. It is also possible to hide "secret" messages within a spoken sentence by changing your tone of voice so that they have an almost "subliminal" effect.

28. If they believe that you have special powers then your job is easy, if they expect to be hypnotised by you then they will be! They are in a strange situation whereas you feel at ease. You have the microphone and are at home upon the stage and therefore you are in charge. You make them feel important, needed and appreciated whilst also conditioning them so that they sincerely believe they are only clever and intelligent if they co-operate with you.

29. You know what's going to happen and they don't so you are already ahead of them. You act in a routine manner as though it always works and it will then work.

30. Ordering them around at the start conditions them to obey you. You are the salesman selling the great idea of hypnosis to them. The sheep effect then makes them follow the leader and try to be a "better" subject than the others upon the stage.

31. Music which suits each routine in the background sets the correct style of scene and has a psychological effect upon them of making it all seem more real and easier to imagine.

32. The subjects who are in a deep trance are kept and used for the, harder routines. You then direct all applause to them and this reward makes them feel good and also conditions them to react throughout.

33. On stage always paint a verbal picture, so that the subjects know what is expected of them. They must know what you are saying as they cannot read your mind. The suggestions you give must also have one meaning only so that they cannot be misinterpreted.

34. A Hypnotist to be successful must be a self-motivated, strong minded, egotistical individual, who is confident in their skills. You must be a good showman and an artist par excellence. A smooth talker, persuasionist, salesman. Actor and adaptable at a seconds notice. In other words you must be able to think on your feet, use your common sense and have the gift of the gab.

35. Hypnosis is co-operation and not confrontation and the nature of your game should be imagination not humiliation.

36. You cannot see hypnosis, you can only see the effects of it. This is my reason for saying that the use of props and music helps to make the whole show more attractive and more believable for both the on stage subjects and also for the watching audience.

Lastly for this part, allow me to explain how Hypnosis works between the subject and the Hypnotist in much the same way as a Bio-feedback machine. Also let me explain briefly how the human mind works, we'll elaborate later on.

THE HUMAN MIND AS I SEE IT

As I see it the human mind is made up of three separate layers making the whole, these three layers are as follows:

1) The conscious mind and/or human will.
2) The analytical and/or critical area.
3) The subconscious and/or imagination

We use the conscious mind to speak etc, the subconscious deals with the automatic actions of our blood circulation and breathing as well as being our imagination area of the mind. And lastly the analytical area analyses all incoming information before being allowed entry and storage in the subconscious mind as truth/fact.

I will now make the analogy of the mind being a computer. The conscious mind is if you like the keyboard, which inputs new information. The analytical area analyses it for any mistakes in much the same way as a spell checker, then the "corrected" data, if of an acceptable nature, is allowed to enter the subconscious mind where it is stored forever in much the same way as storing data onto a floppy disc.

To briefly explain if you told a fully conscious person that when you snapped your fingers they are Elvis and then snapped same said fingers, they would not react! Why? Well simply because the analytical area processes it and then compares it with the memory bank record in the subject's subconscious mind of who they are before rejecting it as it realises the statement to be untrue. All this of course takes only a fraction of a second to occur.

Under Hypnosis the mind and body of the subject relax, and due to the disorientation, confusion and repetition of suggestion the analytical area shuts down or goes to sleep. As such when told that on a snap of the fingers they will be Elvis the mind is then unable to process the information and find out that it is untrue and consequently it is believed to be true. It goes directly into the subconscious as being true and so is acted upon as an automatic reflex action.

If only in a very light state of trance the will of the person may still go into conflict with the imagination or subconscious, but as we stated earlier when the imagination and will are in conflict the imagination always wins. As such they will react and be Elvis or do whatever you have suggested without question.

Just as with any computer, programs placed into the memory which in the long term could be dangerous or more harm than good MUST be cancelled out or erased so that things revert to normality. So it is also with your subjects mind, all suggestions must be completely cancelled out before they leave the venue after the Hypnotic show. Otherwise they will remain in the computers memory bank to be automatically acted upon long into the future! Imagine the scene as the subject is driving home and Elvis comes onto the radio. This triggers off the memory bank association that upon hearing Elvis they must start to dance. They then do so and Crash! This is obviously an extreme example but expressed to implant firmly into your mind the importance of removing all suggestions and commands from your subject's minds except those of a beneficial nature such as in therapy before they leave the room.

You should always aim to leave them feeling refreshed and as good if not better than when they entered the venue that night. If you do this and abide fully by the 1952 Hypnotism Act, the 1989 guidelines and the 1996 Government review and generally put the safety of your volunteers first then you should be a most successful performer. This part contains all the keys you require for Hypnotic success, but I'll end by explaining how the mind is like a Bio-feedback machine.

Observe Figure A and you will see the Hypnotist facing the subject. The final key to a most successful induction is as follows. The Hypnotist suggests things to the subject who in turn accepts and reacts to these verbal suggestions. The Hypnotist then observes the effects of those suggestions and feeds back his observations as new suggestions to the subject. The subject accepts and reacts to these, the Hypnotist observes the effects and then feeds back the observations as new suggestions to the subjects and so the Biofeedback computer effect continues until the subject is in a deep state of trance. In other words the Hypnotist's suggestions are always made up of his observations.

FIGURE A

THE BIOFEEDBACK COMPUTER EFFECT

An example of this so that you fully understand how it works would be as follows. The Hypnotist suggests that the subject will start to breathe deeply and regularly, this is then accepted by the subject and acted upon by them. They then start to breathe more deeply and regularly and perhaps also start to close their eyes. The Hypnotist observes this and then feeds back the observation to the subject as new suggestions along the line of "That's great and as you continue to breathe deeply and regularly, notice how your eyelids are now so heavy and so tired, in fact it's so much easier, just to let them close!" The subject accepts and reacts, the Hypnotist observes and feeds back the observations as new suggestions and so the cycle continues.

This now means that you really do know how to hypnotise someone, as with this technique the wording of your induction must always be ad lib and worded so as to contain your observations and as such capitalise upon them. You would of course at all times be following the basic guidelines of voice tone and speed of suggestions etc. And remember the key words associated by most people with Hypnosis and a trance state are: sleep, relax, drifting, deeper, falling, resting, calm, heavy, tired and all other words associated which mean similar things to these.

Well congratulations you now know more about Stage Hypnosis than most if not all of the "cowboy" Hypnotists who are currently flooding the industry. Now that you have the keys to Hypnotic success, let's look at them all separately and in depth so that your understanding and knowledge of the subject is total. You will have noticed by now I'm sure, that throughout this course, I will repeat many key points several times, the reason for this is that the trade of any Hypnotist is repetition and you can only learn through repetition. As such, this course has been written, not only to be enjoyable to read, but rather in a way that you learn the maximum amount possible in the shortest space of time possible.

<u>**PART TWO**</u>

"BE PREPARED"

You can't see electricity but you wouldn't push your finger into a plug socket because you know that it does exist. In much the same way you can't see hypnosis as it's all in a person's state of mind, however if the subject believes that it exists, then and only then does it genuinely exist! As in reality, all hypnosis is just a state of mind and state of belief!

Your subjects are over 90% of the way to being hypnotised deeply when they step foot onto the stage. This is due to your pre show or consultation preparation and that is what we shall discuss in this part. The preparation which needs to be done beforehand in order to guarantee its success!

Welcome to part two, here we will discuss the elements which when all are combined go some way to placing your potential subjects into a state of mind where they are over 90% hypnotised before they even start! How? Well your reputation as a hypnotist has preceded you; the "induction" of the people starts to happen long before you meet the people. The advertising or recommendations instills the belief of your powers into the subject's minds in advance of the day in question. It also creates within them the expectancy that you, as the great hypnotist, will make them unable to resist and as such will go under instantly! So they are over 90% on their way to being in a deep state of hypnosis when you first meet them.

Let's imagine it's a month before one of my theatre shows, you look in your local newspaper and see an article about me, my show and what a marvelous hypnotist I am. Or you see or hear of someone who has been treated. You start to believe what you have read and as such phone up the box office and order a ticket. A few days later a letter arrives, you open it and YES the tickets you ordered have arrived and so you place them inside your wallet for safe keeping. Upon the ticket it says Jonathan Royle, World's No.1 Hypnotist. This convinces you even more of my skills in an almost subliminal way.

Over the few weeks that follow you mention the forthcoming show to friends, you keep seeing adverts for the show in the local paper, posters around town, adverts on the TV & Radio and in general you keep getting reminders of the show which you are soon to see. Needless to say that all these reminders go some way further to convincing you that I am a master of my craft and must be the best thing since sex was invented. Each time you remove or place things into your wallet you see the tickets and the show returns to your mind yet again.

The night of the performance arrives, you've paid £10 to come and see me, so you expect that the show must be worth this amount which would mean that I can hypnotise people including yourself if I were to pick upon you. You take extra special care to get ready and look smart, just in case you are chosen to go on stage and be hypnotised, which means that you must by now believe you might end up doing this which means in turn it would be easy for me to achieve. You arrive at the venue, the show is a sell-out and people are being turned away. This creates a feeling of excitement and expectation within that the show you are about to see will be the best ever! You enter the foyer and a front of house display board shows my recent national press cuttings and photos taken during other past shows. You take a closer look at this display and see that other normal people, like yourself have been controlled and hypnotised by me. So then you believe 100% fully that as you are just as intelligent as the next man, you to can and will be hypnotised if I should approach you.

You enter the auditorium, the lighting is dim and the background music gentle, relaxing and mysterious such as the music produced by Enigma. You take your seat and stare towards the stage waiting for the hypnotist to start his show. Your expectations are now high and belief almost total. And as we've stated earlier if a subject believes in your powers and expects you to be able to hypnotise them then you will be able to.

The music starts. It is loud and mysterious, such as Thus Spoke Zarathustra from the 2001 Space Odessy soundtrack and recorded within it is my voice over introduction. This introduction may be in two parts as mine is. My intro music is "Are you ready for this?" By Two Unlimited. The track is a disco style tune and I personally have smoke coming off stage whilst coloured disco lights revolve on both sides of the stage sending rays of light shooting around the room like laser beams.

The mid section of the track sounds all weird but changes in tempo and recorded upon this section I have a strange horror movie Orson Wells style disembodied voice which say "Ladies and Gentlemen, welcome to the show! Ask yourself this…… are you ready to witness the most exciting, unusual and amazing show in the world today? Are you ready to let imagination become reality? Are you ready for this?" At this point the music goes back up tempo, but this has had the psychological effect of making them believe this is the best show and the best hypnotist they could ever see in their entire life. The music continues and just before it ends an American style voice says "Ladies and gentlemen, hold onto your seats and leave your misconceptions behind as you welcome live on stage Europe's fastest, funniest and most outrageous hypnotist, the one, the only, the amazing Jonathan Royle!"

You applaud as does everyone else, the atmosphere is electric and I walk out onto the stage to the background (play on) music of "Simply the best" by Tina Turner. My posture is good (dance training helps here). I am smartly dressed in designer clothing although you may feel more at ease wearing an evening suit or tuxedo. Not a hair on my head is out of place, my stage make up gives the impression I have a lovely suntan, I am wearing expensive jewellery and in fact in every way possible I look to be a most confident and successful stage performer. I command the audience's attention instantly by my self confidence and appearance. I act as though I own the place, this is going to be the best show of my life and I must not have a single thought of failure in my head (self-hypnosis is useful here).

From this moment forward I must take the place over and must at all times act as if I am in charge. I must demand instant respect from the audience and I must them dominate them so much that they are in awe of me and have no doubts in their minds that I do indeed know my craft 100% inside out. This is then the point where my opening comedy lines and introductory talk (patter) are made to the audience and details of this follows in the next part.

I then go into the handclasp routine in order to get only the best most suggestive subjects upon the stage. The people who's hands remain together are told to come to the stage as are any other audience members who would like to volunteer and enter my hypnotic world where fantasy becomes reality and there really are NO LIMIT'S. The Two Unlimited song "No Limits" then plays as they come to the stage.

Once upon the stage I immediately start to give them orders in a confident and authoritative voice in order that they feel they must obey me. At this point you may leave their hands locked together or indeed unlock them depending on your style. You move them about the stage, ask them their names, where they come from etc, you get them to change seats in fact it matters little what you get them to do just so long as right from the word go they obey you and know they must do exactly as you demand.

Is the soldier on parade hypnotised to obey every order? Well in a way he is and the same situation is starting to happen here with you and the people on stage. You are ordering people to do certain things and they are unquestionably obeying your every command, which conditions them to continue doing so at all times.

You now explain before proceeding with the induction those people that cannot be hypnotised (see chapter on opening talk). You then also explain that hypnosis is very much a two way thing and that you require the attention and co-operation of the on stage subjects to ensure success. By doing this the ball is now in their court, as, if they don't go into trance and react to your suggestions, then in the eyes of the audience it's their fault and not yours!

You explain that hypnosis is a very relaxing and enjoyable experience and that they will enjoy every second of it! By saying this it makes them want to experience the state and so the whole self hypnosis thing comes into play. Then you explain that you can only hypnotise people with the correct powers of intelligence, imagination and concentration to be a good hypnotic subject and possibly the star of tonight's show. Lastly you say the audience will be laughing with them and not at them and that the audience will applaud to show their appreciation as without the onstage volunteers help and co-operation, there really would be no show.

By saying all this, they feel that if they don't go under, then they are stupid and will look stupid in front of an audience. They also feel they have the chance to be the centre of attention, to be a star for the night and as such they will grab this chance as detailed earlier in this course. They know the audience will appreciate what they do and now any objections they may have had will have gone and your job is literally as easy as saying that when you touch them on the head and say sleep they will immediately close their eyes, relax every muscle in their bodies, fall backwards into your arms and go to sleep….because this is the fastest form of hypnosis known to mankind!

So, you've told them how you expect them to react and you have instilled the belief into them that it will work as you say. Combine all these points with the fact that they want an escape from life, the chance to be a star, plus the fact that you have now on stage only those people most likely to go under (due to handclasp) who have 98% induced themselves before they get upon the stage and I'm sure you'll realise just how easy stage hypnosis really can be.

You must have 100% faith in your abilities though and must feel 100% confident they will sense you are a professional who knows his craft and knows it will work so that in turn they will relax, believe and go into trance. If they don't actually go into a trance they will just play along and try to be the star of the show anyway. So what have you got to lose? Let them do this, as after all the audience won't know and the entertainment value is the most important factor with a stage show.

Some people have one stooge planted in the audience who comes onto the stage at the same time as the genuine volunteers and then they appear to place the stooge into a trance first. The genuine people see him go under and fall to the floor asleep and now their belief in you and your powers is 150% complete. Now the sheep effect comes into play and they follow the leader and do as the stooge did or else they become the odd one out.

To create the funniest situations upon the stage you must always give an air of competition so that the subjects feel they are in competition with each other. They will then respond in better and funnier ways. The remainder of the subjects after the stooge, should you use one (although its not necessary), are then placed into trance using one of the instant induction's detailed later before the group of people as a whole is given the group deepening instructions to ensure they are all in a deep trance.

At this point you give them all the post hypnotic suggestion of: "For the rest of this evening you will react only to the sound of my voice, unless I indicate otherwise I shall only be talking to you if I place my hand upon your shoulder. So in a few moments when I awake you, you'll instantly be wide awake and for the rest of this evening whilst in this building whenever I say sleep to you, you'll instantly renter this state and each and every time you do renter this state you'll go deeper and deeper to sleep. Should for any reason you have to leave this building before the show ends then everything I've said up until that point will be completely cancelled out and you'll be as you were when you arrived here tonight! However each time I awaken you you'll have an overwhelming desire to do whatever I have suggested as an automatic reflex action and finally, you will not go anywhere near the edge of the stage, you'll stay well back and this is because there is an invisible forcefield around the edge of the stage which stops you going close to it. (The first comedy routine suggestion is now given) OK now everyone 1,2, wide awake."

Once all the subjects are induced, deepened to the correct state and have been given the above post hypnotic suggestion, then your comedy routines can begin which of course are limited only by your own imagination and time constraints. At the end of the first half of the show (usually one-hour in theatres) you give the volunteers separate suggestions each of what they are to do in and around the audience in the bar etc during the interval. You then give them all the post hypnotic suggestion that when you say "come and join the party", when you say "come and join the party", they'll all rush up from their seats and return to the stage as quickly and as safely as possible.

The interval then takes place, with a show going on all the time with no actual effort from yourself. Approximately 20 minutes later the audience is returned to their seats and no later than 30 minutes after the interval started the show recommences. The music is again loud and mysterious and as before the smoke, lights and special effects all go a long way to making the show look good. The voice over on your second half intro music introduces you once again as follows "Ladies and Gentlemen, please welcome back live on stage a unique comedy entertainer world renowned hypnotist Jonathan Royle." Then you walk out as before with a good posture but in a change of costume so it adds to the professionalism and show business of the whole thing. You do your second half of the show opening patter and then say "Come and join the party" at which point the subjects race up from their seats and join you on the stage where you question them about what they've been doing in the interval, which gets many laughs. You then put them all back under just by saying the key word "sleep", and your second half is then performed as per your own personal running order of comedy routines.

At the end of the second half of the show, after the final routine, they are all put back under and as a group they are all brought out of trance with all commands given being completely cancelled out in every way. This ensures they leave as they arrived, with no debris in their minds. Everyone lines up; you give them all a free ticket to see your show the next time you're in town as a "thank you" for participating in the show. They are given these both because they didn't see the show and also because it guarantees that you have some good hypnotic subjects at your next show at that venue. The subjects are sent back to the audience and your pitch for audio hypnotherapy tapes is made before saying "if you've enjoyed the show my names Jonathan Royle and if you haven't then my names Paul McKenna" Your "Play off" music of Simply the Best starts as you walk off stage to thunderous applause. The audience then all goes home and they say very good things about you, which ensures a full house at your next show.

Always remember that the very best form of advertising is personal recommendation and/or word of mouth. It is for this reason that it is always good if you can announce on the night of your show the next time you will be appearing at the venue. By so doing the audience will spread the word to their friends and also they will if they have enjoyed the show, purchase a ticket for your next appearance before they leave the venue that night which both gets you the money in early and ensures good attendance.

THE AWAKENING METHOD

"OK everyone just relax and sleep, I'm going to, in a moment count from 1 to 10 and on the count of 10 you will all be completely wide awake. There will be no side effects whatsoever and in fact you will feel better than you did when you entered this theatre tonight. All the things I've suggested to you will be completely cancelled out and no longer have any effect. In other words, you'll walk out of this building tonight feeling just as good if not better than when you arrived. Most of all, you will be wide-awake, full of energy and 100% normal in every way. 1, 2, 3, lighter and brighter. 4,5,6, coming up out of it now and beginning to breathe more normally, 7, almost as though your eyes are being washed by pure spring water. 8, feeling full of energy and optimism now as everything I've suggested tonight is with immediate effect erased from your memory banks. 9, full alertness and consciousness now returning and on 10 your wide awake, wakey wakey rise and shine!"

Well that's how the preparation works, the layout of a standard hypnotic theatre show and all that occurs prior to them being hypnotised to get them into the correct state of mind. It is also how my two and a half hour theatre stage show is structured. As the old saying goes, "If you follow a way that's tried, tested and proven to work then it will save a lot of trial and error on your part". Once again I will repeat one of the best pieces of advice in this entire course. If you want to be a stage hypnotist then watch as many hypnotists at work as possible, see you in part three!

PART THREE

"KNOW YOUR LINES"

The man who said flattery will get you nowhere obviously knew how powerful it was and wanted to keep it to himself! Flattery will get you everywhere in life, in therapy and on stage.

In this business it really is a case of "its not what you know but who you know", so try and go where the right people are and "accidentally" bump into them.

If you've got to stay in a town overnight, stay in the best Five Star hotel even if it costs more than you can really afford! It is in places such as this that you have a far better chance of meeting people who can be of help to your career. So although it's a big expense, in the long term it's a major investment and will pay you dividends.

Also remember these two show business adages. "The show must go on!" and "Always leave the audience wanting more!" There is of course the very true saying also of "It's not what you do but the way that you do it that matters" and this is the thing which will make you stand out from other hypnotists both in the eyes of the audience and potential bookers!

Welcome to part three. Here I will give you examples of the patter which I use in my shows and also examples of comedy gags relating to hypnosis which you may wish to include in your own patter when writing the script for your own show. You do not have my permission to copy my show word for word as it is detailed within this course for example only. Although to the audience it's not obvious what you are saying has been learnt word perfect parrot fashion this is actually the case and for good reason too.

As a hypnotist, you must be confident, decisive, and straight to the point and shouldn't make any mistakes. By scripting as much of your show as possible you are far less likely to have "gaps" appear in what you say and do. And you can then be sure you'll be saying all that you need to in the least number of words possible and as such will appear far more confident and decisive. The examples given in this chapter are all ones that I either use at the time of writing or ones that I've used earlier in my career as part of my stage shows. Rest assured they all have the psychological effect of getting your potential subjects into a state of mind where they will co-operate as easily as is humanly possible.

<u>OPENING PATTER FOR THEATRES & LARGE VENUES</u>

"Thank you, thank you and thank you too. Thank you very much indeed ladies and gentlemen for that truly overwhelming reception and welcome to what's going to be for most of you I'm sure, a truly interesting, informative and entertaining hour or so. Now the reason that I say most of you is because obviously tonight many of you will be hypnotised and for those of you who are hypnotised it will be a very relaxing, enjoyable if somewhat slightly unusual experience.

Now although you'll hear me say the word sleep rather a lot tonight, none of you will actually ever be asleep or at least I hope you won't. If you're hypnotised you'll be fully aware of everything that's going on around you at all times, you'll just have this overwhelming desire to do almost everything that I say. Now the reason I say almost everything I say is because it is impossible, despite what you may have read in the media to make anyone say or do anything which would contradict their morals or their values. So what I'm ideally looking for tonight are about a dozen or so people with no morals and with no values and then I'm sure we can all have a great show! Seriously though, although I say I want a dozen or so people to fill these chairs ideally I want about 40 or 50 people to come up to the stage and then we can pick out those with the best imaginations.

Actually to be truthful in an ideal world I'd hypnotise you all go to the bar, get drunk and then come back in an hour, wake you all up and tell you you'd all enjoyed a really wonderful show! Now basically, virtually everybody can be hypnotised which is actually very true indeed. Every single one of you here tonight can be hypnotised, but it's not always possible for me to hypnotise everyone that comes on stage right at the start and that's mainly due to the short time of space available as I'm sure you'll appreciate! Having said that of course it is virtually impossible to hypnotise anyone who does not wish to be hypnotised, so when I ask for volunteers, you have to come up here on stage with the idea of letting yourself go, relaxing and giving it a try. If you come on stage with an open mind that's all that really matters, the other things of course is that you can't hypnotise anyone who is drunk and the reason for this is that drunk people already think they are hypnotised! But I'm sure we won't have any problems there. And finally I can't hypnotise anyone who's asthmatic, epileptic, clinically depressed, suffering from any heart condition or indeed any pregnant women, although if your not pregnant see me after the show and we can sort that one out. Also I can't hypnotise the insane because despite popular belief in order to be a good hypnotic subject you need good powers of intelligence, imagination and concentration. Now I am aware of the fact that there are some families in the audience here this evening with younger children. This is very much a family show and I only mention this because when I ask for volunteers I would prefer it if the really young ones didn't come up to be hypnotised. It's not that there's any rule or anything it's just purely and simply that I hate kids! So if the really young ones could stay in their seats that would be much better all round. Are there any in by the way? (Wave at them) Hello, that was just a little joke by the way I didn't mean anything by it OK? (Pause) Jolly good, Father Christmas is dead.

Now I think that we've all got the gist of the idea now and I also think that covers just about everything that I wanted to say to you, so what I'd like you all to do now is take part in a little experiment which involves you all, even the people sitting upstairs in the cheap seats! Incidentally are you all right in the balcony? Well you won't be for long, it's loose!

LOCKED HANDS PATTER

"Now all that's going to happen here is that when I say one, you'll put your hands straight out in front of you like so. When I say two you'll join your hands together, fingers interlocked, palms pressed tightly together and then you'll squeeze your hands together just as tightly as you can. And when I say three you'll just close your eyes and concentrate upon your hands. Now all that will happen with this experiment is, that if you concentrate, which I'm sure you will, then you'll find that your hands keep getting tighter and tighter all the time. In fact many of you will find that your hands get so tight that they will begin to shake violently like this (shake own hands to and fro). If this does happen to you, don't worry its perfectly natural, it happens all the time, you won't go blind and it won't last for very long! Now you may laugh at that bit, but there's a guy there with the big glasses and he knows exactly what I'm talking about don't you? OK, now remember this is just a little experiment to find out which of you have got good enough powers of intelligence, imagination and concentration to be a good hypnotic subject and possibly the star of tonight's show. So now is the time to put down your handbags and your purses and if the women could do the same that would be a great start. So here we go now, on ONE, hands out in front of you. TWO, join your hands together, fingers interlocked, palms pressed tightly together, as tightly as you possibly can, so that the fingers of the left hand are pressed firmly against the back of the right hand and so that the fingers of the right hand are pressed firmly against the back of your left hand. And on THREE, just close your eyes and concentrate on your hands and the sound of my voice.

(At this point Jean Michelle Jarre's Oxygene music starts to play)

FOUR, you can feel them getting tighter now, really concentrate it's almost as though your hands are stuck together with the worlds strongest superglue. FIVE, Your hands getting tighter and tighter with every breath you take every noise that you hear and every word that I say, tighter and tighter. SIX, they are getting tighter and tighter, and the tighter they get the more they will shake and the more they shake the tighter they will get. Seven, Eight, Nine, they're getting extremely tight now, tighter and tighter. TEN as you listen only to my voice and the sound of the music your hands are getting one hundred times tighter all the time. 11,12,13, They're getting much tighter now. 14, 15, hands getting tighter and tighter all the time now as they shake more with each second that passes by. 16, 17, 18, now lift your hands up above your heads, in the air now getting tighter and tighter all the time. 19, getting much, much tighter now as each second passes by so quickly and on 20, good now wherever you are, open your eyes and concentrate on me and me alone for a few moments. Now even if your hands are only slightly tight at this moment it does not matter, what I would like you to do now though is this. With your hands above your head, stand up in front of the chair your sitting in so that we can all have a good look at each other. Come on up, up, up, good that's much better. OK now hands in the air getting tighter and tighter and tighter. Now wherever you are, move out into the nearest aisle to you and walk this way up to the stage and we'll see you all up here in about a minute's time.

(The Star Wars theme tune then plays them up to the stage)

Right, now here we have a fair selection of perfect strangers, well actually they're not perfect, but by the look of them they are strange. First of all if one or two of you are feeling a little apprehensive about what's going to happen tonight, I'd like to assure you that whatever else happens tonight, I won't be making anyone run around the stage like a chicken or getting anyone to take their clothes off or anything like that! (Here turn to the audience wink at them and smile as if lying) Seriously though, fundamentally speaking you won't be asked to do anything, which contradicts your morals or your values. So firstly if there are any Estate Agents in, I won't be asking you to tell the truth and secondly if there are any Sunday Sport readers in I'll explain what fundamentally means after the show. For the next few minutes though, just stare directly at your hands not at me or anywhere else. Each time I count to three your hands will continue to get tighter and tighter all the time. 1,2,3 (click fingers) look straight at your hands and every time I count 1,2,3, they will continue to get even tighter. So 1,2,3, tighter and tighter now, so tight they'll start to shake and the harder you try to stop them shaking the more they are going to shake and quiver violently! Getting tighter and tighter now 1,2,3 tighter all the time. Really concentrate and think of nothing but your hands 1,2,3 tighter and tighter. OK all stand where you are, feet together, 1,2,3 tighter and tighter 1,2,3. 1,2,3. 1,2,3 tighter and tighter."

SPECIAL NOTE

At this point you question the participants, names, where they live, jobs, have they been hypnotised before etc. and at all opportunities use normal one liner jokes for comedy impact. This entertains the audience and also gives you time to work out which will be the best subjects by observing who's hands are shaking most and who seems to be concentrating on their hands and following your instructions most. Then it's back into the patter as follows: "OK right, well we'll start with you then sir, (the best subject whose hands are shaking most) by the way you don't mind me calling you sir do you? After all it's only in fun!"

FALLING BACKWARDS INDUCTION ON SUBJECT A

Feet together, hands against your chest and tilt your head well back and close your eyes. I'd like you to take a nice deep breath in, and then out, nice deep breaths, gets fresh air and oxygen into the blood stream and helps you to relax. Now when I count backwards from 3 down to 1, this time you're going to feel yourself falling gently backwards into my arms, but I won't let you fall and hurt yourself, you'll just go into a beautifully relaxed state when I count from 3 down to 1. 3,2,1, falling back, back and sleeep (draw out the word sleep).

FALLING BACKWARDS ON SECOND SUBJECT

"OK, now you know what's going to happen and you know you'll be completely safe at all times. So feet together, hands against your chest (for subjects with hands not together say hands by your sides), tilt your head well back and close your eyes whilst breathing at all times deeply in through your nose and then out through your mouth. 3, relaxing every muscle in your body from the tips of your toes to the tips of your fingers. 2, the deeper you go the better you feel and the better you feel the deeper you go and on 1, falling back, falling back and sleeeeep!"

FALLING BACKWARDS ON REST OF SUBJECTS

"OK, you've all got the idea now so you're next. Feet together, hands against your chest (or by your side) tilt your head well back, close your eyes and breathe in deeply and regularly. On 3, relaxing, 2, relaxing and on 1, falling back, back, back to sleeep!"

THE WAY TO CONTINUE

Then from the remaining subjects with hands locked together pick as many as you need to make up the numbers who you feel using the information which I will detail later will make good subjects and then place them into trance by this or any other suitable method. Now you need to get everyone's hands separate so you can do this and at the same time deepen the state of trance they are in a little. To do this say "I'm now speaking to everyone upon the stage, in a few moments I shall take hold of your hands and the moment I do, they will immediately separate. I will then let your arms fall down by your side and as I do you'll feel yourself sink down into a 100 times deeper and 100 times more relaxing state of relaxation!" You then follow this up by going round all the subjects, separating their hands and as you drop their arms down by their sides you say "Deeper and deeper to sleep!" Its now time for the group deepening of the induction so that everyone will then be in a deep enough state of trance for the show to continue successfully.

GROUP INDUCTION DEEPENING

"OK, now everyone listen only to the sound of my voice, as I count backwards from 10 down to 1 you'll find that with each count down it's like a step further down on a staircase to deep satisfying relaxation. So on 10, the deeper you go the better you feel and the better you feel the deeper you will go. On 9, deeper and deeper now as each second passes by so quickly. 8, now every muscle in the whole of your body from the tips of your toes to the tips of your fingers becoming so limp, so loose and so relaxed as they now feel so heavy and tired. 7, deeper and deeper still. 6, 5, 4. From now on, no noises will distract you whatsoever in fact they will simply send you deeper and deeper to sleep, even the sound of my voice will send you deeper and deeper to sleep. 3, should you have to leave this building tonight unexpectedly for any reason then everything I've said will automatically be cancelled out and you will return to normal in every way. 2, Deeper and deeper to sleep. Throughout the show you'll avoid going anywhere near the edge of the stage for your own safety. In fact it's as if there's an invisible force field stopping you from going near the edge of the stage as you relax more with every breath you take, every noise you hear and every word that I say. And on 1, from now on I'm only talking to you if I tap you on the shoulder or indicate otherwise. For the rest of this evenings show, whenever I say 1, 2, wide awake, you'll instantly be wide awake and have an overwhelming desire to do anything I say as an automatic reflex action and whenever I say sleep, as quickly as that, (snap fingers) a snap of my fingers, you'll instantly renter this state except each time you renter it, it will be 100 times more relaxing and enjoyable for you!"

SUGGESTIONS FOR THE FIRST ROUTINE

At this point everyone is under hypnosis and the state has been deepened to a level ideal for the show to continue. The routines can now begin as whenever you have given them a suggestion to carry out, you need only say 1,2, wide awake and they will then awaken and carry out your instructions. Then when you wish the routine to end just say "OK everyone look at me and…. Sleep!" they will then return to trance and be ready for the next suggestion of the show.

END OF THE SHOW'S FIRST HALF

The routines continue until its time for the interval (usually one hour from the show starting). You can then give everyone a separate suggestion to act upon during the interval so that the show effectively continues within the audience before saying "OK everyone when I awaken you in a few moments, you will return to the audience and carry out the suggestions given to you a few moments ago. However the very moment that you hear me say come and join the party! The moment you hear me say 'come and join the party', you'll return to the stage area and will still be carrying out your suggestions until I say otherwise and will, the very moment I say 'sleep' return to this beautifully relaxing state. OK now everyone 1,2, wide awake!" At this point the subjects are returned to the audience and the interval takes place.

SECOND HALF OPENING PATTER

"Welcome back ladies and gentlemen, now as you've probably already guessed, with hypnosis almost anything could happen. All that happens when you are hypnotised is that the imagination is enhanced by 10 times, maybe as much as a hundred times so that what is one minute purely imaginary, the next minute seems very real indeed and I'm sure you'll see many more examples in this the second half of the show. So I'd just like to say…. Come and join the party! Come and join the party!" (At this point the people under hypnosis will return to the stage and after some comedy banter about what they have been doing during the interval you say 'sleep', and they return to trance and the comedy routines continue as normal until the end of the show).

AWAKENING THEM FROM THE TRANCE

At the start of the second half of the show you may wish to demonstrate the world record high speed hypnosis method as detailed later, in which case you'd do the guaranteed locked hands test, as explained later, before demonstrating the high speed induction, again as explained later. The only other thing you must remember is to awaken everyone fully from trance at the end of the show and indeed this was explained fully with word for word patter in the previous chapter.

SOME EXTRA NOTES AND ADVICE

Once everyone has been hypnotised and the trance deepened, everyone is awoken and then given a seat to sit in for the rest of the show. The moment they sit on the seat you snap your fingers and say sleep and return to trance they will. The comedy routine suggestions are given to them with their eyes closed and when you say 1,2, wide-awake they will then awaken and react to the suggestions as instructed. It is also possible to tell them to carry out the suggestions immediately with their eyes tightly closed at all times and then you are able to say "1,2, wide awake" to let them realise what a compromising position they are in. You can also whilst they are reacting to one suggestion and are "awake" get their attention, look directly at them and give them an immediate change of suggestion without first returning them to sleep. For example they see the audience as being nude and you look directly at them and say the moment I click my fingers they will now all look like elephants and indeed the moment you click your fingers they will react in this different way.

A huge list of suitable family and adults only routines is given later in this course, it's just a matter of choosing those you feel are best for you. Don't forget also that suggestions can be given either to specific individuals by stating you are only talking to the person who you are touching on the shoulder or to everyone by saying I'm talking to everyone on the stage. You can of course also get either the men or women to react by saying I'm talking only to the men or whatever is relevant for what you wish to suggest. See a stage hypnotist at work and you'll see with your own eyes the numerous different ways and times in which the suggestions can be given to them to carry out.

END OF THE SHOW PATTER

"Well unfortunately we've almost come to the end of the show, but before we do end, can I just thank you all for being such a wonderful audience and may I also ask you to tell your friends if you enjoyed tonight's show.

Please do come again next time as every show is different, people react in different ways and of course we also include some new routines from time to time. Anyone interested in how to stop smoking, lose weight or gain confidence amongst other things should see our range of hypnotherapy tapes which will be on sale in the foyer after the show. But for now let's have one final routine" (then go into the world's greatest strippers routine).

NOTES

At the end of this final routine put them all back under and do the awakening method as detailed in the previous chapter and of course suggest also that the moment they wake up they will wonder what they are doing and will get dressed as quickly as possible! Then everyone is returned to the audience as you leave the stage by saying "If you've enjoyed the show tonight my names Jonathan Royle and if you haven't then my names Paul McKenna, thank you and goodnight!" You then leave the stage as your "theme" music plays you off and the house lights go back to normal in the venue as they have been dimmed throughout.

A COMPLETE SCRIPT

What I have just detailed is the complete step by step script to get you on stage, explain everything, get them laughing and relaxed, lock their hands together, induce and deepen the trance state, implant the post hypnotic suggestions, how to give the comedy routine suggestions, awakening them from the trance along with patter for both halves of the show and for the end of the show.

Use it as a guideline to word your own personal script, which should of course suit your individual personality. Obviously you have to just ad-lib the patter with regards to each of the comedy routines although seeing a stage hypnotist in action will illustrate examples to you and teach you all that is needed to know on this subject. But basically, give them the suggestion of what to do, awaken them and they do it, so in fact there is very little else to say here. Listed below are some one liner jokes all on the subject of stage hypnotism and/or those that can be used within your chosen routines.

Although I give a word for word example of my stage show patter, I do advise you to construct your own using the advice and guidance within the next few chapters. It is always better to be the first Jonathan Royle rather than the next copy of him! Although to start with it will without doubt aid your success to emulate me and other stage hypnotists, in the long term you are well advised to devise your own patter and as such not get labelled as a copy. Patter which you devise yourself will also suit your style, personality and manner much better as well.

HYPNOTIC GAGS & GAGS FOR ROUTINES

A lot of people think that hypnotism comes from the brain, well they're wrong it doesn't, it comes from the hip.

Is this safe? Is this safe? Is the pope Jewish?

Seriously though I'd like to assure you that the chances of this going wrong twice in one week are very small indeed.

Hypnosis is just a very relaxing experience, rather like having a joint of Moroccan Black!
I'm both a mind reader and a hypnotist, which means I read minds and put people to sleep, I don't like the way I said that.

Several people have asked me tonight if hypnosis can be used to improve your chances with the opposite sex. Well I was going to speak a little on the subject later but I've got a date with Jennifer Lopez.

Well, there are several different states of hypnosis, she's in a light state, he's in a medium state and she's in one helluva state.

I always ask women if they want to go under because if they say yes I know I'll soon be on top.

I'm a Jewish hypnotist, so I'll put you into a trance and steal your cigars.

Now there is no need to worry about the on stage volunteers, they will no doubt enjoy the show more than you. They've certainly got the best seat in the house.

All these people behind me have great imaginations, in fact they'd probably put the headline writers of the Sunday Sport to shame.

Now if you want to come up here you can always slip into something more comfortable, an altered state of consciousness perhaps?

If you'd like to be hypnotised, mesmerised, pulverised, pasteurised, sterilised (pause) Circum…….stances being as they are the best thing you could do is come up to the stage.

OK. Just tickle horsy under the chin, did he like that? Well he should have done your sat on him the wrong way round.

When you wake up you will not hit the hypnotist, I repeat you will not hit the hypnotist.
I hate it when my shows are really successful, there is never anyone left awake to applaud my act.

If I were a mind reader, I'd be offering you a refund Sir!

I actually managed to do this last week, it's just a shame I wasn't watching what I was doing at the time.

Some of you will be getting the impression that I haven't done this before, well I have its just that I couldn't do it the last time either.

You might be laughing at the volunteers now, but in an hours time you might wish that you'd slept through the entire show.

People tend to do strange things when they are asleep, I always imagine I am a Red Indian. Perhaps its because I have to sleep with an old battle-axe?

I tried to hypnotise my wife last week, she's got a speech impediment she can't say no.

I played Glasgow last week, the audience was full of insomniacs, evidently tickets for my show were cheaper than Valium.

When you wake up, the show will be over, I bet your glad you paid for your ticket now.

Now if your hands are stuck together you would be well advised to come up to the stage as if you don't your hands will be like this for three weeks, then they will turn blue and drop off.

This is all a case of mind over matter, if you don't mind then I don't matter.

What's your name? Correct!

What's your name? I was called that when I was a girl!

(Heckler) Quite funny Sir, only quite funny that's why I'm stood up here and your stood down there.

Next time you go to the loo Sir, you will get stuck to the seat for an hour.

Was that a round of applause or has someone put the chips in?
A lot of people say to me Alex how did you become a hypnotist, but I'm sure the question you'll be asking after tonight is why?

I've always been weird since the day I was born when I came out of the woman in the bed next to my mum.

This act is very educational, you'll go home tonight and say well that taught me a lesson.

We've been saving this chair for you Sir, for Rigormortis to set in.

You don't mind if I call you Sir do you? After all it's only in fun!

(Bingo routine) 6 and 9, excellent position.

(Send subject back to crowd) OK just go and join the other rejects.

You will not be made to do anything you don't want to do, but you will find that you want to do everything.

You may as well laugh now it doesn't get much better.

(Martians sketch) Nanu, Nanu! OK just go and join the earthlings.

(In love with hypnotist) When she awakens the more I click my fingers the more she'll fall in love with me. In fact would you excuse me a moment whilst we go back stage and I click my fingers a lot?

(Nude glasses) When you look through the glasses you'll see all the men in the nude but the hypnotist is the only one with anything of decent size.

(Nude glasses) Marks out of ten for presentation?

(In love with hypnotist) These are the perks of the job, if you want to learn how to do this Sir, I'll teach you after but it will cost you £500.

I'm good at putting people to sleep but not as good as a politician's speech.

What do you do for a living? (Taxman) Well in that case your hands are getting a Million times tighter.

(They keep moving when returned to Sleep) Well that just goes to prove that Duracell out last any other brand of battery.

(Weird reactions) Don't worry he's just excited about being up here, that's the kind of guy he is, a prat.

Hypnosis is a state like we all drift into everyday, for example like when we're reading a book or drinking our tea and don't hear someone talking to us or indeed like watching Emmerdale Farm.

(Prior to Falling Back) He looks just like a thunderbird's puppet. (Then as he falls backwards you pretend to cut the invisible strings, and then as he's awoken and stand up the Thunderbirds theme music starts to play)

Behind me are our 12 victims, oh sorry, Volunteers.

(Punter with loud clothes) There must be a Ford Cortina outside with no seat covers.

A lot of people find that if they drink coffee they can't sleep, well I'm the opposite if I'm asleep I can't drink coffee.

(Say to a man) OK. Just stare into my eyes, my goodness your attractive do you find me beautiful?

One night I dreamed I was awake and then I woke up and found I was asleep.

One night I dreamed I was Julian Clary, it was my own fault I fell asleep on a camp bed.

Talk about hypnotised, did you hear about the Politician who dreamed he was doing a speech in The House of Lords, then he woke up and found he was.

Scientist's say we only use 10% of our brainpower, well if that's true what do we do with the other 56%?

(Woman stands up when men should) Don't worry she's got a slight identity crisis, she's the one who entertains the men!

You'll do anything that the stage crew tell you to do when you wake up, you'll bend over backwards to help them in fact you'll have to.

Fall back and I'll catch you (let them fall) Whoops I lied.

(Put subject under by him staring at the microphone and then wave it to the audience as you say) Your all nervous now aren't you?

(Man has just fallen back asleep, now say to person next to him) That scared the living daylights out of you didn't it?

(Cardboard Razor Blade) I want to show you something that's very close to my heart; it's my liver.

OK Sir just move up a seat, I might be able to get a lovely young lady to sit next to you. Although looking at you I think not!

(As they get up off stage after falling backwards) Don't worry we did get the drivers name and we got his number.

What are you doing down there? (Pause) Oh I see getting up!
(Make noise like bad back) Oh dear you'll have to see the doctor about that Sir.

(Hippie Guy) Wow mans my heads exploding! Peace, Love and Brown rice.

You can go and sit in that seat now so we can switch it on.

It's OK Sir, we did sweep the floor before we started.

SOME GENERAL NOTES ON COMEDY

Basically it's up to you and the style you adopt as a performer to whether you use lots of one liner jokes in your act. In general though it does help to enhance the show if you have a good repertoire of one liners to suit every possible occasion. You can then make a joke here and there as you find out the subjects names, occupations, where they live etc. On a weekly basis you are advised to buy The Stage & TV newspaper which can be ordered each Thursday from W H Smith's. Under the classified adverts section you will find several comedy writers advertising their services. It's from these sources that you can obtain material of use in the aforementioned ways and they can even write you original gags on the subject of hypnotism.

My personal advice to you would be have a good stock of one liners to cover up any mistakes etc. If you can be a great comedian, your job as a hypnotist will be that much easier. Always remember that people relax when they laugh and also remember that the likes of Bruce Forsyth and Michael Barrymore grab people from their audiences and get them to do the most outrageous things without ever using hypnosis. If you can learn to get an audience in the palm of your hand, to get them to relax and then to do anything that you say, then either you're a hypnotist or an experienced comedian.

Always remember on stage that entertainment value comes first and the hypnosis element comes last, after all the audience has paid to be entertained. Lastly, remember that the best possible teacher in life is experience, but the next best teacher is observation, so go and see as many stage hypnotists at work live as possible then you'll see in action how the contents of this course do work and how they are put to use in a practical situation.

<u>**PART FOUR**</u>

RAPPORT, OBSERVATION, RECOGNITION AND LEADERSHIP!

You have been offered the knowledge and wisdom required to act upon the opportunity to profit from being a stage hypnotist! But as Sir Winston Churchill so rightly said and I quote:

"Most people will at some time in their life stumble over opportunity. Unfortunately for them, most will just pick themselves up, dust themselves off and carry on as if nothing had ever happened."

Another very old and famous saying from the sales industry, which I'll quote, is:

"Nobody ever got seriously rich working for somebody else!"

And Lastly:

"I'd sooner have 1% of the profits of 100 men than 100% of the profits of just one man!" John Paul Getty (Multi-Billionaire)

Hi, welcome back again! Well let's deal in this chapter with rapport, observation, recognition and leadership. These are the four stages of inducing a hypnotic trance state. All are lead by the subject and merely followed by you the hypnotist. I shall take each step one at a time and lead you through the techniques involved. However never forget that there is no substitute for practice and practical application! And after this, there is no substitute for real live stage shows or consulting room experience and if possible a little of both. Whether you practice on friends, relatives or colleagues matters little but practice you must do!

RAPPORT

The Oxford English dictionary defines rapport as relationship or communication, especially when useful and harmonious! This itself is a perfect description of the first stage of induction. The concept of rapport is not unknown to you. You see it around you all the time, in fact you are already an expert at it, yes you are! Take a look at your friends and family, at people in the street, at parties or in the bars and you will see people in rapport and also people who are quite definitely not in rapport.

A young mother or father with child, lovers looking into each others eyes, old friends comfortable in each others company, two supporters of the same football team recalling the high points of the match, the three people in the corner discussing their mutual concern about political matters and the two drunks who are at each others throats, these are all examples of how you have spotted if people are in rapport (or not) in the past.

Now wait a minute, there is something missing here isn't there? I was talking about and you were thinking about something that we could not possibly have observed, namely thought processes. When we see people together we can't read their minds can we? We can only observe their bodies and actions and listen to their voices. We don't know if the young lovers are really in love or if they are both secretly having affairs. We couldn't possibly tell if the two old friends are secretly plotting to rob each other or if one of the political discussion group is actually bored to death. What we base our assumptions on are the obvious signs of rapport, the smiles, the laughter, the physical closeness, the relaxed stances, in short its down to body language and voice tone.

Most of our daily communication is non verbal or tonal. That is to say, the way we move our bodies, change our facial expressions and raise or lower our voices communicates more than the actual words themselves do. This is what we have been watching and/or observing all these years and from this we have all become experts at reading peoples minds. I said you are expert at rapport and indeed you are, so much so, you cannot only use your body to mean much more than you say but you can even lie with it.

Imagine this situation. I am willing to bet you have done something similar to this many hundreds of times in the past, perhaps without even noticing it yourself. There is someone you need to impress, a potential employer or the bank manager. Someone from whom you need, but do not like. It may be a situation or an act that you feel is beneath your dignity, asking for a raise or a loan, or maybe trying to convince a policeman that although you shot through a red light you really are a responsible person that can be trusted to never do it again. At times like this your body sings out like an orchestra, your intent and meaning can be read like a neon sign from a dozen yards away, if you watched yourself on a video you would be astonished at just how brilliant you are, and all the time you probably didn't even know you were doing it!

In the hypnotic sense, rapport is exactly the same. Just as unconscious, just as easy and just as natural. Let us examine the mechanics and the purpose of it. The first necessity of rapport is "sameness". I would like to take you back to the two old friends we met earlier. How did you tell they were old friends and not just passing acquaintances? It was their "sameness", they were at "one", they sat facing each other, they spoke in the same tone of voice. If one whispered the other followed suit, if one laughed the other laughed, if one sat with his arms on the table or slouched back and relaxed so would the other. Always they looked into each other's eyes and paid attention. This much you could see but if they were genuinely friendly there would be other things happening that you could not see. Their thought processes would be exactly the same. They would be thinking consciously of the subject under discussion but subconsciously they would be examining each other and every examination of "sameness" would reinforce the belief within their subconscious that they are liked and trusted. Their breathing would become synchronised and their heart beats the same. The tonal qualities of their voices would stay within the same range. They would look into each others eyes at the same time without any obvious signal being given, they are becoming psychologically one, at least as far as is possible.

Before you start to think that I am now going into the realms of hocus-pocus let me assure you that I am not! There was an experiment carried out many years ago, one which would quite rightly be illegal today. Two Oxen were tied together at birth, they were connected at the neck, legs and tail so that they stood, walked and slept for many years side to side and could not move except in unison. When the bonds were removed some years later they naturally enough felt very insecure about this new situation. The bond between them was so strong that they still walked, ate and moved as one for many years after the fastenings were removed. Stopping for food and water at the same time, walking, stopping and turning heads together all as if still tied together. Bonding is as normal and natural in humans as it is in all animals.

The bond between families and friends is as strong as the tethers that those poor Oxen were subjected to, but I hear you cry: how is this of use in the hypnotic induction process? "Sameness" is the key! Get onto the subject's own level, don't try and impress or bully. Talk to them in their own style of language, be intellectual with intellectuals and be plain and simple with others. Move as they do, breathe as they do. Observe their body language and respond accordingly. People naturally like and trust people who appear to be the same as them, those who look into their eyes and communicate!

If hypnotism can be summed up in a single small phrase then it is: "The art of communication and the avoidance of conflict!" The greatest sales people in the world are those who have learnt or have naturally the gift of sameness. This is something that you can try for yourself today. Go out and be with someone else whilst being someone else. The signs now that I have alerted you to them are glaringly obvious. One thing to remember though and that is sameness is NOT mimicry. In fact nothing is more likely to get you a punch in the eye than mimicking exactly what a complete stranger does. Be subtle, listen carefully, and note what he or she does physically out of the corner of your eye and copy it a few seconds later. Only copy what is obviously unintentional body language and not their deliberate actions. If your subject is smiling, smile too, but if he is tapping nervously on the table or has a nervous twitch in his eye then leave well alone. Match movement with movement, voice tone with voice tone, language with language, attitude with attitude. But do not attempt to imitate them exactly. Do all of this in a laid back manner and be non-aggressive at all times. Be sympathetic, be caring but never be patronising or condescending. Listen to what they are saying and always remember you have two ears and only one mouth so use them in these proportions. Avoid confrontation and contradiction, agree with what they say or say nothing at all. Praise the praiseworthy thoughts and ideas he or she is imparting and let stupidity and inaccuracy pass over your head unnoticed.

Everyone's natural instinct is to join in conversations, have their voices heard and their opinions too. They also wish to contribute to, or control the situation. But just for once put these quite normal and natural desires to one side, just for the sake of a single experiment. Listen to the other person's view and let that person take the lead. I promise you a very eye opening experience, which is also extremely satisfying, so go on, go and try it! You'll be astounded. For some this technique takes no more than a couple of hours to hone and polish but for others it can take months to undo a lifetime of habit, but it does work for everyone given time and genuine application. Remember it is you that you are trying to change at this stage not others. If you gain nothing else from this course then you will have been given the gift of friendship and ease in the company of others. By the way these are also good methods to use when picking up members of the opposite sex!

In a hypnotic induction the first thing to do is establish rapport. A nice friendly relaxed atmosphere, "sameness" is apparent to you both and you are communicating and feeling on the same level as the client. The subject trusts you and is confident to be placed into your hands, if this trust is not established, continue to work on it until it is. When you first start out, no doubt you will try to induce friends and acquaintances. Well YES, it is easier to establish rapport with them but it is also harder to establish trust in your abilities as a hypnotist. After all they know you are new to the subject and that you only bought this course recently. They will say things like "go on then hypnotise me!" and then sit there waiting for you to cast a spell over them. Be prepared for this, be calm, maintain the sameness, explain that it takes some time to hypnotise people and that you are new to the subject (only say this to people who already know the truth) and that you wish to proceed slowly. Make it a bit of a joke, you should both be enjoying yourselves.

A professional established stage and/or therapeutic hypnotist does not have these problems of confidence and nor will you when your credentials have been established. Experienced hypnotists obtain rapport instantly and then recognising that the time is right, simply instruct the subject to "go into a trance now!" for them and me it's easy (sometimes). The subject knows that he is going to be hypnotised, has paid for a ticket to see the show or for the therapy session, there is no doubt in his mind that he will succumb, so they do, its all down to the power of the moment. Rapport should establish three things as follows: 1) Trust 2) Comfort and 3) Belief. You are then ready to progress to the next stage, which is:

OBSERVATION

By now you will have sharpened your eye as to the body movements of others. Probably for the first time in your life you will really be taking notice of those that talk to you and those you talk to. Observation is an acute version of this. You must be aware of every single movement because these are the tools you will use to induce the first stage of hypnosis. Having established rapport you must now connect even further with the mind of the subject. I mentioned earlier that each stage of the hypnotic induction process is lead by the subject, this is a case in point. You must show them that you are able to feel what they feel, that you are sharing the same experience with them. In a way this is just sameness but is at a much deeper level. But how can you do this considering you are not a mind reader? Well you don't have to be, you just have to be a body reader. The following is an example of the opening words of a verbal induction. See if you can spot how it's done. It shouldn't be hard for a keen observer like you. Remember these are not magic words that will work for all people in all circumstances but they are typical of a keen and observant hypnotist at work.

"Just sit down and relax, lie back if that's more comfortable. That's right, feel your body being comfortably supported by the couch and the weight of your head sinking down into the cushions. Let the stress in your arms and legs flow effortlessly out as you relax completely and become calm, serene and composed. Take your time there is no rush as you feel relaxation flooding your entire body." Some of the language used here might seem a little strange, the phrasing a little unusual even. But pay no attention to that at present, these are things which I will explain later. What I want you to consider now is the subject matter of what is said. At first it may seem that the subject is relaxation, but look again and bear in mind that we are looking at observation in this section. Go on, go back and read it again.

Can you see all the observations? The subject looked uncomfortable sitting up, fell back with a sigh and exhaled deeply when her head touched the cushions, she looked a little hurried and anxious and so had to be reassured, her arms and legs looked stiff and straight with toes pointing straight up and fingers clenched, in short she did not look comfortable in this situation and needed reassurance. The hypnotist (that's you) having obtained rapport, now establishes that they are sharing the same experience! That he has an insight into the subject's mind, knows what she is feeling and is a part of it.

If you now take the trouble to go back and read those words again you will see that it truly is the subject that is leading and not the hypnotist. By using observations which are feedback to the subject as suggestions, as well as rapport, you start to enter the subject's mind and are then able to control it.

RECOGNITION

The subject will slowly begin to recognise that you are capable of understanding her thoughts. Her arms and hands are stiff for example and you observe this without being told. To her the experience of tense fingers is only a thought, she does not know how obvious it is to the trained observer. She is well aware that you are not reading her mind, after all she is not stupid, but the level of contact between you both is becoming more mental and less verbal. As this link is strengthened you can suggest and control more easily.

LEADERSHIP

You will have noticed in the earlier extract that there are some strange links and connections where different sentences that are not really inter-connected are joined together in a cumbersome way. "Let the stress in your arms and legs flow effortlessly out as you relax completely and become calm, serene and composed." You are aware that the hypnotist's words are only a response to his observations. He has seen a physical tension in the arms and legs and is trying to use it to enter the subject's mind. So why not just say "I can tell your legs are tense?" Would this not have the same effect? NO! For one thing it would be far too obvious. The subject's mind would be trying to figure out how you did know, and lets face it, it wouldn't be too hard for her to figure out would it? And secondly by giving her a puzzle to sort out you are asking her to think alone and not be guided by you. This "guidance" is "leadership" in the hypnotic sense.

There are two things going on, firstly you are addressing the subject's mind and secondly you are leading her in the direction you want, which is relaxation! Relaxation is not necessary or even important in inducing hypnosis, but it is what the subject expects and this is helpful. It also relaxes the belief mechanism to obvious benefit. The way in which this works is a little complex and will take a page or two to explain, so please bear with me. You cannot become expert without understanding this method of induction as it is the most basic and commonly used.

Stress is an ancient response, sometimes called the "Fight or Flight" response. When our ancestors were still living in caves there were essentially two types of people…the quick and the dead! When suddenly faced with danger, perhaps whilst partaking of some pleasant and relaxing pastime like sleeping or eating, there had to be an instant and profound reaction. If a wild animal or some member of another tribe attacked them without warning then the entire body would have to be put on a "war footing" those that responded well lived and those slow died! It is not surprising that this particular process of instant and permanent natural selection had a profound effect on the human race.

The mechanics of stress, or the fight or flight response, is to flood the body with adrenaline, increase blood pressure, make immediately available resources of energy, stop any unnecessary functions like digestion, the energy of which at that time can be put to better use elsewhere, fill the muscles with Oxygen and get ready to fight to the death or run like hell! But what has this got to do with you and me today? Well the mechanism still exists and would still work today if called upon to do so. If a mugger or a rapist suddenly confronted you, the threat would create the exact same physical reaction as just detailed.

But just analyse that for a moment, as a mugger is a person who looks much like any other person. They have one head and two eyes, two ears etc. The sight of a person would not normally trigger such a profound effect. Even a shady, wild looking individual if he just passed by you in the street would not produce such a reaction, so what is the trigger? It is your conscious mind that sets things into motion. You see him and compare his actions against the files in your memory banks and he matches one marked "danger" and it is then that things start into motion. Once you see that it is not his actual moves or words that trigger stress but in fact your analysis of and reaction to them, it is far easier to see how more commonplace stress is and how it is triggered. Your mind will push the stress button every time that you are threatened, even if it is only financially, emotionally or in any other way.

The stress function cannot be switched off as easily as it is on. You are prepared to fight but normally do not. While it is true to say that it would ease your stress considerably if you could punch your boss in the eye every time he denied you promotion it is not recommended if you wish to keep your liberty. So the chemicals keep on bubbling around your system causing all kinds of problems, sometimes for day, weeks or months on end, with each stressful event compounding the effect upon your central nervous system.

What has all this to do with hypnosis? During stress your conscious mind is racing, checking everything, analysing all things, checking memory files and sorting out all new information. The entire system is on full alert. If you remember the ancient origins of stress you can then understand why this is so. In a situation where you have to be killed or kill it is your subconscious mind that is checking for every possible opportunity to strike. Checking your opponents every move or action in order to prepare a defence, looking for chances to flee or find a weapon whilst all the time controlling and moving your body in response to this immediate and very real danger. Even under only slight stress it is firing on all cylinders at 110% efficiency. It is, don't forget, this part of the minds operation that you are trying to bypass in order to make direct contact with the subconscious.

In this modern world we are all stressed, to some greater or lesser extent, most of the time therefore you don't have a hope of bypassing the belief system at least that is while the defences are up and checking every detail. Just as the mind can control the stress reactions of the body, the body can influence the mind. Don't believe me? Let's try a little experiment. Without doing anything special or putting this course down or moving I want you to do one thing for me - SMILE! No don't grin that inane little smirk with no real feeling in it, smile with your whole face, a realistic smile as if you were posing for a photo to be sent to a loved one and keep smiling for a full ten seconds. 1,2,3,4,5,6,7,8,9,10, strange how your mood has lifted isn't it? While you are stressed your body is tense. It remains tense until it is exhausted (and have killed your enemy) the system works like this:

Body still stressed EQUALS enemy still attacking
Enemy still alive EQUALS need more stress
More stress EQUALS more bodily tension
Body still stressed EQUALS enemy still attacking etc!

These are not just ideas of mine, I am trying to explain to you in written terms, the chemical reaction which is going on in your body during stress. It is a cycle that feeds on itself and all the stressful stimuli. The cycle can be broken in your hypnotic subject and it has to be broken if you are to quieten his or her conscious mind and its belief system. Physical relaxation will do this. Look at how the above cycle changes now that I have inserted an element of physical relaxation.

Relaxation EQUALS less stress
Body not stressed EQUALS enemy gone or defeated
No enemy EQUALS no need for stress
Less stress EQUALS less bodily tension
Body relaxed EQUALS mind can now rest

Remember that these are not the subject's conscious thoughts but a written description of mass interlinked chemical and nervous reaction in their body. Through physical relaxation comes mental relaxation, a lowering of the defences of the conscious mind (belief and filing system). A good way to imagine the conscious defences is to liken them to a guard. Yes that's right a soldier or security guard. Lull it into a false sense of security (relaxation) and then create a subtle diversion (suggestions) before you slip passed without even being noticed.

It sounds like a tall order does it not, controlling a person's innermost defence? That is until you remember that we are all slipping in and out of trances all the time. In your life there must have been times when you couldn't sleep or a friend or loved one has come to you for advice on the same problem and what did you say? Count Sheep! There is hardly a person alive who has not tried this or advised others to do so. This is a bypassing of and a controlling of the conscious mind and a giving up to the subconscious. The image of a sheep is a soft image to most people, that is to say anyone who has not actually seen them up close. We think of them as soft, cuddly and totally unthreatening. They are also completely unexciting. Counting wolves or spiders simply would not do. The job of counting is boring and dull to the extreme. It's so dull it is actually a subconscious activity, you just bring up the file marked counting and the system is fully automatic.

To prove automatic counting, remember that time when you were counting something and your attention was distracted or your mind wandered. You lost count didn't you? We have all had this experience, countless times, this is why we count something that we have to imagine such as sheep and not just numbers. The visualisation of the sheep leaping over a fence is just interesting enough to distract your thoughts away from the exam tomorrow or whatever it is that is keeping you awake. The act of counting has no natural end, like reciting a poem has and so your consciousness is then centred on a soft, pleasant, unthreatening image. The worry/stress is put to one side and you consequently fall asleep at long last. I can hear you all shouting but I've tried counting sheep and it didn't work.

Well it's true to say these techniques are not fool proof and although they work for everyone they do so at different times in their lives. Incidentally if you do have trouble sleeping, due to worries that are so strong that the image of the sheep is not distracting enough, then try counting backwards from 1000, if you get to 500 and are still not asleep then count from there backwards in threes or sevens. If that doesn't work then try subtracting six and three quarters each time. Sooner or later you will find something distracting enough to quieten the problem which is keeping you awake and as such will go to sleep. Bear this in mind and you'll always have a good nights sleep for the rest of your life. The conscious mind can only think of one thing at a time, so make it something that does not trouble you!

Now back to the plot, as with the sheep, the distraction of a swinging watch, flashing light or moving microphone is used to concentrate the mind of the subject away from the defence and then the hypnotist's suggestions seep more easily into the subconscious. Tone of voice is also essential and you'll discover in the next chapter to say certain words with a slightly different tonal quality, more slowly or at a lower pitch so that a new message entirely comes across in an almost subliminal way. Yes it's possible to hide "subliminal" messages within normal spoken sentences even during normal conversation and then the "subliminal" sections will be acted upon. So basically, leadership is the process of taking control of the situation and using what you observe to best advantage by including it within your verbal suggestions.

PART FIVE

PRINCIPLES OF VERBAL PSYCHOLOGY

Suggestions can be both of a positive and negative nature, always aim to make your suggestions positive.

To briefly illustrate how strong a negative suggestion can be, imagine this scenario. A young child climbs onto a wall whilst their mother talks to a friend. The young child starts to run along back and forwards on top of the wall. Suddenly the child's mother turns round and sees her son and shouts out "be careful or you will fall!" The child in turn falls off the wall and gets hurt.

You see in the above example, until told that he could fall, the child did not know it was possible. The mother said "Be careful or **YOU WILL FALL!**" and indeed the negative suggestion of you will fall was then acted upon.

Now this chapter may appear to be very haphazard and of little point. However the point I shall be making and be trying to implant into your mind through the writings of this chapter is that every single word that you say in your role as a hypnotist is of utmost importance. Things, which may appear like casual statements, can and usually do have a strong psychological effect on your audience, potential subjects or already hypnotised volunteers.

Not only do the words you say have great importance, but even more so the way in which you say them matters also. For example if you said "OK now just close your eyes then sleep and relax" to a subject in a raised tone of voice as if shouting, do you really think they would relax? Of course not, however if it was said slowly, in a low tone of voice with each of the words being drawn out then your chances of success would be somewhat better. As a general rule of thumb, sleep/relaxation style suggestions should be given in a slow, deep, monotonous tone of voice with words drawn out and suggesting a downwards (sleepy) motion.

For awakening style suggestions a faster, higher tone of voice with inflection/tone changes would be used and words suggesting an upward (awakening) motion should be used at all times. Monotony and repetition is the trade of the hypnotist. Although, of the two, repetition is by far more important, as whether you sing it, shout it or even whisper it, if it is repeated enough then it will start to have an effect upon the person. So repeat, repeat and repeat some more!

Learn to use your voice. It is a most powerful tool both on stage, in the consulting room and in everyday life. Listen to people when they speak and you will notice a lot can be learned about their emotions just by the way they are speaking. Are they happy? Sad? Upset? or domineering? Well observe, listen and learn, you will soon uncover the secrets that lie within each person's tone of voice. When proficient at this with the people that you know well, you'll be able to tell when they are lying or holding something back. In order to help you exercise your voice so that you can use it in a monotone or in a commanding way as you would when giving a subject commands, I have included two little exercises below which you must do daily on a regular basis until you become aware how you speak and how to use your voice more effectively.

Firstly here is a poem, which to start with I want you to say with emotion just as the poet would mean it to have been said. When proficient at that, learn to say it in a monotone and then add a commanding overlay to that monotone.

EXAMPLE:

I wandered lonely as a cloud that floats on high or vale and hill. When all at once I saw a crowd, a host of golden daffodil.

WORDSWORTH WROTE IT WITH FEELING

I wandered…………lonely as a cloud……that……floats on high……or vale and hill……….when all at once……I saw a crowd……..a host of golden daffodil!

PAUSE AT THE DOTTED SPACES TO ADD FEELING TO VOICE

The next exercise must be spoken in a monotonous yet commanding manner of speech:

You are tired……..very tired……you want to go to sleep……you cannot keep awake…….you are so tired that you must sleep……….your eyes are tired……you cannot keep them open……you are so tired and sleepy……tired and sleepy…..tired and sleepy……..all you want to do is sleep………sleep……deep……deep sleep!

NOTE:

Repeat that over and over again until you know it off by heart. Master the commanding and decisive tone of voice and you will then be on the way to success as a hypnotist. Remember the craft of any hypnotist on stage or in therapy is suggestion. Yes that's right, repeated suggestion followed by cadence! What's cadence? Simple answer, that old fashioned sleep suggestion is nothing but cadence. Cadence is rhythm and rhythm is powerful.

Remember the story about soldiers marching, who break step to cross over a wooden bridge, so that the cadence of the march will not build up resonance in the structure and cause it to collapse. Just as I mentioned earlier you can tell a lot about a person's emotions and state of mind through their tone of voice. So in the same way the subjects upon the stage who you wish to hypnotise can also tell a lot about you by your tone of voice as well.

By now I will have said numerous times that as a hypnotist you must have 100% confidence in yourself and your abilities. Indecision will show both in your body language and your tone of voice. As a hypnotist you must be decisive which means everything will be suggested and spoken in the least number of words possible. You must also appear commanding and confident that any suggestions you give will be enacted upon by the subjects. Remember your subjects are told what to do by suggestions being repeated and also remember:

SUGGESTION CORRECTLY EXPRESSED IS HYPNOSIS

On stage my definition of "correctly" expressed is that it must be spoken in a commanding tone of voice, whereas in therapy it must be commanding with an air of empathy. Remember, as a hypnotist you are not asking people to do things, you must ORDER them to do things. You must therefore speak clearly and simplistically as does the majority of the population so that there is no doubt in the subject's mind what it is you expect of them. Back to cadence again. Do you know how to chant like the mobs do at football matches? A good piece of poetry is nothing but cadence, cadence is a rhythmic beat… one, two, three, four, up two, three, four etc. Repeat this giving exactly the same intonation to each word and then you have mastered cadence.

Positive and negative suggestions are things which you already use in your everyday life without a second thought. Always be positive where possible in the future! A verbal statement of a negative nature can ruin live's, for example parents often turn their brilliant children into dunces by always telling them that they will never be successful because they are dim and should try harder. How much better it would have been to praise the child on all the good things that it did, the child would be happier, feel better about themselves and go on to achieve far more in life! I repeat, always be positive in all that you say and do.

The words most spoken by a hypnotist are: I, You, Sleep and Awake. "I" meaning I am dominant, "You" meaning the subject you are talking to or the hypnotised group as a whole. The other two words explain themselves. Soon you will speak this way too. You will no doubt have noticed that I have written this course in the style in which I speak, in a dominant manner, but simple like a child. Remember also and I've said this before but it is worth repeating again, your subjects must ALWAYS understand what you are saying, never talk down to them but do speak in a most simplistic manner.

Your commands must always be clear and decisive, if they are not so, they could be interpreted in a way which could be detrimental to your subjects. For example "Would you like to sit in the chair?" This is in fact a question and not a command, what should really have been said is "Sit down in the chair that is directly behind you." This last example is a command and has only one possible interpretation. Make sure all your suggestions are commands with only one interpretation both on stage and in therapy, as you must always give one meaning only commands.

Remember also to use the language that all can always understand. Always be extremely careful what you say when your subjects are in trance, a casual word said by you might be taken as a command by one or more of your subjects, which as a direct result, they may then act upon now or in the future. Your voice must at all times be decisive, NEVER ever sound unsure of yourself, never whinge, your voice is your personality on stage and in everyday life or therapy.

I will also say again that to learn anything in life you must keep on repeating it until you get it 100% right. In much the same way you must keep on repeating those sleep suggestions until the subject goes into a trance.

On stage, words are your paintbrush, even more so when giving the subject suggestions, so see what happens when you use bold precise strokes. By this I mean always paint a verbal picture with your words when giving commands so that the subjects know exactly what is expected of them. They must always know what you mean, as they are not psychic.

For example I might say the following: "In a few moments when I awaken you it will be 4pm in the afternoon, you'll be sat in your deck chairs on a sunny Spanish beach and it's lovely and warm. In front of you is a calm blue sea and you can hear the birds as they fly overhead, your feet are firmly on the sand and when you awaken it will be getting hotter and hotter all the time so you'll have to rub that suntan lotion in as quickly as you can because the quicker you rub it in the cooler you will become!"

With this example I have painted a picture with my words which in turn will paint a picture in their imagination. As we said earlier, when the imagination and the will are in conflict the imagination will always win. So here too they will really believe the scenarios presented to them and act upon it to the full. Now imagine if I'd just said "When I awaken you, you're on a beach and it's hot." They could have been on wet mud, pebbles, in fact anything that their imaginations dreamed up as being reality to them at that time. So remember you must ALWAYS paint a picture with our words and set the scene of the play which our subjects are to act out clearly in their mind before we awaken them to perform their tasks.

To briefly define hypnotism it is "The art of communication and the avoidance of conflict!" Now I hope you understand just how important your voice really is, as all hypnosis is just a form of effective communication. Tone of voice is essential in all communication. It is possible through the way you speak to hide secret (subliminal) messages in a spoken sentence just by changing the tone of your voice.

Although this may sound a bit like science fiction, allow me to demonstrate. You might say to a subject in hypnosis "As you lie there comfortably feeling the weight of your body being supported by the couch you are wondering how it is possible that you will go into a trance." Now obviously this is said in a monotone, you will also be at the same time establishing rapport, observation, recognition and leadership as detailed in the previous chapter. Now if you were to say certain words with a slightly different tonal quality, more slowly or at a lower/higher pitch then another message entirely comes across to the subject's subconscious mind and as such is accepted and acted upon without their conscious mind even realising what has happened.

Incidentally this works during normal everyday conversation also, its just a case of making what you actually want the person to do seem like part of an innocent sentence so that when the subliminal voice change technique is used the event occurs and they think its their own idea!

In the following example I have underlined the words which are spoken in a different more commanding pitch/tone of voice. "As you lie there comfortably feeling the weight of your body being supported by the couch you are wondering how it is possible that <u>you will go into a trance.</u>" The subconscious accepts "You will go into a trance" as a direct command but the subject does not realise this as they just assume it to be a casual part of the sentence. What is happening here is that the reality mechanisms are being bypassed and the subconscious mind is taking in the information unaided. It isn't as discerning as the conscious and it wasn't designed to be, so the ideas not only go directly in without being checked but are also acted upon without question.

[The use of subliminal messages is ideal for longer therapeutic inductions. This is covered in more detail in the hypnotherapy course.]

IT IS FRIGHTENING JUST HOW EASY IT IS TO HYPNOTISE PEOPLE WHO VOLUNTEER AND WANT IT TO HAPPEN!

To conclude this chapter on verbal psychology I shall give examples of "phrases" I have at one time or another used in my patter during shows when I was at the start of my career and was forced to work pubs and clubs. These venues are much harder to work than theatres and it's also much harder to hypnotise people in these venues as when all is said and done they are there to drink beer and you come second. Whereas in a theatre you come first and the beer is only available in the interval. So here are some example phrases and also the psychological reason why each statement is said in this way.

"You came here tonight of your own free will and you remain at your own risk"

(This covers you if anyone is daft enough to try and sue you.)

"I am here tonight to hypnotise you, yes you! You are the stars of the show not me, I'm just here to see that you entertain your friends."

(This flatters them because they think they are to be the stars and it motivates them to co-operate.)

"Everyone can be hypnotised given enough time, however, tonight my time is limited and I shall concentrate on those who are willing to be hypnotised and can both concentrate and co-operate!"

(This makes a logical excuse for not hypnotising everyone, so therefore you will not be questioned when returning unsuitable volunteers to the audience.)

"Allow me to point out that no harm will come to anyone on stage, in actual fact they will all enjoy themselves, in fact many times I find that those that did not volunteer wish they had by the end of the show."

(This reassures them that they will come to no harm. I also add that I never embarrass anyone, as I want them to come back again! Some hypnotists think that to embarrass people is funny, well it is not! Especially when it is in front of friends and in an area where they live and work. Yes it is easy to shock and embarrass but it is not funny!)

"A lot of you sitting down there saying that you will not come up had better watch out, now you have heard my voice many of you could find yourselves waking up on stage anyway so don't bother hanging back when I ask for volunteers!"

(This can and usually does have the effect of getting you more volunteers to take part and as I've found, can also be so strong that some people fall "asleep" where they are sitting in the audience whilst the show is occurring as they really believe what you have just said! If this happens for you then just wake them up, get them to the stage and use them in the show.)

"You must be intelligent, strong minded and willing or you cannot be hypnotised. Some of the people we cannot hypnotise are very young children, mental defectives or alcoholics, and by the look of these tables I'd say there is a lot of the last group in tonight!"

(When you tell them they must be intelligent this both gets a laugh and also brings the I.I.C. syndrome into effect. Also note that as this phrase is said as I walk around the concert room sending the fear of God up everyone making the belief syndrome even greater, it also gives you a chance to see the audience close up. Eye contact and a smile can reassure those that look over nervous. From a comedy angle, if a youngish female is around I will pat her on the head as I say very young children. For mental defectives, I pat someone on the head who is very well dressed or the person who is in charge. And after saying alcoholics I look at the tables and say it whilst looking at someone (not too big) with a load of beer glasses in front of them! On occasion you can add even more comedy to this situation by saying, "start the car" or "can I go and get my fee now then go home?")

"Some of those who did not come up will wish they had, your friends will be talking to you for the next year and if you are wise you will get them to buy the drinks before you say anything!"

(This gives them an incentive to take part in the show namely FREE drinks)

"You might just find yourself upon the stage without knowing it, so I'd advise you when I do ask for volunteers to come up of your own accord at least that way you'll know why you're up here!"

(This takes the belief and expectancy thing another stage further, which leads to self-hypnosis within their minds)

"Do not at any time interfere with my subjects, they are not to be held responsible for their actions but you are for yours!"

(This has warned the audience in a nice way not to try and mess up the show or else.)

"I now require some volunteers, so to start with I'd like 5 or 6 gorgeous girls to come up on stage, now the reason I ask for the girls first is that from experience I've found them more daring than the men!"

(This both helps get more volunteers and sets off a competition between the males and females to be the best subjects, which of course leads to a funnier show)

SOME FINAL ADVICE

The last example given helps to get you volunteers easily. The women get up willingly to display that they do have more courage than the men and then obviously the men retaliate and want to participate in order that they look better than the women. So here, with a casual statement, you have brought the "battle of the sexes" into play and there will be an air of competition between the onstage volunteers, which helps ensure your shows success. A little note on the side is this.

Try to seat them so that any close friends, lovers or family members are NOT next to each other and as such cannot distract each other in any manner. As a general rule of thumb in a family show seat them boy, girl, boy, girl. This psychologically reminds them how they used to be seated at school and in turn this reminds them that just as they had to obey their teacher, so they have to obey you to.

As a hypnotist you must learn most of what you will say in the show word-perfect parrot fashion. Although obviously it must not sound like you've done this to the listening audience, to them it's new! In ordinary everyday conversation, one may be forgiven for forgetting the proper words to use, but there is absolutely no excuse for a hypnotist. You are meant to be an expert who knows his/her subject inside out, as such you cannot when giving suggestions with a stammer, stutter or a search around in your mind for the correct words to use. All you say must be precise, it must fully and completely express the suggestion it intends to convey. It must also be constantly recurring so that the expression of it becomes monotonous, for monotony is, as you know by now the great allay of suggestion.

Well that almost concludes this chapter on "verbal psychology" hopefully by now you will have realised that when used correctly your voice is a most powerful tool, which can have a most powerful effect upon people. My final example of how powerful the voice can be is to point out that the style of voice used by a Sergeant Major gets people to obey his every order whereas a doctor's tone of voice reassures you that everything will be OK! So I'll end this chapter by reminding you of one most important thing:

Every effect has a cause and every cause has an effect, see you in the next chapter!

PART 6

PRINCIPLES OF PHYSICAL PSYCHOLOGY

What we say verbally is only a minute percentage of what we are always communicating to others. It behoves us as hypnotists to have an understanding of non-verbal communication and body language. So for this chapter I intend to explain the basic points of this subject to you. After reading it, you would be well advised to train yourself to be aware of all your body movements in order to ensure that your non-verbal style of communication matches the message of what you are saying verbally.

Upon the stage you must always appear a most confident and dominant performer in your role as stage hypnotist. This means that both your verbal and non-verbal language must transmit the same message to the audience and that message must be the one that I've just outlined above. How many times for example have you heard someone say yes when asked a question and yet they are shaking their head negatively in contradiction to what they have said? Well in this example the true message was NO, and they were obviously lying, otherwise their body language would have coincided with their verbal speech and not contradict it.

Have you ever met someone, taken one look and then decided you want to hit that person? I bet unbeknown to them they were transmitting very negative attitudes through their body language. Remember your physical behaviour is made up from your motives, thoughts, attitudes and feelings of an emotional nature and it is this behaviour that people see. Your behaviour and your appearance combined are the only bits of you that other people can see. It is therefore logical that other people's impressions of you will be based on the behaviour they see, as they have nothing else to analyse you on except this behaviour and your personal appearance.

Your behaviour is like a transmitter, sending out signals to the people who you are dealing with, the signals you send through your body-language are vital because they influence the reactions of the other person and the faith they have in you and your abilities. Remember that behaviour breeds behaviour, also remember that at least 70% of communication is non-verbal and falls within the realms of body language. So it would behove us to at least have a basic understanding of the subject for use on stage, in therapy, or even in our everyday lives. Examples of ways in which non-verbal messages are communicated are as follows:

Vocal pitch and emphasis, speed of speech, breathing, posture, stance, facial expressions, eye contact, eye movements, pupil size, distances and territories, gestures, movements, clothing, dress, status symbols, choice of words and jargon amongst many others.

The most significant features of non-verbal communication are:

Body-language (which is seen/observed)
Voice (Which is heard/listened to)

The body language aspect includes movements, posture, sitting position, use of the arms. Facial expressions, eye-movements, handshake, way of walking, distance from others, style of dress etc.

So remember your success or failure depends on the mastery of body language and the degree to which your words and body language convey the same message that you are trying to transmit. At any given moment your brain can assume an attitude and communicate this to various parts of your body thus promptly responding with specific actions and expressions (body language). The unseen attitude will then have been conveyed to your potential subject without you even speaking and if this is of a negative nature, then you may find that they lose faith in your powers!

A dancer is trained to, at all times, know exactly what their body is doing physically and as a hypnotist, you must train your body in the same way. If you didn't and were for example slouching around the stage looking depressed, do you really think the show that night would go well for you? So as a general rule of thumb, your verbal and visual behaviours must compliment each other 100%. Now for some examples of conscious body language signals to set your mind thinking on others:

1) A raised, clenched fist = A threat.

2) A raised hand or finger = A request to speak.
3) A finger to the mouth = Be quiet.
4) Pointing to the clock = Time to stop.
5) Cupping the hand behind the ear = Speak up please.

Now follow a few examples of unconscious body language signals to set you're mind thinking on the many others which there are:

1) Dilation of the eyes = Interest aroused.
2) Raised shoulders = Tense.
3) Touching the nose = Uncertain.
4) Tilting the head to one side = Interested.
5) Arms and legs crossed = Defensive.
6) Touching of watchstrap = Impatient.

7) Hands behind the head = Feels confident/superior.

By the way, it is the unconscious body language signals which are the most interesting and significant when interpreting other people's moods, attitudes and intentions as often they will say one thing verbally whilst they actually mean another which is shown through their body language. These body signals will always transmit to you the true picture of what they mean. However, do remember when reading body language that you cannot just look at one detail and draw a conclusion from it. In order to get a reasonably good picture of another person's thoughts and feelings from their body language, you should try to assess the body signals as a whole and see them within the context of the present situation as it arises.

Generally speaking, in order to be accurate, at least three signals should be pointing in the same direction. In short, if you observe people a bit and use your common sense it will become quite easy in a short space of time to become a master of body language reading. There are of course many books on this subject which you could buy or better still borrow for free from your local library which will tell you far more than I am able to tell you here.

Confident people such as you must appear such at all times, consequently, you should always look people directly in the eyes and never break eye contact with them. Don't blink your eyes and thrust your chin forward.

You should keep your hands and arms away from your face and if standing, should have them down by your sides or together behind you. If standing up, be bold and upright with your back totally straight at all times and if seated, lean back with legs out in front of you. When standing in one place, don't fidget and then you will appear a most confident and relaxed person, in control of both their mind and their body. Now in order that you know the signs to look for, which indicate a friendly and co-operative subject with whom you should achieve great success, I will detail some of the most important signs to look for.

FACE AND HEAD

Looks at the other persons face, smiles a lot, nods head as other person is talking to them, looks both interested and directly at you whilst talking.

HANDS AND ARMS

Have open hands, hand goes up to face occasionally, uncrossed arms when sitting down.

BODY

Uncrossed legs when sitting down, leans slightly forward, moves closer to other person who is talking.

REACTIONS

Will immediately do as you ask without question, will appear happy to help you, seems to be concentrating hard on all the suggestions you give and carries out any other instructions without objection or delay.

The reason I have given only brief examples is that by far the best way to learn anything is through practical experience. Therefore spend some time in cafes, pubs and other public environments observing peoples body language as they react in different ways and say different things. Very rapidly you will become a master of body language interpretation.

Obviously, experience of life and on stage will tend to give you a "sixth" sense almost, as it becomes automatic to pick out the subjects whose body language indicates that they should react well to your suggestions. Also another very important point is that a persons name is to them the sweetest and most important word in the entire English language. It is also easier to get people to do things if you call them by name. Many excellent books are available on memory systems and as such you have no excuse for forgetting the names of your on stage subjects! You could however make life easier and have an assistant who writes all the volunteers first names onto white self adhesive labels which can then be stuck to the subjects upper clothing as a constant visual reminder of their names throughout the show.

Although you can hold your radio microphone close to the subjects when they are speaking during a comedy routine so that they can be heard clearly by the audience, it is much better to have the stage miked up with mikes in the fly's (above the stage). Also have mikes at the footlights (front of stage), between them, these microphones will pick up all the speech of the on stage subjects and as a result, the audience will be able to hear the at all times unless they are whispering of course! Another alternative is to kit them out at the start of the show with their own clip on tie clip radio microphone which at least one well known stage hypnotist always does.

Anyway back to the plot and the secret of how to never break eye contact. To do this you simply look them not in the eye, but instead stare at the bridge of their nose. To the subject it appears that you are staring them directly in the eye and as they will always have to break eye contact first this will make them feel very uncomfortable (inferior) and as such confirm that you are the person in authority who must be obeyed. When a subject is talking to you always look directly at their lips and this way they can never catch your gaze unless you allow them to. Once again, you are in the dominant position at all times.

Another way, although longer and harder to achieve, which can be used to stop you ever having to break eye contact and also to stop your eyelids fluttering too much in a nervous manner is to practise staring at a point on the wall in your living room. Now practise this until you are able to gaze at one spot without your eyes watering or tending to close. It could take a long time, but once you have mastered this you will never again have to break eye contact and doing it this way you will genuinely be staring them directly in the eyes! This ability to fix a gaze on anyone or anything for long periods of time without your eyelids fluttering excessively is a most mysterious and unnerving ability to have. Also look in the mirror and practise so that you can adopt a penetrating gaze of a stare with both your eyes and facial expression whenever you so wish. Of course, it is this stare which you would use to help induce the subjects into a trance.

I'll move next onto the subject of image, that is how you're physical body looks and the state of health you are in. Now you may be thinking what has this got to do with being a hypnotist? In fact it is very relevant indeed, as for example would you visit a smoker to stop smoking? Would you visit a fat person to lose weight? Of course you wouldn't and in just the same way, as a hypnotist, it does little for your credibility to be a smoker, to be overweight or to be dressed in cheap clothing. So stop smoking if you do it, lose some weight if you're a little on the large size and buy the best outfit that money can possibly buy so that you look like a million dollars. If you can't afford a real Rolex then a fake one, which looks convincing will do. The psychology behind this from a subject's point of view is that if you are dressed in expensive gear then you must have loads of money and to have lots of money you must be good at your job and so you must be a good hypnotist. And as I've said numerous times now, if they believe in you and your powers then your job will be easy due to belief and expectancy!

A little note on the side, if you're a non-smoking person of an average weight don't be surprised if you sell far more of your hypnotherapy tapes after the show. Believe me this in itself can be very profitable with over £9-00 per tape (when sold at £10) profit you only need to sell to a small proportion of the audience and you can enhance your appearance fee in this way. Your face and skin are also part of your physical appearance so make sure you treat them well.

To sum up in a few words, make sure that from tip to toe, teeth to fingernails and all in between, that all aspects of your physical appearance are clean, smart and tidy and project that successful image which you require.

As this chapter is called physical psychology I will now reveal a secret which many hypnotists use but have for a long while kept secret. They place their hands gently on the subject's shoulders and say sleep? Or do they? Well my experience has shown me (I'll explain how I discovered this in a moment) that although the hand appears to be gently resting on the subjects shoulder, in actual fact the fingers are pressing firmly into the small gap under the bone at the front of the shoulder (you will find it with a little practise). When a little pressure is applied here it can be quite painful, however if you then tilt your head forward onto your chest, as you would if entering trance on stage then the pain suddenly disappears due to the position which your body is now in!

This can very quickly become a conditioned response rather like Pavlov's dogs, and as such each time you just apply a little pressure at this point as you command sleep, the person by then having been conditioned to realise what will happen concludes that in order to feel no pain they should immediately close their eyes and let their heads flop down onto their chests!

How did I discover this? Well, prior to becoming a hypnotist, I did a lot of research and some of this took the form of going to hypnotism shows, volunteering and then playing along as if hypnotised so that I could then get an idea of what went on from the stage situation point of view. Were stage whispers (talking off mike) used? Were other forms of trickery used? Well the answer to both these questions is - yes they were used, in abundance alongside the principles of genuine stage hypnotism.

This is something that you can do, but please don't make life difficult for the hypnotist, do exactly as they say and in return you will be rewarded by learning a great deal. I had this conditioned pain response ploy used upon me by a quite well known Blackpool hypnotist and I noticed that he was only using it on the subjects who he could tell were not genuinely under hypnosis. As a kind of non-verbal warning to play along as they were doing. Not to be awkward, or else they would pay for it! Believe me, it worked very well for him indeed and since then has worked well for me also.

Now it's time to dispel a long time misconception. As lots of people believe that if you swing a watch in front of their eyes and say sleep then they will go into trance. Well indeed, if they believe and expect this to happen, then it would become 100% total reality and would be the quickest induction you could use on such a person with a belief system like this! However all that the actions of staring at the swinging watch does or the point on the wall or the bright spotlight is to strain the small muscles at the corners of their eyes and also to blur their vision out of focus. These are natural physical effects, which are ordinarily caused by staring at one fixed point for a long time. However the hypnotist capitalises upon this by suggesting that the eyes will get strained, vision will blur and so on. So when these natural effects occur to them, the subjects believe them to be due to your suggestions and allow themselves to slip into trance more readily. Although this has been quite a short chapter you will find through experience that it has been a most important one too!

<u>**PART SEVEN**</u>

WHAT IS HYPNOSIS?

Derived from the Greek word "Hypnos" meaning sleep, Hypnosis is seen as being a power when in fact it is, as the Oxford English Dictionary says. "A form of communication where suggestions can be given most effectively by one person to then be carried out be the receiver of those suggestions." The answer I give when asked this question of what is hypnosis? Is the one which I learnt from Delavar's training manual "The Hypnotists Bible" and it goes like this:

Hypnosis is that small moment in time when the Ego gives way to the I.D. and vice versa. With hypnosis, we can extend that fraction of a nano second into a period of time as long as we like. We are then at this time in communication with both the Ego and the Id. We have the Ego, that is you (when awake) and the I.D. (you when asleep). To clarify further, the I.D. controls your body all the time but has no control over the Ego, whereas the Ego has no real control over the body, only the emotions are affected by it. You breathe, think, taste, smell, feel pain, keep your heart beating and so on only because the I.D. is there to see to it! The Ego is the part, which makes you walk down the street with a swagger because you feel you are the best thing since sex was invented. It is also your Ego that allows you to go on stage as the world's No.1 hypnotist or invite clients into your consulting room. We need both the Ego and the I.D. However they cannot both be in charge at the same time, so we say the Ego when awake and the I.D. when asleep. OK so this is true but what is hypnosis? Well the I.D. can always overrule the Ego, Ego awake and I.D. when asleep. So this then really is an explanation of what hypnosis is or what happens when it occurs.

Now there comes a time twice a day (normally) when the Ego and the I.D.

need to communicate with each other, can you remember going to sleep? Can you remember waking up? (Nobody can!) Before you go to sleep or awaken there is a transitional period of a few seconds. That period is the time when the Ego and the I.D. give instructions to each other, the only time when they can if you like come together. To get to this period, we always dream, we drift off to sleep and awaken with a dream also (It acts as a distraction for the mind as in the hypnotic induction process). It is this transitional period when the Ego and the I.D. are exchanging dominant positions and it momentarily confuses the brain function. This is what the hypnotist uses and his induction methods if you like, merely extending this transitional period from a few seconds into very long periods of time and it is this we now call the hypnotic state.

A few extra points on the side, under hypnosis (deep relaxation) the I.D. can take full control of all the bodily functions, but the Ego is still in a watchful state as it never likes to give up full control. During sleep of a normal kind, the I.D. has a free hand to repair some of the damage caused by the uncaring Ego. In a hypnotic trance we do not cut off the supply of Oxygen to the brain as happens in normal sleep, we do in fact go straight to the dividing line between the Ego and the I.D. so that the subject is neither awake nor asleep. They are in that mid point between the two points/states. It's this midpoint which is hypnosis. In layman's terms I will now explain how this state (in trance) feels and also what its like/what it is.

WHAT IS A TRANCE STATE?

Nobody really knows, there are many theories, however in scientific terms a trance is measurable by changes in brain activity and behaviour. Auto-suggestion, Yoga, meditation and self-hypnosis all induce a trance state. The reason why the trance state is so hard to understand is because they are so commonplace that it is hard to tell when you are in one or not. The closest I can come to an explanation of a trance state is the state in which the mind selects what it is consciously going to pay attention to. For example when you are watching a Western on TV, you are not sitting in your living room observing an electronic device, you have suspended disbelief and if it is a good film for long periods of time you will feel that you are actually in Dodge City observing those gunslingers in action! You are ignoring the sound of the traffic outside your window because it is not part of the story, you are unaware that you leg has gone to sleep or that the dog has just chewed its way through the newspaper, this then is a trance state.

A Boxer is hit many times during a bout but only the really hard blows hurt. All the little jabs and ineffective punches that would under normal conditions hurt the boxer as much as you and I go by unnoticed. The Boxer is concentrating on his opponent's moves and actions to the exclusion of all else, even pain! This too is a trance state.

Another example is a good driver, one who does not consciously think about the physical act of driving, changing gear, moving pedals and so on, but instead concentrates on the road ahead and the other drivers around them. He/She has turned the driving over to the subconscious and this too is a trance state.

When so engrossed in a book that you don't even hear a person's offer of a drink, this too is yet another example of a trance state. All of these examples are trance states and all of them are normal and safe. If the adverts come on whilst watching TV, the bell goes off during the boxing match, or the car engine makes a funny noise whilst driving, you simply change your focus of attention from the trance state to the new scenario. You are in fact fully aware and awake at all times, just as the hypnotic subjects on stage and/or in therapy are. You are under nobodies "control" but your own, you have not become deaf or had any of your senses dulled and above all the transition is so quick that it goes by unnoticed. I'm sure you will have experienced many such examples in your life in the past and so you see you already know from personal experience what a trance state is and what it feels like to be in one.

In the hypnotic trance state you can still be fully aware of your surroundings and situation, the only real difference is that you are no longer in control of the switch which operates the normal automatic control systems. You have willingly and happily given this power to another. Many people who have been hypnotised, especially those who have only been under a low key influence, for example like when being told to stop smoking, will feel that they have been tricked because they have not yet lost full consciousness. If only they knew that hypnosis is a state of heightened awareness.

This feeling of having been tricked is due to their own misconceptions and preconceived ideas of what hypnosis is all about. They often complain to their friends "What a rip off the whole thing was" yet they never again touch another cigarette.

One way to imagine how the mind works is to imagine it as an art gallery full of beautiful pictures. As a person is walking through it, the gallery is the subconscious mind and the person the conscious. As the person looks upon a picture, he is all absorbed by its beauty and form, but all the other pictures are still there. They are just not being paid attention to at this time. If you think of the conscious mind as the real you (your personality), the part of your mind that thinks in language, then you are misleading yourself. You are in fact far more complex that that! Let us imagine what you are doing right now whilst reading this course. First your eyes are scanning the page and the meaning of the words are coming into your brain. You are not consciously thinking A is for apple, N is for nightie, D is for daisy and so on, instead you just read the word AND. These other things were committed to your subconscious mind and became conditioned into you so that they now work as an automatic reflex action and all this was learnt as a child. What happened is your conscious mind decided to sit and read the course and to open a channel to your subconscious mind, to the bit in the "computer file" marked "reading and how to do it". This in itself is a trance state (a distraction of the conscious mind) which your conscious mind was in until I alerted you to the situation.

Also until I alerted you to the situation, your conscious mind was lost amongst all these new ideas that I am sharing with you. Therefore you are not thinking about the gas bill or next Sunday's weather, you have not either considered your surroundings at all or the fact that you may be standing or sitting. It could in fact be argued in a very real sense, that I have hypnotised you or induced a trance state into you without us even meeting in person, for what has just been described is the essence of the hypnotic induction process.

One person's control of another's conscious mind by keeping it occupied with but one thought. That is what hypnosis is, not all that frightening now is it?

During hypnosis, it is the belief system and processes which must be overruled and controlled. Now the only way one person can control another persons belief mechanism is to bypass it completely and that is what hypnosis enables us to achieve. This is what allows us to convince subjects they are Elvis or Madonna. Because the belief system is not being consulted, it does not realise the discrepancy with fact and as such is not objecting to the command, as would usually be the case. If the belief mechanism were to check with the subconscious, it would find that it has been temporarily reprogrammed. The hypnotist bypasses the belief and understanding systems (reality safeguards) in the mind of another and influences the subconscious mind directly.

This is hypnosis at its simplest form. Just as when counting sheep in your mind at night to promote sleep, the distraction of the swinging watch, flashing light or moving hand is used to concentrate the mind of the subject away from defence so that they relax. Once they have relaxed, the hypnotist's words will seep more easily into the subconscious where they will then be enacted. Basically speaking, hypnosis is easy to achieve through fixation of attention and distraction of the subject's mind away from what they are doing. It is the thinking behind the words you say and the flexibility and ingenuity you have as a hypnotist that matters.

You may have seen a trance induced or been hypnotised yourself and been amazed at just how simple it really is. It may have followed the almost comical form of "go to sleep, you are in my power!" etc. But the true power of the hypnotist lies within the mind of the subject and the words and/or actions used are not dictated in advance but are lead by the actions and reactions of the subject. It is this understanding that makes a major difference to the success you will achieve.

In the mind of the subject, it is the "Belief and Expectancy" which matters most. Now it shouldn't take too much common sense, after all I've told you, to see that what I've said is all actually 100% true. Now, if the words were all important and you could induce a trance simply by uttering them, then the entire audience would fall under the spell and act in the same way at the same time at each and every show you did which of course is not the case in reality.

In reality, hypnosis occurs due to a persons belief and expectancy and as we mentioned earlier the best kept secret of all is that all hypnosis is really just self-hypnosis, with us just acting as directors of the trance state. Now its time for a very brief history lesson:

Hypnosis is a condition in which willpower and a person's consciousness is suspended but other functions remain unimpaired. The subject of hypnosis is then exceptionally suggestible to suggestion, may be made insensible to pain and will carry out instructions (post hypnotic suggestions) at once or long after being awakened from the trance. Discovered by Anton Fredrich Mesmer (1733-1815), an Austrian physician who claimed he could reduce people to a trance like state by applying a technique he called Animal Magnetism. The subject's willpower being entirely subordinated by his own.

The police expelled him from Vienna and he created a sensation with stage and public demonstrations when he moved to Paris in 1778. But again in 1785 he was denounced as a charlatan despite his obvious powers. He was really just an early experimenter in what we now call hypnotism or hypnosis. It was however at the time called Mesmerism and was called this for many years afterwards also.

A surgeon by the name of James Esdaile Braid then, many years on, studied Mesmer's work and coined the name hypnosis from the Greek word Hypnos meaning sleep and so a whole new life was given to the suggestion technique. James E. Braid performed operations with only hypnosis as the anaesthetic and brought it as a science almost to the attention of the medical profession.

Another key peg in the development of hypnosis and its use in medicine and psychotherapy was Milton Erikson who's great books are available on general sale and publications authored by, or co-authored by this man are unreservedly recommended to all students of this course. From a stage performance point of view it was Peter Casson who made stage hypnosis so popular back in the 50's although obviously many Music Hall performers had been doing it for many years prior to this. It was due to Mr.

Casson that the 1952 Hypnotism act was implemented, otherwise stage hypnotism shows may have been banned completely in England in 1952 no thanks to the actions of an American hypnotist called Ralph Slater who brought the industry into disrepute and for this we have a lot to thank Peter Casson for.

In more recent years there have been people such as Paul McKenna, Andrew Newton, Ken Webster, Peter Powers and myself presenting hypnosis on TV to millions of people at one time, bringing it to a much wider audience and so making stage hypnotism shows more popular than they have ever been.

So all in all, its roots are set many years ago and it's an art that is tried, tested and proven to work. Well let me rephrase that. Hypnosis is a skill anyone can learn, but the practice of it is an art which can only be learnt through practical experience. Just as anyone can play a piano this does not automatically make them a great concert pianist and in the same way it follows that each and every hypnotist will have a different level of skill and only those with the highest skill levels could be classed as the concert pianists of stage hypnotism.

In 1952, the hypnotism act was introduced (amended 1972) to protect the citizens of the UK from the humiliating, dangerous and pornographic stage hypnotists who gave the subject a bad name for many years. Other similar laws were passed in countless other countries at about the same time. Now licenses must be sought for any public show and strict controls and regular inspections are now normal procedure. Stage hypnotism is now a safe and highly recommended form of family entertainment, performed by the skilled without trickery and watched by the enthralled without embarrassment.

Hypnotism is a form of power over people, and any power when misused can be dangerous. This knowledge, like any other knowledge is given in trust to you, to be looked after, used for the good of all and shared with other like-minded people. Most importantly let me state that nobody has ever come to any harm under hypnosis or as a direct/indirect result of it despite what may have been said in the media (during 1993/1994) about the tragic death of one Sharon Tabarn, the daughter of Margaret Harper some five hours after a stage hypnotism show conducted by Andrew

Vincent at the Roebuck Public house in Leyland (Preston) Lancs. Despite the fact that several people including her family and so called experts who should have known better, including top Hypnotherapist Derek Crussal, backed up Mrs. Harper's allegations of death by hypnosis and formed (C.A.S.H) The Campaign Against Stage Hypnotists she did in fact die due to natural causes.

Well the real truth as I understand it and it has been related to me is as follows. The coroners report, the pathologists report and all other expert reports concluded that her death was due to natural causes and has no connection whatsoever to the hypnotism show or the hypnotic trance state. In fact I am led to believe by what I have recently heard that excessive traces of alcohol and chemicals (not just prolactin) were found in her bloodstream and it is now generally believed within the industry that this is why she died tragically in her sleep by choking on her own vomit. So despite the false impression given by the mass media there was no connection whatsoever between hypnosis and the death of Sharon Tabarn and in fact there is no recorded case in history backed up with proper facts and evidence of anyone ever dying due to hypnosis.

Always remember that hypnosis is a totally harmless state, which is why as detailed earlier, it is a natural part of our everyday lives. At this point it would be interesting to note that in 1989 the government attached model conditions to the granting of licences for hypnotism shows, and then in 1995 the government appointed an expert committee to investigate if stage hypnotism posed a threat to the public and as such should it be banned? Then as a result of the 1995 investigation declaring that stage hypnotism posed no serious risk to the public, the 1996 Government review on stage hypnosis came into force along with a revised set of model conditions to be attached to the issuing of licences. A full copy of the 1952 act, the 1989 Guidelines, the 1995 safety report and the 1996 Government review and revised conditions are included along with a letter from the Home Office in a separate chapter within this training course and you are advised to become fully conversant with the contents of all these documents in order that your shows and practices are 100% legal at all times.

Following the laws by the letter and providing proof of public liability insurance, details of your past three successful shows and a copy of your membership certificate should almost certainly always result in you being granted licences with ease. If however you do encounter problems do not hesitate to contact us and we will be pleased to assist.

So to return to the subject in hand, hypnotism is the effect of the thoughts, feelings, imagination and will of each particular subject. When the subject's mind is in agreement with the mind of the hypnotist, according to a given suggestion, then this is hypnosis. Take a look in your dictionary and the definition of hypnosis will no doubt mention sleep, it is a sleep like state, a trance if you like, in which the condition of the subject becomes passive and the subconscious mind accepts the hypnotists suggestions, providing of course that these fall within their moral code. Very briefly put, hypnotism is a psychological method of selling an idea by an operator (the hypnotist) to a subject under certain conditions. These conditions can be divided under two headings:

1) Conditions applying to the operator (hypnotist).
2) Conditions applying to the subject

It is also interesting to note that it is now an accepted fact that a subject under the influence of hypnotism will only carry out the hypnotist's requests when they are not against their morals or internal beliefs. This is not, to be honest, strictly true as in fact once a person has given their consent to be hypnotised and is under hypnosis they can be made to do anything you wish just so long as the suggestion is phrased correctly. By correctly, I mean worded so that to the subject it appears that they will be carrying out a perfectly pleasant act which ties in with their morals, but which has the end result of them doing as you wish.

An example is. The person would not pick up a loaded gun and shoot someone at your command under normal conditions. But if you convinced them they are four years old, playing cowboys and indians and that it's a cap gun which they will use to shoot the big bad chief indian, then they would carry out what seemed to them something normal, but which would actually result in them committing murder. For this reason, you should ALWAYS think very carefully before giving suggestions.

You should by now, realise that when a subject enters hypnosis, although they may themselves not believe this to be the case, (remember belief and expectancy) they are in fact going under by means of their own free will.

They co-operate with you the hypnotist, to bring about this state of mind which is actually self-hypnosis.

POSITIVE THINKING IS A MOST POSITIVE FORCE

AND

CONFIDENCE BEGETS CONFIDENCE

From your point of view, the key secret of hypnosis is the faith in your abilities is the means and confidence is the weapon of execution.

IT HAS GOT TO BE IN THE MIND FIRST BEFORE IT CAN BECOME AN ACTION LATER

So quite simply, make sure all the suggestions you give are clear so that they do go into the mind first and then become actions late. Another important point is to always be enthusiastic in whatever you are doing then you will automatically become more successful as a result.

ENTHUSIASM IS ESSENTIAL - A NEVER TIRING ENTHUSIASM

Now, so that any fear of failure you may still have can be forgotten, allow me to state what is a very true fact indeed and that is:

Anyone can, if they so desire, become a competent professional stage hypnotist. The only qualities which are 100% necessary are an outgoing personality and the ability to force ones own personality onto others as described in this course which you now hold in your hands. The only difference between you and the majority of people on planet earth is that you have, I assume a desire to practice the art of stage hypnotism and also an inner belief that you can do it! You should by now have the self confidence that by the end of this course you will be able to, without doubt present your own stage hypnotism shows. Basically speaking all hypnotic inductions and trance deepening's have the following characteristics:

A) The subject's attention and concentration is focused upon one stimulus or a range of limited stimuli. You can ask the subject to gaze at a bright light or at a spot on the wall or ceiling, at the tip of your finger or indeed at their clasped hands. The subject could even be just concentrating on the sound of the hypnotist's voice or the regular beat of a metronome. The subject can focus upon feelings in their body or the ebb and flow of their own breath to mention just a few possible examples. The key secret here is to have the subject focused and concentrated upon one thing and make it seem important at all times.

B) The hypnotist repeats continuously, suggestions of relaxation, letting go, sleep, heaviness, calmness, going down deeper and deeper etc.

C) The coupling of A & B combined, e.g. focusing their attention by a suggestion. For example, with each breath you take you are letting go more and more, as your eyes are getting heavier and heavier you find yourself drifting down deeper and deeper, or, each time your hands shake more rapidly, so in turn you drift deeper and deeper to sleep. These are all good examples of how to do this.

These three key points are present in one form or another in all the induction and deepening methods that you will ever encounter or indeed will ever use. Remember that the power of hypnosis does not lie within the hypnotist, but rather the real power is within the minds of the subjects. The hypnotist just utilises the simple techniques within this course to unlock that power, and here I refer once more to the principle of belief and expectancy within the subject's mind. Another important rule to remember so that you realise that hypnosis really is as easy as I've made it appear is that when an idea takes root in the subconscious mind, then it must show up later in the motor (psychical) actions of that person. This brings me back to the rule that when the imagination and the will are in conflict the imagination (subconscious) will always win.

BE SIMPLE POSITIVE AND DIRECT IN ALL THAT YOU DO

AND

WHAT THE MIND PERCEIVES THE BODY ACHIEVES

To explain, let me put it this way. Once a person under hypnosis perceives that what a hypnotist suggests will take place, (Coue's law of reversed effort) then whatever else is suggested will have a stronger influence upon that person with even greater ease than the previous suggestion. The suggestion that everything will be cancelled out of their minds at the end of the show and that they will be just as they were when they entered the building is given, as you will recall at the very end of the show, a show in which volunteers have responded in a way that you wanted them to many times and so you need have no worries that they will also respond to your suggestions to awaken them and to cancel out previous suggestions before they leave the venue. This is itself a logical illustration of the rule I have just mentioned above.

Another clever ploy is after giving a subject a suggestion to act upon, before "awakening" them to act upon it, you say to them "Now just nod your head if you understand." As long as they nod their head you need have no worries, as you can then be certain they have both heard and accepted what you have just suggested and as a result it will be acted upon as 100% total reality.

COUE'S LAW OF REVERSED EFFORT

The French physician Emile Coue (d.1926) who was most famous for the short positive thinking statement of "Every day in every way I am getting better and better" was well aware that the subconscious mind was directly responsible for the imaginative processes of each and every one of us. If you imagine that you are going to feel uncomfortable and ill at ease when you have that meeting with the boss later, then a suggestion/idea will take root in your subconscious mind and therefore must show in your motor actions. Consequently when you arrive at the meeting the harder you try to relax, the more the idea will pop back into your head and will occur in reality and you will feel uncomfortable and ill at ease.

Emile Coue teaches that no matter how hard we try to consciously stop something from happening, whenever a persons imagination grasps hold of an idea, then the conscious will stands no chance whatsoever of exerting any control over the situation because as we know already "When the imagination and the will are in conflict the imagination will always win." So the law of reversed effort means that any conscious effort that is used is reversed into the exact opposite.

FEAR AN EVENT HAPPENING AND IT INEVITABLY WILL

So due to the law of reversed effort as detailed above, we are able to achieve any things in our role as a stage hypnotist. For example when doing the handclasp test to lock the subject's hands together we say after all the suggestions have been given:

"OK, now just **TRY** to separate your hands, but the harder you **TRY** the more they will stick together!"

Because the idea has taken root in the imagination that their hands will be locked together, the law of reversed effort comes into play here to ensure as reality that their hands do indeed stay locked together. The way the last statement of **TRY** to separate your hands is worded is also very clever and has an extremely strong psychological effect.

The word **try** is in fact a very strong suggestion within a suggestion so to speak. It means that you believe their hands are now locked together and as such they cannot possibly separate them, but they can try anyway! In other words it implies in the one word **try,** that should they bother to try and separate their hands then they will be unable to do so. This technique of using the word **try** in this manner, along with the law of reversed effort can be used after many other suggestions, the wording of which you can devise yourself but remember to always paint a word picture of the end result you desire. So some other examples of how this ploy can be used are as follows:

A) OK, now just **TRY** to say your name, but the more you **TRY** the more you will be unable to remember it.

B) OK, now just **TRY** to open your eyes, but the more you **TRY** the more they will remain stuck together.

C) OK, now just **TRY** to lift up the chair, but the harder you **TRY** the more you will be unable to lift it.

The technique I have just detailed is more powerful than you could ever imagine. Using it, you can lock people's hands together, make their arms or legs rigid, stick their eyes together and much more, all just by using the suggestions that these things will occur and then by using the word **try** and the law of reversed effort to ensure that they don't. As all these things are done without actual so called hypnosis, the subject is fully awake and conscious at all times. Hence these things are often called suggestibility tests. This is known in the trade as conscious hypnosis or waking state hypnosis.

In general, those people who react readily to such suggestibility tests will make excellent hypnotic subjects and can be placed into trance with the greatest of ease. Experiment with this and you will see what I mean as you should never forget that practical experience is the best teacher in life. Always have 100% confidence in yourself and your skills because if you fear failure, remember the law of reversed effort which states that if you fear an event happening then inevitably it will.

One last most important point for this chapter and that is to say that don't forget that doing one actual show will teach you far more through practical experience than this or any other course ever could teach you. A close second to this is that participating in stage shows will also teach you far more than just reading this course ever can, although now you will obviously be able to observe with far more expertise. Don't forget also that just like myself and every other person in this industry you can never, and will never know all that there is to know on this subject as new developments and discoveries are made daily. So you will never stop learning if you want to become a really expert professional hypnotist.

<u>REVERSE PSYCHOLOGY</u>

Reverse psychology works in much the same way as Coue's law of reversed effort and I will mention it only briefly herein. You can of course find detailed explanations of it in any practical psychology book available from your local library. My one main example of how it does work is this. When I was a boy and at school one day the hardest lad in the entire school started to pick on me and call me names etc. Believing in the law of reverse psychology I started to criticise him back (this in itself shocked him), then when he threatened to hit me if I didn't shut up, instead of shutting up I said "OK then just TRY and hit me!" He just stood there for a minute and did nothing, then he said "Be careful or I will hit you!" To which I replied "Why wait a minute try to hit me now if you can!" He then just looked bemused by my reaction and after calling me a complete prat walked off without so much as touching me. You see I'd said exactly the REVERSE of what he would have expected me to say in such a situation and this use of reverse psychology combined with the law of reversed effort helped me to avoid a good bashing that day. When you say something which is the exact reverse of what people would expect you to say in a given situation it stuns them and this shock makes them unable to think clearly or indeed be able to carry out the original actions they had planned as in this example.

PART EIGHT

SUGGESTIBILITY TESTS

"I want you to imagine in your minds eye that I've just cut a lemon into two halves. I have then picked up one half of this bitter, sour, horrible, juicy lemon and placed it into my mouth at which time I've sucked all the bitter, sour juice from inside it and now all that bitter, sour, citric lemon juice is now running down my throat!"

"OK now, TRY to whistle! I bet you can't, in fact I bet your mouth is now awash with saliva making the action of whistling impossible. In fact if you truly imagined what I suggested for you, this will indeed have occurred in reality and by the way this is an example of a most simple suggestibility test!"

THIS IS AN EXAMPLE OF THE POWER OF SUGGESTION

In this short chapter we will deal with the subject of suggestibility tests. All of these work due to the word **TRY** as detailed in the previous chapter and indeed also due to the law of reversed effort, an element of pure suggestion and the person's ability to be suggestible to this comes into play also. These suggestibility tests are used whilst the subject is fully conscious at the start of your act or therapy session if desired in order that you can easily and quickly decide which of the people will make the best hypnotic subjects.

Some hypnotists perform these tests upon the entire audience at once and then ask those it works on to come forward to the stage and these people are then narrowed down to the best subjects who are then used in the show. Others who are more confident of their skills ask for volunteers to come up to the stage and then they do the tests only on those onstage volunteers, the logic behind this being that one sincere volunteer is worth one hundred pressed men. So either way should be most successful for you if presented correctly, confidently and believably.

I would however in your early days advise you to do these tests upon the entire audience, as then the law of averages will be in your favour. Don't forget, the more people there are in your audience by far the more chance you have of getting more people under hypnosis. It really is all just a numbers game at the end of the day. Incidentally, as in your early days you will be working in pubs and clubs to audiences of about 80 to 150 people you will not have the advantage of 2000 people in a theatre to choose your subjects from and so in these situations the suggestibility tests are an essential part of your show and should be done on the entire audience.

When your career develops and you move onto larger capacity venues, you will then be able to safely and confidently ask for volunteers who wish to be hypnotised to come forward to the stage before you have even done any suggestibility tests. Once upon the stage these volunteers are subjected to the tests and the best reacting subjects are singled out to be hypnotised. Remember that in a theatre which seats 1000 to 2000 people when you ask for volunteers at the start you will get around 80 to 100 people coming up to the stage. Not only does this look dramatic and impressive to the rest of the audience, but also effectively it means your volunteers each of who is worth a hundred pressed men wants to be hypnotised.

In a theatre situation, you will have almost as many volunteers on stage as would be in the entire audience during the early days of your career in pubs and small clubs! So you see it really is all down to the law of averages and the numbers game. In general your shows will always be more successful in large capacity venues such as night-clubs and theatres than those held in pubs and social clubs. Don't let this deter you though, as upon having read this course you **WILL** be able to do an excellent show in pubs and clubs until you progress to the larger venues. The only problem, or should I say difference there is really between working in a pub and a theatre, is that in a theatre they have paid to come and see you and so you are the main thing of importance and alcohol comes second and will only be available in the interval anyway!

WHEREAS IN A PUBLIC HOUSE

They have come to have a few pints and you the poor entertainer have got to work really hard to keep their attention. Also in pubs it is not wise to let your show start too late as, due to the drinking and the fact people who are drunk cannot be hypnotised, it is wise your show starts before they have all had one to many to drink.

Some of the components that make up these suggestibility tests or the induction's which follow later are of a physiological and/or physical nature. In other words, in many of the cases if you got them to do as I describe then it would be physically impossible to separate their hands or open their eyes even without the verbal suggestion element coming into play!

However as these tests are all presented in a manner which makes the subject believe that whatever occurs is due to our suggestions, when these things do occur for whatever reason whether physical, physiological or suggestion, the subject comes to believe that it was all due to your suggestions and so will more readily accept and react to any future "genuine" suggestions that we may give them.

In other cases such as in the inductions detailed later, due to natural physiological causes, they may be made to feel dizzy or disorientated and because we know this always happens and is a natural feeling we can suggest that it will happen before it actually does happen of its own accord. Then when it does occur, as indeed it will, the subject always believes our verbal suggestions to have been the cause of what they now are feeling and/or experiencing and so in turn this compounds their belief in our powers even more and from that moment any "genuine" suggestions will always get a successful response as the subject is now conditioned to belief they will and expect they will work and so in turn they will.

So hopefully, you now see that little known naturally occurring phenomenon are used by the hypnotist to make the subject experience strange sensations which the subject then connects to your suggestions and as a direct result, increases their belief in your powers and takes them further down into the trance state.

Examine closely all the suggestibility tests and induction's which I teach you and you will, without fail, see that each one has an element of it either being guaranteed to happen or of some part, feeling or sensation being guaranteed to occur which the subject then comes to believe are due to your verbal suggestions and in turn cements into their mind the belief and expectancy that all future suggestions will indeed be 100% effective also.

These suggestibility tests also get the subjects to focus their attention and concentration onto one thing which of course you will also command them to do later when inducing the trance state. This conditions them to react in a certain way when asked certain things and makes your overall job easier. So I suppose we should really call these suggestibility tests pre-induction's or light induction's as when anyone is focusing or concentrating on one thing they are in effect in a very light hypnotic state. This is because the key element of trance is fixation of attention and concentration on one point of focus.

It almost goes without saying that the people who's hands lock together are better subjects than those whose don't! So what? Well in a pub or club situation you will probably have only about 8 or 10 people come up with their hands locked together and so it would be wise here to hypnotise as many of these as possible before asking for other volunteers if needed. On theatre shows however you will have loads of people with their hands locked together so how do you choose which will be the best subjects to use? Well very obviously those people whose hands are shaking violently as opposed to just locked together are by far the most suggestible subjects, as indeed they have so far reacted better to your suggestions than anyone else. To narrow down the numbers even more remember always that one volunteer is worth a hundred pressed men so first of all return anyone to the audience who does not wish to remain there.

Next you would of course eliminate people who seem drunk or high on drugs, people who appear under the age of 18, anyone who looks petrified being on stage and lastly if there are enough people on stage with their hands locked together those people who just volunteered without their hands being locked together. However, where numbers are smaller than usual, the volunteers without hands locked together are used as potential hypnotic subjects also.

From the remainder, the "handshakers" are excellent subjects. Next, those people who have been hypnotised before on stage or by a therapist are easy to place into trance also and then it's a matter of observation. Although experience of performing will give you an almost sixth sense of who to pick here follow some important signs to look for which are indicative of a potentially good subject.

Those that take what you say seriously and appear to concentrate on things when you tell them to, appear to do as you say when you tell them to and generally seem sincere in their efforts will also make excellent subjects. The reason for this being that hypnosis is co-operation and not confrontation. Also during your initial banter/patter with the on stage volunteers, the answers they give to your questions will on many occasions give you an indication of who will make a good subject and who won't! For example those who have been hypnotised before in the past can usually be made to enter trance just by commanding them to close their eyes and Sleep!

If the people have been hypnotised successfully before, even if it was not by you, then as they have entered the state of trance before, know how it feels and know what to expect and how to react they will make the most excellent of subjects and can be placed instantly back into trance as their belief and expectancy in the powers of hypnosis is 100% complete and based on prior practical experience of being hypnotised. They have experienced the state of hypnosis before so they know it exists and now they just need a catalyst if you like, to renter the state and you serve this purpose for them. With these kind of people it is often as easy as snapping your fingers in front of their face and saying sleep to make them enter trance with ease.

So what actual visual clues are there that people are indeed doing as you suggest and taking it all seriously? Well basically, it's a case of using your common sense here. If they do as you say the moment that you suggest it, then obviously they are taking it seriously and are concentrating on your instructions and so in turn are a potentially very good subject. For example, if you suggest that their hands are getting tighter and tighter together all the time and you can visually see that their hands are turning red with the pressure they are using to squeeze their hands together then obviously they are reacting well to your suggestions.

Having given you all this guidance, it is however true to say that the selection of who to use is something that each person must master for themselves through practical experience. Body language plays a part; those that will be good subjects will usually have similar patterns of body language which of course you will learn through hands on practical experience. Basically however, having used the correct patter to open the show and due to all the other psychological elements in our favour as discussed earlier, if you are adaptable and suit your induction to the personality of your subject then you can hypnotise given enough time **<u>EVERY PERSON</u>** that steps onto your stage.

Anyway, enough about what the suggestibility test is used for or how to spot potentially good subjects, lets now explain a few actual suggestibility tests, which can be used to narrow down the selection process. This is all "Waking State" hypnosis if you like and does demonstrate to the watching and participating audience that all suggestion correctly expressed does have a most powerful effect.

THE ARM DROP TEST

This test, if used at all, is used right at the start to find which people in the audience are already in a nicely relaxed state and as such would make potentially good subjects for use upon the stage, it also shows you which members of the audience are able to relax when they want to, as once again these type of people make excellent subjects.

You get everyone to close their left hand into a fist and then to extend their left forefinger so that it points up in the air. They are then told to place the lower part of their right arm (near the wrist) resting upon the top of their extended left forefinger. They are told to allow the full weight of their right arm to be supported by the forefinger of their left hand. Next they are told to relax every muscle in their bodies and especially in their right arm so that all the weight of the right arm rests upon the left forefinger. You explain that you will now count to three and that on the count of three they are to pull their left forefinger away from under their right arm rapidly. You count 1,2,3, and on the count of three they take their fingers away. The people who are able to relax best and have followed your instructions to the letter will find that having allowed the weight of their right arm to rest fully upon the left fingertip, that upon removal of the left hand's finger, their right arm will immediately fall into their laps like a sack of potatoes.

Their arm will have fallen, as it will be limp, loose, relaxed and heavy and that's what you are looking for, the people who have relaxed easily in this manner. Those who did not react due to not relaxing enough will probably have remained with their right arm still suspended in the air upon removal of the finger or at least it would have fallen far more slowly into their laps than the really suggestible people.

So in this test the idea is just to see who can relax quickly when asked to and indeed those people whose hands fell into their laps rapidly have passed this test with flying colours! This one is not a suggestibility test as such it's more a way to see who follows your instructions to the letter and who can relax easily. I would therefore use at least one actual suggestibility test such as the handclasp after this experiment prior to inducing the Trance State in order to ensure success.

FINGERS CLOSING TEST

This is a suggestibility text of a natural type. By "Natural Type" I mean that what occurs would do anyway for most people automatically without any suggestions, so it's a physical trick, if you like, but this instills more belief into them prior to the handclasp test. You ask them to interlock their fingers so that the fingers of the left hand are against the back of the right hand, and the fingers of the left hand are against the back of the left hand. Palms pressed tightly together and thumbs resting on top of their interlocked fingers just as in the handclasp text, which is fully detailed with complete explanation and patter in the "Know your lines" chapter of this course.

You then ask them to extend their two forefingers, so that the tips of each outstretched finger are touching. They are then told to separate the tips of the fingers by about an inch and a half, and lastly they are told to stare directly at you and not at their hands. You yourself have got your hands in the same position as their hands, as you suggest that by the count of 3 their fingers will be touching just as they were beforehand, that should the try to keep them apart then the fingers will just draw nearer and nearer together. You then count as follows:-

1. It's almost as though there are strong magnets on the tips of your fingers, drawing them together, more and more, bringing them nearer together.
2. They are getting so close now, that they are almost touching as those magnets become so powerful and pull your fingertips together. And on,

3. The magnets are so powerful that your fingertips are now touching.

As you do this, you close your own two fingers together slowly, so that by the time you say the number three, your own fingertips are touching. Many will take this as a non verbal suggestion that their own fingers are getting closer together.

You then get the people whose fingertips were touching by the count of three to place a hand up. This makes it easier for you to gauge the response level which with this test is usually extremely high. At the end of the fingers closing test, you can then go into:

THE HANDCLASP TEST

The way to do this is fully detailed in the "Know your Lines" part, so it is not necessary to repeat it all.

I will however, mention how it can be used differently when working in smaller venues where there is not enough room to have lots of people coming to join you on the performance area.

In these cases, you would carry out the test as described in the earlier chapter until you have counted up to 20 and given all the suggestions. At this point, you would say, "OK now, everyone, still believing in the worlds strongest superglue which sticks your hands tightly together, I'd like you to try and separate your hands (law of reversed effort takes effect here), but you'll find the harder you try to separate them the more they will stick together tightly. OK, now, try. (give them a few seconds then say) Right, that's enough, just relax your hands now and stop trying." Those people whose hands are now still stuck together I'd like you to stand up, because if you don't, your hands will be like this for three weeks, when they'll turn blue and drop off. Also anyone else who just found their hands difficult to separate who wishes to experience the state of hypnosis, please come this way towards me.

In this way of using the text, obviously fewer people will end up with hands locked together. However, it solves the limited space problem. Those whose hands are shaking are usually the best subjects, those with hands just locked together, next best and those whose hands separate, but it was harder to do than usual come next in order of preference and lastly, those people who just volunteered to take part anyway. Remember though, as with anything in life, there will always be exceptions to the rules and as such, you must always use your common sense and learn to think on your feet.

In all methods of using the test, here is how to separate their hands for them. You simply suggest that the moment you tap them on the back of the hands their hands will spring apart, as if two magnets were repelling each other. You then go round to each person whose hands you wish to separate and touch them on the back of the hands, whilst at the same time, saying to each of them, "its O.K. now you can separate your hands, you CAN separate your hands."

Just as imagination allowed them to stick together due to suggestion, so it will also allow them to part due to suggestion. Usually most people would separate all the subject's hands and then do the induction's on them. As you will have noticed in the "Know you Lines" chapter, on large theatre shows only, I separate their hands straight away, if I wish to return them to the audience, or, if I wish to use one of the inductions from the next chapter which requires them to have their hands separate at the time. Otherwise, I would place them into trance via the falling backwards induction, using the patter as detailed in "Know your Lines". Their hands would still be locked together and they would be held against their chest area. This being to case, the top half of their body would now be much heavier than the rest of their body, and, as such, they are now going to find it much harder to stop themselves falling backwards into your arms, when you start the induction of falling backwards.

Once on the floor with their eyes closed, I would suggest to them, that their eyes will remain tightly closed at all times until I say otherwise and then, that when I take hold of their arms, their hands will immediately separate. The moment you have said this you take hold of their arms, one in each hand and say, "OK just separate your hands now." The moment they separate their hands, you use this as an opportunity to deepen the light trance they are in by saying, "The moment I drop your arms to the floor, it will not disturb you, in fact, it will serve to send you deeper to sleep, 10 times deeper to sleep" (then drop their arms to floor as you say) "Sleep and Relax".

LIGHT AND HEAVY HANDS TEST

With this test, the audience is told to close their eyes and extend their two arms out straight in front of themselves at the same level. You now suggest to them that their left hand has got a pile of heavy books upon it, which are so heavy, that their hand is being pushed downwards.

You then suggest that tied to the middle finger of their right hand is a large helium filled balloon which is pulling their right hand high up into the air, as it floats ever upwards. You keep suggesting things along these lines that the left hand holds the heavy books and right hand is being pulled up into the air by the helium balloon.

You will find that people who are really open to suggestion, will allow their arms to react accordingly. As such, their left hand will move downwards, as if a heavy pile of books is upon it, and their right hand will move upwards, as if tied to a helium filled balloon. You then tell everyone to open their eyes, and many will be amazed to find that their arms are now in very different positions with a huge gap between them both.

THE PERFUME BOTTLE TEST

You remove a fancy cut glass bottle from your pocket and explain that it contains the most powerfully scented perfume in the world. You state that, in a few moments, you will remove the lid of the bottle and allow the scent to travel around the room for everyone to smell, as it really is that strong. You tell everyone to raise their hand into the air the second they smell the scent come their way, which, as it's so potent, will take only a few seconds.

The bottle's lid is then removed and the people start to raise their hands, once several hands are in the air you explain that the power of suggestion has worked upon them, and in fact the bottle contains nothing more than water, with a little added food colouring. You then drink the contents to prove your point and people will be amazed as they will swear they smelt the scent travel around the room, trust me, this does, if presented convincingly, work.

WARM FINGERS TEXT

This is sometimes used prior to the handclasp text. You have them place their arms outstretched in front of them, and get them to place their hands flat against each other, you then command them to start rubbing their hands backwards and forwards against each other, as quickly as they can. You say you'll count from 3 to 1. All the time they are to keep rubbing their hands together and, if they concentrate, then by the count of 1 their hands will be getting hot and sticky, as if coated with superglue. You then say 3, getting hotter and hotter, 2, the hotter they get, the more sticky they become, and the more sticky they become, the hotter they will get, and on 1, just interlock your fingers like this (you then demonstrate how they should put their hands for the handclasp test, which you immediately go into). OK everyone, as you hold your hands interlocked the warmth and stickiness you felt, is already locking them tightly together (you then go into normal patter for handclasp).

Now just to explain briefly, the idea of his test is that if you rub your hands back and forth against each other rapidly, they do indeed become hot and sticky. But, as this is so obvious, people don't realise this to be the case and attribute it to your suggestions, which not only gives them a greater belief in your powers, but as they feel their hands are hot and sticky, do not be surprised if it becomes easier for them to believe that there is super glue on their hands, sticking them together tightly.

THE ORDER OF TESTS TO BE DONE

So, in your very early days when you lack confidence in yourself, you may wish to use all the tests, if you do however, please ensure you do them rapidly, as you're meant to be a dynamic showman and not a boring lecturer. So the order of tests would go:

1   Arm drop text

2   Finger closing test

3   Warm fingers test

4   Handclasp test

5   Actual induction of Hypnotic Trance

The psychology behind them being placed in this order being that:

1   ARMDROP TEST

This shows you which can relax easily and quickly, and which do exactly as you tell them to, it's just a relaxation exercise; however it gets them used to doing as you say.

2   THE FINGERS CLOSING TEST

It is natural for the fingers to close together anyway and, you will have a high success rate with this, the success of it then increasing their belief in your powers.

3   WARM FINGERS TEST

This takes but a matter of seconds to do prior to the handclasp and should, as just described, take the belief in your powers, another step further.

4   THE HANDCLASP TEST

By now they BELIEVE in you, and EXPECT it to work, so you should have a high success rate here.

5   THE ACTUAL INDUCTION

As the people you are using, have probably reacted successfully to tests 1, 2, 3 and 4, you can be sure as they are now conditioned to do as you say, they will enter the Hypnotic Trance.

GAIN PRACTICAL EXPERIENCE A.S.A.P

Do as many shows as possible, as soon as possible and once you've gained confidence in your skills, you will then be able to speed up the whole process. By then, just coming onto the stage, doing your opening talk and then going straight into the handclasp test from which you induce the Hypnotic Trance state in your volunteers.

The only thing which you may not quite have now, which will enable you to do this, is 100% faith in yourself and your new skill. But, if you have already got this faith, then start out like a master and just proceed as if you're a very experienced hypnotist (after all the audience doesn't know). I will end this chapter by telling you of a "Handclasp" style test in which it is, if they do as you say, physically impossible for 99% of people to separate their hands. This art which is unknown to the general public means:

A   You are guaranteed a high percentage of people who can't separate their hands when asked to try, and

B   It ensures that their belief in your powers is then greatened, so that it becomes extremely easy to place them into the trance state.

I personally use this method of "Handclasp" at the start of the second half of my theatre show, in order to get some new people upon the stage, whom I can then use to demonstrate how I am able to place between 12 and 40 people or more into trance in less than sixty seconds. Have fun using it, it's also a great way to quickly establish your credentials and a volunteers belief in you when at a party etc. before placing them into trance to demonstrate your art.

THE GUARANTEED HANDCLASP TEST

With this you stretch your arms out with palms facing yourself. Fingers wide open and thumbs up in the air. Bend wrist, so that although arms are out stretched, palms are facing your body. Interlock your fingers and push in together as closely as you can. Turn thumbs towards you, until back of your hands are facing you. Now push arms out hard, until elbows crack, and push your palms away from you as much as you can. Now I will count to three, and on the count of three, your hands will be stuck fast together, and in fact, the harder you try to pull them apart, the more they will stick together tight so on 1, staring directly at the backs of your hands as they stick together, tighter and tighter. 2, just lift your hands up above your head now and push your palms up towards the clouds, as high up into the sky as you possibly can and on 3, keep pushing your hands up high into the sky, and now just try to separate your hands, the harder you try, they stick tighter together.

(GIVE THEM A FEW SECONDS THEN SAY)

OK, just relax and keep your hands together as they are until I say otherwise. OK, everyone, firstly I'd like you all to stand up where you are so that we can all have a good look at each other, now walk this way, towards the stage, and I promise you, I will not keep you up here if you don't want to take part.

At this point, loads of people will come towards the stage and as they do so you say: "OK everyone, the moment I touch your hands, they will immediately spring apart and it will feel as though you've received a slight harmless electric shock in your arms."

You then quickly, go to each person and knock the underside of their arms firmly and sharply, so that their hands do indeed spring apart. For anyone who still keeps their hands together, just get them to reverse the procedure which got their hands into this position in the first place. From those who do come up to have their hands separated, you ask for volunteers to take part in a quick 3 minute test after which they may return to the audience. You get between 12 to 24 people to come up, dependant on the stage size etc. and the rest of the people are now returned to the audience to a round of applause.

It is at this point, that the 12 to 24 people are lined up in a straight line, when you can follow the details in the next chapter, in order to be able to place all of them into a trance in less than sixty seconds. That's about 2 to 3 seconds per person only to get them into an instant deep hypnotic trance. And that's where this chapter ends. In the next chapter, I will reveal what you have all been waiting for, and that's the secrets of the actual induction methods used to place people into trance. So hold onto your seats and leave your misconceptions behind, as we enter the hypnotic world, where there really are NO LIMITS.

PART NINE

INDUCTION METHODS

The simplest things are usually the most effective in life and hypnosis is no exception. The process of hypnosis is so easy to carry out, that, for most, it's hard to believe it works and yet, that's exactly the reason why it's so effective, as people believe you must be doing something complicated to place them into trance. But you should have learnt the true secret off by heart now and that's the fact it's all down to belief and expectancy and following the simple steps, which I am explaining to you in this course, then success will be yours.

Well welcome to the chapter which you've been waiting for, how to place people into the hypnotic Trance. By now, you will have hopefully assimilated all the other knowledge which I have revealed to you, if not, then please go back to page one, read through it all again and digest until you do understand what I've said. As you must understand what I've said in order to understand how these hypnotic inductions actually do work.

Basically speaking, the success of the hypnotic induction relies on the belief and expectancy within the mind of your potential hypnotic subject. All the other elements of the suggestibility test, your opening patter and the fact that people are already 90% on the way to already being hypnotised before they step onto the stage, due to your advertising etc. also help in a huge way.

If you have followed all these points and the subjects on stage or in your consulting room believe you are a professional hypnotist, with the skill to place them into trance and they also expect whatever you do to work, then as hard as it is to believe at this moment in time, it will work.

So step A is the belief and expectancy within the volunteer's mind. Step B, of disorientation and confusion is catered for in the way which these hypnotic inductions have been designed. They themselves, if carried out as instructed, will either confuse them, disorientate them, or in some way do both. When this element is combined with step C of suggestion and repetition, you will almost always get the end result of relaxation and sleep, which of course is step D.

So follow the guidelines and you'll have great success with your hypnotic inductions. There are two general rules of thumb I should mention at this point, and these are also applicable to every hypnotist on earth.

1   The more confident you are in your own skills and talents, the more successful you will be as a result in all that you do. As it says in the bible "As a man thinketh so he becomes"

2   The more experience you get of actually hypnotising people, the faster and more effective your induction methods will become and the greater a percentage of people upon the stage you will be able to get into a trance easily and effectively.

So practise, practise and practise some more. Remember this though, don't try it out on family and friends and expect a huge success, as they knew you when you weren't a hypnotist, so that most vital element of belief and expectancy will not be there.

Instead practise on new faces in bars etc. in conversation say what you do, and present them with one of your business cards to establish belief and expectancy and ask if the group wants a free demonstration, then go ahead and practise your skills. But remember this, you are the only one that will know this is the first time you've ever done this, as far as they are concerned, you've been doing it for years and are a true master of your craft. So once again belief and expectancy come into play here.

Anyway, I've tried to dispel any doubts which you may still have and hopefully I've done that, if not, you'll have to pluck up the courage to try it all out and then hindsight will tell you that what I'm teaching you is 100% true in every way.

As a hypnotist, the most important thing you could possibly need is supreme self-confidence, so here goes with an induction method which can be used very successfully on stage.

FALLING BACKWARD INDUCTION

You get the subject to stand with both feet together on the floor, hands down by their sides unless this is being done after the locked hands in which case they are told to place their hands closely against their chest. This means there is then more weight at the upper area of their body and they are even more likely to fall back than usual. You stand to the left of them and place your right foot flat against the back of their heels so it can act as a pivot if required. Your right hand middle finger pushes onto their forehead, as you say, "and tilt your head well back as you close your eyes." You have now still got your right middle finger on the centre of their forehead, just above the bridge of their nose, as you count from one to three and give the suggestions of relaxing and falling back, as I will describe in a moment, you draw your middle finger lightly across the centre of the subjects forehead, so that by the count of 3 it is almost ready to slide towards the top of their head. This acts as a non-verbal suggestion to fall backwards, and believe me, even without the verbal suggestions, it usually has the effect of the person falling backwards.

When you have given your suggestions and the person starts to fall back, all you need do is lower your right arm from their head, down to their upper back area and just cushion their fall back so they don't hurt themselves. In actual fact, you are just lowering them down onto the floor at which point they will be in the hypnotic trance.

On some occasions, if I feel it is a difficult subject, I will prior to getting them to tilt their head back and close their eyes, get them to take some really deep breaths in, hold them a few seconds and then out. This has the effect of slightly "hyper-ventilating" them. This means that when you tilt their head back and tell them to close their eyes, they will then feel a little dizzy already and this brings the self-hypnosis angle into play again. This will occur even more strongly if you, as they breathe deeply, knock them with your right hand on their back at the place where their lungs are. This has the extra effect of knocking them off balance and disorientating them even more.

Remember, that you must read these instructions several times and get it clear in your own mind the whole process of physical actions and verbal suggestions, as they should take just a few seconds from starting point to the point at which they are lying upon the floor in trance. From a verbal point of view, the whole lot would go as follows:

"OK sir (or madam). Just stand there, feet together, hands down by your side (or hands against your chest). Tilt your head well back and close your eyes. I'd like you to take nice deep regular breaths in, hold them a few seconds and then breathe out as this will help you to relax more quickly. In a few moments, I'm going to count from 1 to 3 and on the count of 3, when I say sleep, you will feel yourself falling back, but I won't let you fall and hurt yourself, instead you'll just fall into a beautifully relaxed state.

1.   The deeper you go the better you will feel and the better you feel the deeper you will go.
2.   You can feel yourself falling backwards now into a beautifully relaxed sleeplike state.
3.   SLEEP (They fall) falling back, back, back and sleep and relax."

THEY WILL NOW BE IN THE HYPNOTIC TRANCE

If the subject does not start to fall of their own accord, you can always use the fact that your feet against the back of their heels acts as a pivot to tip them back gently, so that to the audience it appears as if they have just fallen back into your arms. Another point worth mentioning is that on the count of three, you immediately remove your hand from their head and tap them firmly on the back as you say SLEEP. This has the effect of knocking them even more off balance and as a result they then fall backwards into your arms. So your next step is to get your wife or husband and use them to practice the actions on, until you can do them without hesitation, then you will have one of the quickest and most effective inductions that there is available to you.

The great thing with this induction on a theatre stage is that all the volunteers can be lined up in a straight row and one by one, after each other, they can be placed into trance using this method. Once all of them are upon the floor under your spell so to speak, you then proceed by deepening the level of trance for the whole group at once, which makes it slicker and quicker. In this case, the volunteers would be face on to the audience and they fall backwards away from the audience. As with all the induction methods, which I will explain to you in this chapter, I will tell you the basics, and your own common sense would tell you the rest. For example, in a funny shaped venue, you might have to have the subjects standing sideways onto the audience before making them fall backwards. This is really an excellent induction to use. It's quick, safe and works well, I wish you much luck with it.

FALLING FORWARDS INDUCTION

This is, in essence, almost identical to the falling backward induction, except that they fall forwards. The reason it works is the same, and even without belief and expectancy being considered, if this is done correctly, then people will feel themselves falling forwards into your arms. You stand facing the subject, they have their hands down by their sides, stand up straight rigid, feet together and stare directly into your eyes. They are told to keep staring directly into your eyes at all times and then you proceed as follows:

Verbally you say something such as, "I'm going to count backwards from 3 to 1 and on each descending number you'll feel yourself falling forwards, but I won't let you fall and hurt yourself, instead you'll just fall into a beautifully relaxed, dreamy, sleeplike state. So,

3, the deeper you go the better you will feel and the better you feel, the deeper you will go.

2, You can feel yourself falling forwards, more with every breath you take, ever noise you hear and every word that I say.

And on 1, you can feel yourself falling forwards, falling forwards, forwards and to sleep."

As you say this or similar, the physical element is as follows:

From the moment you start talking, your fingers of each hand are placed firmly, flatly and gently on the sides of their head in line with their forehead. As you talk you are gently pulling your fingers forwards in a smooth motion towards yourself and this has the effect of both distracting them and also disorientating them a little. But, perhaps more importantly, as your fingers are firmly against their head, it has the effect of gently pulling their head forwards towards you, and also acts as a non verbal suggestion to do the same. This as a result will mean their body will follow suit and they will start to move forwards. At the same time to promote this further, you take one small step backwards, as you count each number and as they are to stare into your eyes at all times, it will have the effect of their eyes following yours, and as such their body will move forwards more.

Also bend your legs slightly as you get nearer to the count of one, so that your eye level becomes lower. This means that to keep their eyes in line with yours, they have to lean over slightly and when they do, they will reach that point of no return, and will suddenly be falling forwards into your arms. You must catch them and then very gently lay them upon the floor, so that their head is to one side.

Combine all this with belief and expectancy and the shock element of you commanding SLEEP, just as they reach that point of no return and now I'm sure you'll be able to understand why this induction works so well.

THE FLOATING ARM INDUCTION

For this induction, have the subject sitting in a chair, feet together and hands resting upon their lap, with eyes tightly closed. You then proceed as I will detail in a second, although you'll have to adapt things for each person. The method of this induction is to first get them to lift up their middle finger of the right hand, due to suggestion, then to allow their hand to lift up, followed by their arm. The moment their arm has floated up to their face and touches their nose, it will instantly fall back into their lap and they drift into an instant deep relaxing sleep.

This is really all down to suggestion, and is a 100% genuine induction. The standard phrases, which are used by all hypnotists and which are detailed at the end of this chapter, are inserted at appropriate points, to relax them even more. This will give you a brief idea of what to say, but this is really a case of what suits your personality, you now know it's all down to suggestion and what you want to achieve, so now here's an idea of what to say.

"As you breathe deeply and relax more with every breath you take, every noise you hear and with every word I say, you'll notice that the deeper you go over the next few minutes, the better you will feel and the better you feel, the deeper you will go. I'd like you to concentrate on your right hand middle finger, and as you do, just notice how it almost feels like a helium balloon is tied onto it making it so light, so light, that it no longer wishes to remain resting upon your lap. And just notice that with each breath you take and ever noise you hear, your finger now becomes so light with that helium balloon attached, that it is lifting up off your lap and up into the air. Now just imagine that helium filled balloon, floating up higher and higher into the air, and as it does your hand is starting to rise up, up off you lap and into the air, as it's now so light, as light as air, in fact, so light it floats up higher into the air. (Proceed in this fashion until their hand is up off their lap, and starts moving upwards) You now notice that as your hand floats up higher, being pulled up higher into the air all the time by the helium filled balloon, that your arm is now so light and follows suit. (Continue in the same vein, until their finger, hand and arm are up in the air). Now just notice that your hand is floating towards your face, nearer and nearer to your nose, all the time (Continue in this vein etc.) And realise now, that the moment your finger touches your nose, your hand will suddenly become as heavy as lead, will fall instantly down back into your lap, and you'll sink instantly into a state of relaxation 100 times deeper and 100 times more enjoyable than that which you are already in." (Continue in this vein etc).

If you follow this basic outline, they will do as you intend and the moment their arm falls back onto their lap, you will also have a visual indication that they have now entered trance. Remember, paint a picture with your words, leave no doubt in their minds what you wish to occur and as such belief, expectancy and the power of suggestion will do the rest.

EYES GLUED TOGETHER INDUCTION

This can be done with the subject standing up straight, hands down by their side and eyes closed, or whilst they are sitting down, feet together with hands on their lap and eyes closed.

You place your right hand middle finger, firmly onto the central area of the head, just above the top of their forehead. You explain that they must imagine, that there is a hole in their head at the point where they can feel your fingertip and as such, they are to stare through the hole in their head and up at your fingertip. To do this they will have to push their eyeballs upwards underneath their eyelids.

Once in this position, you then suggest that by the count of one their eyes will be stuck together and the harder they try to separate them, the more they will stick. As long as you make it clear that even when you ask them to try and open their eyes that they must in actual fact keep staring upwards with their eyes as if staring through the hole in their head, then this will work. The reason for this, being that when your eyeballs are in this position it becomes physically impossible to open your eyes anyway.

The subject will believe his failure in opening his eyes is due to your suggestions, and then so that it comes very unexpectedly, you suddenly tilt the subjects head forward onto their chest as you say, "Eyes tightly closed at all times and just sleep". They will remain like this now until you command to them otherwise, obviously the trance will be deepened along with everyone else a little later on into the act.

INSTANT INDUCTION

Here follows the wording of a very effective and quick, induction method. Having finally got you subjects lined up on the stage, you begin in a very strong and commanding voice, "Close your eyes, begin go breathe deeply and regularly, you will find that your eyes will begin to stick together. They will become tightly stuck; in fact, you cannot open your eyes. Then walk up and down the line speaking to each person in turn. Try if you want to, but you cannot open yours eyes." (Each of them tries and can't, they believe they are now under hypnosis and shock themselves into a deep trance).

Then continue up the line saying "And neither can you, or you, or you, etc. In fact the harder you try the more they stick together and the more you enter trance. OK, now everyone, eyes stuck together, but your feet are now stuck to the floor, yes your feet are stuck, rigid to the floor, you cannot move from where you are standing, however hard you try. OK just try and move from where you are standing, but the harder you try the more your feet are stuck solidly to the floor, (continue for a few seconds, then say). Relax, relax, stop trying and relax as you go down completely into trance. In fact, from this moment forward, you will listen to and respond only to my voice. Whenever I say, 1, 2, wide-awake you will instantly be wide-awake, and do whatever I have told you to do. In fact, you'll carry out everything I say as an automatic reflex action. And whenever I say SLEEP, as quickly as this, (snap fingers) a snap of the fingers, you will instantly return into a deep sleep, but each time you re-enter it, for you it will be 100 times deeper and 100 times more enjoyable."

Now whenever you say sleep, they will re-enter the trance state, but each time they will go deeper and deeper into trance. It is for this reason, that the harder to do routines are left until near the end of the act, as by then everyone will have gone in and out of trance several times and now will be so deep that almost anything is possible. A last word here, and that's the simple fact that as a hypnotist who wishes to master rapid and instantaneous inductions, you must have 100% faith and confidence in yourself to be a success.

HYPNOTIZING HECKLERS (CEREBRAL ANOXIA)

Allow me to point out here and now, that this method is included for information purposes only, I would never, ever dream of using it myself and anyone who does try it, does so at their own risk. THIS CAN KILL PEOPLE. BE WARNED. Do you know what Cerabral Anoxia is? Well it usually means a dead person, dead from a lack of oxygen to the brain. You may be asking what has that got to do with you? Well, it is very easy to render someone unconscious by pressure on the Carotoid Arteries, leading to the brain. Even until a few years ago some stupid idiots would pass this off as a quick way to hypnotise people, or a way to hypnotise hecklers, even today, the odd person uses it, but if I were you, I would not even contemplate its use.

Under many byelaws, laws of a country etc. its use is now forbidden. In fact, part of a permission to perform in the UK will read that only psychological methods may be used to induce hypnosis. Well, cerebral anoxia, is what they are referring to here. It is absolutely forbidden to be used in any circumstances, and any reputable person would never dream of using it on someone.

However, should you ever come across a "new method" from someone which resembles this, you will be aware of its existence and avoid it at all costs. Here's how it is done for information purposes only.

Stand in front of your subject, then place the fingers of each hand at the side of their neck, just below the ears and slightly towards their throat. Do this with their head tilted way, way back. Whilst in this position your fingers should now be directly over the large veins in the neck. There is one on each side of their neck, you can often see them, and if not, you can feel them very easily as they pulsate and throb beneath your fingers. Press gently on those veins, but also firmly at the same time. Now ask the person to breath deeply, keep the pressure on until the person goes limp, if the word sleep is shouted at this time, as far as the crowd watching will be concerned you have just placed that person under hypnosis. The moment they start to go limp remove all pressure and allow them to fall to the floor or back into their chair, like a sack of potatoes.

However, should you accidentally keep the pressure on a few seconds later, the person may end up dead or a cabbage for life, with permanent brain damage. You could be arrested for murder, at the least manslaughter. If you did not kill them you can be convicted of attempted murder or assault, with intention to endanger life, or grievous bodily harm. So the golden rule here is ***never, never, ever attempt this technique on anyone at anytime***. Should you ever see someone use this method then please report them and we will investigate, as anyone using this method is not fit to call themselves a hypnotist.

This by the way is what is known in the trade as the "Carotid Artery Induction" and yet as I'm sure you've realised, it has nothing to do with hypnosis and, as such, should not be used.

THE CRAIG WILLIAMS MICROPHONE INDUCTION

This is an induction method, which is excellent and a very good up and coming hypnotist, by the name of Craig Williams, has made it a masterpiece in his hands. Anyway, here goes with the technical inside information on how it's done.

This induction is very quick and looks amazing to the audience, it is usually done whilst the subjects hands are still locked together. You get the subject to stand so that you're both facing each other, and yet, at the same time are both sideways on to the audience so that they get a good view. You tell the subject to stretch out their arms, straight out in front of themselves, this means that the distance between you must be such that it gives them room to do this. You take hold of their right arm with your left hand and make sure that you have a firm grip upon it. In your own right hand, you have got hold of the microphone. You explain that they should stare at the top of the microphone at all times and for no reason whatsoever should they remove their eyes from it.

You also instill into them the belief and expectancy that the moment the microphone taps them on the head they will instantly relax every muscle in their body from the tips of their toes to the tips of their fingers and that their eyes will immediately shut and remain closed until you say otherwise. You then hold the microphone, which is in your right hand up in the air as high as you can comfortably hold it. It is held at a slanted angle, pointing towards the subject's forehead. They have been told to stare at the top of the mike at all times and in order to do this, as the microphone is above their eye line they will have to strain their eyes in order to do this and here, once again, the belief factor will be taken a step further by the strange sensation which the will feel in their eyes.

You then count backwards from three to one and use the standard phrases as you would in the falling backwards induction etc. With of course the addition that the moment the microphone touches their head, they'll fall back into a relaxed dreamy sleeplike state, as you won't let them fall and hurt themselves, and of course their eyes will instantly shut and remain closed until you say otherwise. Then on each descending number you bring the mike closer towards their eyes, so that by the count of one, and the word sleep, the microphone will tap them upon the head and act as the trigger to enter hypnosis.

Also to keep their eyes upon the top of the mike as it gets closer to their head, they will have to tilt their head backwards a little. As they do so, if you take a small step towards them, then they will start to fall backwards anyway, but as you have a firm grip of their arm you don't let them fall, instead you just allow them to lower to the ground in a smooth, steady motion.

With the combination of belief, expectancy, suggestion, eye strain and visual disorientation, plus the added element that they will, if you do this correctly, start to fall backwards anyway, means that you now have in your armoury of techniques, a most powerful and quick induction, which should only take about 30 seconds from start to finish.

Once again, as with all things detailed in this course, experience will teach you more in one show, than any book, video or audiotape ever could. A last point here is, that should you wish to place a person under hypnosis with this method whose hands are not locked together then for the sake of the induction just have them clasp their hands in to the correct position, then, in both cases, the moment they are in trance and lying upon the floor, you can separate their hands for them and so suggest that as you drop their arms down by their sides, they will sink 100 times deeper in trance, so it even has a built in trance deepening method.

THE BODY FLOP INDUCTION

For this dramatic looking induction, your subject is sitting in a chair with a low back. This is so that you will be able to push the upper area of their body forwards by leaning against their back area, so obviously if the chair back was too high then this would not be possible.

They are sitting in the chair, upright with feet and legs together, so that their feet are flat upon the floor, and their arms and hands are rested upon their lap, with palms facing upwards. You then get them to close their eyes and at this point you must be standing directly behind them and the chair in which they are sitting. You place a hand upon each of their shoulders in a relaxed fashion and then say something along these lines.

"OK, (subjects name here) just relax. I'd like you to take nice deep, regular breaths so you can relax a little quicker and I'll keep my hands upon your shoulders so that we can get our rhythm of breathing into alignment. (Here pacing, leading and rapport come into play strongly).

I'm going to count backwards from 3 to 1 and on each descending number, you will find that the deeper you go, the better you will feel, and the better you feel, the deeper you will go. The moment that I say sleep, you will instantly drift into a deeply relaxed sleeplike state. OK (their name) here goes.

Three: With every breath you take, every noise that you hear and every word that I say, you are relaxing more and more as you concentrate only on your rhythm of breathing which is now so deep and regular.

Two: Every muscle in your body becoming so heavy and so tired, each muscle now so limp, so loose and so relaxed, as you go deeper and deeper. And on……

One: Sleep, deeper, deeper and deeper to sleep."

Whilst this is being said you are massaging their shoulders which is a great stress reliever and will help them to relax very quickly, it also acts as a distraction for their mind. As you are coming to the words "And on one", prior to saying the trigger word sleep (drawn out), this is the point of importance. At this moment in time you must rest your chest area against their back lightly, as you lean over them from behind, very smoothly, but very quickly, your hands now move off the subjects shoulders and down to their lap ready for the sudden physical element which shocks them into hypnosis. As you say the word sleep (which is drawn out), your hands lift their arms up off their lap and sweep them off, so that they quickly fall off and down besides them hanging in mid air, at exactly the same time you lean forward so that your chest area pushes the upper area of their body over and their head flops down almost into their own lap.

This, by the way, must be practiced so that you can carry out both actions simultaneously. This is a disorientation method par excellence, as one minute they are being massaged on the shoulders and the next second they are simultaneously flopping forwards with their head falling towards their own lap and their arms have fallen off their lap at exactly the same time. This strange combination of distractions for the mind acts as the trigger and into hypnosis they do go rapidly. To the audience it looks so impressive, as the subject suddenly seems to flop forward in their chair like a rag doll as you command sleep.

THE LOCKED HANDS INDUCTION

This is an instantaneous induction method which one of my hypnotic tutors Mr. Peter J Fox has a great success with and which I have seen him use many times. This is 100% reliant on belief, expectancy and your supreme self-confidence as are all instantaneous induction techniques, which you will ever use.

In practice you get a subject, lock their hands together and just a few seconds later after you've said, "OK, just try and separate your hands, but the harder you try the more they will stick." You suddenly, whilst facing the subject, place your right arm on the back of their neck and pull them gently towards you, with the end result of their head being rested upon your shoulder. This is done at exactly the same moment as you unexpectedly say in a loud and commanding voice, "just sleep and relax, going deeper and deeper to sleep".

As their mind is already on something else, it's already distracted (see keys to hypnosis) and with the shock element of suddenly moving towards you and commanded to sleep and very quickly followed up with commands to go deeper etc., it also acts as a disorientation and confusion method. The moment they do have their head against your shoulder, you must follow up immediately with a quick trance deepening method, as explained elsewhere.

Then you awaken them, get them to sit down and the moment their bum touches the seat you click your fingers in front of their eyes and say sleep, and back under they will go. This induction works because of the shock element being so unexpected at the time it occurs and as they have been trying to separate their hands with no success they have no reason to disbelieve any further commands as such they will be acted upon instantly.

THE HANDWAVE INSTANT INDUCTION

This is the method which I have both used myself and have also seen Paul McKenna use with great success. You ask you're on stage subjects, if any of them have been hypnotised before. Those who answer yes are asked when and by whom, you remember this information and then place 2 or 3 people into a trance with inductions such as falling backwards etc. During this, the people who have been hypnotised before are watching and this takes the belief and expectancy concept one step further. As, don't forget, it's easier to hypnotise someone rapidly when they've just seen you place other people into trance, and as such know that you can do the same to them. You then return to the subjects who have been placed under hypnosis before and ask three quick questions.

1   Do you wish to enter this lovely dreamy state of hypnosis tonight? (YES)
2   Can you remember that the moment you enter hypnosis, your eyes close, and your heavy head falls forward onto your chest and you breathe deeply and listen only to the sound of my voice? (YES)
3   Well (their name) in that case, may I have your permission to use the fastest form of hypnosis known to man, to make you instantly re-enter this lovely dreamy sleep like state? (YES)

The moment he/she has said yes to answer all three questions, you immediately, without any time delay at all, so that it comes as a complete shock, just do as follows:

"Well in that case (their name)just sleep and relax."

As you say this, your right hand is lifted up in front of their face and as you command sleep, in a raised tone of voice, your right hand moves in a downwards motion in front of their face, so that the fingers are outstretched and move down from above head, past their eyes and downwards, which in itself, is a powerful non verbal suggestion of sleep. It also gives them something to psychologically connect entering the trance state to and something for them to believe in. Remember, that as they've been under hypnosis before, they know exactly how to react and your three questions prior to the instant induction have done two things.

A. It has psychologically conditioned them to enter the trance state immediately that you say the word sleep.

B. It has acted as a brief reminder to them of how to act in trance. If they have been under before and have answered yes honestly to the three questions that you ask, then you can be sure that they will instantly enter trance.

Someone who has been hypnotised before is, by far the best type of person on whom to do instantaneous inductions, as they know how to act in trance and their belief is 100% complete, as they have experienced it first hand. Also, as a general rule of thumb, the more recently they have been hypnotised, the more easily that they can be made re-enter trance. I'm sure you can now see why you need to have enormous confidence in your abilities in order to make instant inductions work.

HANDSHAKE INSTANT INDUCTION

Before I describe how this induction is presented, allow me to make this point. As long as the subjects' belief and expectancy in your powers is totally 100% complete and as long as you truly have tremendous confidence in your skills and this is transmitted to the subjects through your actions etc., they will then both expect what you do to work and also know that you expect it to work. As such the Handwave and Handshake instant inductions can be done without asking any questions. In fact, the moment a subject said that they had been under before, then you could just say:

"Well in that case, (their name) Just sleep and relax"

The hand movement, handshake or whatever was being used as the trigger would be just the same and of course, your voice must sound commanding and demanding. However, the point which I am trying to make here is, done with belief, they will instantly re-enter trance without any additional psychological conditioning. This even applies to "Hypnotic Virgins" who have never, ever entered trance before, as long as their belief is total, then when you command them to sleep, they would do so however the induction had been presented as it's just the trigger word, sleep, which they expect to hear to make them enter the state and, if this is what they believe, then for them, it's very true indeed. You of course would only use instant inductions on the most susceptible subjects (see elsewhere) this means the odds are then even greater in your favour of it working.

Anyway, to the handshake induction. This really is as simple as it sounds, you approach a subject who you have observed will be very susceptible after having unlocked their shaking hands etc. You ask their name, and upon their reply you extend your right hand as though ready to shake hands as you say:

"Nice to meet you (their name)"
Still holding their hand as though ready to shake hands you quickly say
"Have you ever been hypnotised before (their name)?"
Then, whatever answer he/she gives you, immediately follow up by saying
"Is it OK with you (their name) if I hypnotise you right now, instantly?"
If they answer yes, it's an easy subject and all you need do is just say
"In that case (their name), just sleep."

As you say the word sleep, you lift their arm into the air slightly, and then move it down rapidly towards their lap, as you command in a loud voice, "sleep." This hand (downwards) movement acts as a non verbal suggestion of sleep and that's why this is called the handshake induction, as the audience just sees you go up to a subject, shake that persons hand and say "sleep" and at that moment the person has gone under your spell. Incidentally, I have found from experience, that the downwards motion of the handshake is more effective when made on an outbreath of the subject (as they breathe out), all suggestions of relaxation and sleep are more effective also when made as the subject breathes out, as this psychologically implies letting go etc.

This induction, can of course, with confidence and experience, be done in the way which is used by experienced hypnotists. In our version, we simply go up to a subject, ask their name, the moment they reply, we extend our hand and clasp theirs and then do the handshake motion, as we say "Ok (their name), just sleep and relax." This is all so sudden for the subject, that it shocks them into trance and they connect entry of trance to the handshake. Lastly, if the person says no when you ask if they will allow you to hypnotise them quickly, you simply reply by saying "Well in that case (their name), I can't be bothered wasting my time on you. Sleep". Because he feels he has one up on you by saying no, he suddenly feels small when you say you can't be bothered wasting your time with him and here, the shock/surprise factor comes in, as you shake his hand and in a raised voice command him to sleep. As with all instant inductions, they do work but only if you have enough confidence.

CAN'T BE BOTHERED WITH YOU INDUCTION

This induction only works, because what you do comes as a real shock to the subject and because you do it with such faith, confidence and conviction, that they will instantly enter the trance. They sense your confidence and as such, belief and expectancy again comes into play. They would of course have just seen you place other people into trance and will be waiting, anticipating, almost rearing, when you'll come and do the same thing to them.

Proceed like this. You do an induction such as the falling backwards technique and prior to this you've had several susceptible subjects stand directly in front of their chairs, which you've said they will sit in. They are standing right next to the chair, so that when made to fall back they will fall into the chair, and not fall and hurt themselves. You have just placed someone into trance, and now walk along the line as if deciding whom to pick to hypnotise next. As you do this you must stare directly into each person's eyes and send the fear of God into them. You walk along the line and when you reach the subject whom you are going to use this induction upon, you stop for a moment which you did not do with the others, you say nothing and just stare at him for a couple of seconds, this will scare him to death, he will be so relieved 2 seconds later when you continue along the line, that he will relax more, and let his defences down. You then come back along the line, and the moment you reach him, your right palm is pushed against his forehead, and he falls back into his chair as you simultaneously say in a loud and commanding voice. "Oh, I can't be bothered with you, Sleep." This will come as such a shock, especially when he thought he had escaped.

It works due to shock, belief and expectancy, in short, it's the power of the moment and the power of the unexpected which will make him close his eyes as he's seen the others do (he's been conditioned), and he then enters trance. Although I shall give you several more presentation examples for inductions, the bottom line is, that if belief and expectancy are 100% total, then any trigger can be used to make them enter the trance instantly. Remember this and you can always adapt to suit any venue, audience or show situation.

AEROPLANE INDUCTION

The moment you have just placed someone into trance, you turn to the person sitting next to him or her and say, "you wouldn't do anything daft like that, would you?" They, of course say no. You then tell them to watch the microphone as the moment is taps them upon the head, their heavy eyes will shut tightly, their head will fall forwards onto their chest and they'll breathe deeply as they go to sleep. You then hold the mike in front of their face as if it is about to tap their head, then suddenly, for a few seconds prior to unexpected tapping them upon the head with the mike and commanding sleep, you move the mike up, down, sideways etc. and make funny noises as if the mike is an airplane. This will cause the audience to laugh and the person upon the stage to think you're crazy, but as the beliefs already there and he expects to go under when the mike hits his head, guess what? As such he will go under.

This "aeroplane" gag, can also be used when the person has already been placed under hypnosis and you just want to add a little variation, so, instead of using the trigger word sleep for them to re enter trance, you use the aeroplane induction which takes only a few seconds and helps add an extra little comedy elements to the proceedings.

Another comical way to make two people re enter trance, is to apparently knock their two heads together and then they go back to sleep. Of course, the real reason they've gone back under is because you've used a stage whisper to put them back under by quickly and audibly to them (but not through the mike) saying sleep. To the audience however it looks hilarious, as you appear to knock two people's heads together and they then re enter trance instantly.

Yet another comical way you make them re enter trance is to say to them "You wouldn't go to sleep if you slapped yourself across the face would you?" (They say no) "Of course you wouldn't. I'll tell you what though, give it a try." He then slaps himself across the face and as he does, so instantly re enters trance, he would do anyway, but if in doubt, use a stage whisper to say sleep to ensure that he goes under as he slaps his own face. These few ideas are all very simple to put into use and all looks hilarious to the audience and as entertainment is the key thing on stage you are onto a winner here

THE FINGER STARE INDUCTION

This is also a very quick induction and should take no more than 40 to 50 seconds to have the person enter a deep trance state.

They should be sitting on a chair, feet together firmly flat on the floor, upright and looking directly at you, the hypnotist. Their arms and hands being rested upon their lap with palms upwards, you then proceed as follows. You extend your own right arm and then extend your own right hand index finger, whilst the rest of the hand remains like a clenched fist. This extended finger is then held slightly above the level of the subject's eyes and a few inches away from them so that they must strain their eyes to look upwards at your fingertip.

You explain that you want them to stare at all times at your fingertip. They must not move their head, only their eyes in order to follow the route which your fingertip will take. When you are sure that they have understood this full you say something such as:

"In a few moments, I shall count from 3 to 1, and by the count of one you'll notice your eyelids will be so heavy and tired, in fact the harder you try to keep them open the more they will want to remain shut. The moment that I say sleep, and tap you upon the head, you'll instantly drift into a deep, relaxing, dreamlike state. So on 3, the deeper you go, the better you will feel, and the better you feel, the deeper you will go. On 2, you can feel your eyes starting to strain as they get so heavy and so tired, it's so much easier to just relax and let go. And on 1, eyes closing tightly now, as with every breath you take, every noise you hear and every word I say, you go deeper and deeper to sleep. Now that you're asleep, in a few moments I am going to tap you on the head. The moment I do, you'll sink instantly 100 times deeper into trance, so just sleep (here head is tapped) and go deeper."

As they start off staring at your fingertip, which is above their eye line, the key here is to strain their eyes as much as possible, as quickly as possible. To do this in a steady motion, during the count from 3 down to 1, you move your fingers both nearer to them (they go cross eyed etc) and at the same time in a downwards motion. So on 3 it starts above their eye line, on 2 in line with their nose and 1 in line with their chin, which means by this time, as they will still be trying to keep their eyes on your finger, their eye lids will have shut naturally anyway, and because their eyes have been very strained, it's so much easier to leave them shut as you say sleep. Without pausing you follow this up immediately, with the quick trance deepening method, of telling them that the moment you tap their head they will go 100 times deeper into trance, you then tap their head and remove your finger quickly, as you say sleep and go deeper. This usually has the effect of pushing their head back a bit, they resist and as such push forward onto your fingertip with their forehead and then you suddenly remove your finger as you say sleep and go deeper, which means that their head then falls down onto their chest. If this does not occur, you can literally just place your hand upon their shoulder, as you say, "and your head is now so heavy, it falls down onto your chest." Whilst saying this, you simply use your fingers as a lever against the front and back or their neck to make them move their head down against their chest. In practice, the whole induction takes between 40 to 60 seconds maximum.

THE SWAYING HANDCLAP INDUCTION

For this induction you have the subject standing just in front of their chair. Their legs and feet are together, hands down by their sides, eyes shut and they must breathe deeply in through their nose and out through their mouth. You then say something such as:

"As you stand here, with your eyes closed, you notice that with each and every breath that you take your body is relaxing more each second that passes by. I'd like you to relax completely, so I'm going to gently sway you backwards and forwards in rhythm with your rate of breathing." (This you then actually do) "So breathe in and out, in and out."(They are swayed back and forward in time with their breathing) "Don't forget that the moment I tell you to, your whole body will relax, your eyes will remain tightly closed and you'll enter a sleep like state."

Throughout all this talking, you've been progressively swaying them further backwards and forwards, so much so, that if you were to set them off swaying backwards again and did not stop them falling with your hand, then they would indeed, fall backwards into their chair, or at least it would be very difficult to stop themselves. You capitalise upon this fact, and the moment you've said, "and you'll enter a sleep like state," you have timed this as you will be ready to set them back on their swaying backwards direction movement. The moment they are moving backwards, you clap your hands by the person's ear, as you simultaneously and very loudly command sleep. This is immediately followed in a quieter tone of voice by, "and going deeper, and deeper to sleep." As you clap in the direction they are going anyway, the sheer shock of the noise knocks them off balance and they'll fall all the way back into their chair, it also quite literally shocks them into hypnosis.

THE PROGRESSIVE RELAXATION INDUCTION

This induction, as the title suggests, is a slower, more progressive style. It is the type of induction which can be suitably used in the therapists consulting rooms, as well as upon the performance stage. In a stage situation, it is usually used to hypnotise a group of several people simultaneously so although it takes longer, you are actually placing several people into trance at once, therefore overall, there isn't too much difference time wise. For these styles of inductions the subjects must be sitting on their chairs, feet together and flat on the floor, with hands and arms resting upon their laps, with palms facing upwards and they should be sitting up straight, as comfortably as is possible. You will find that the wording for such an induction (with added subliminal effects) is in the verbal psychology chapter of this book, and basically, it just relies upon the principles of rapport, observation, recognition and leadership, which are also described in full elsewhere.

What you say to the subject/s will be different each time and dictated by the way in which the subject/s react to you suggestions. (Always use what the majority do as your guide). Of course the standard phrases, which all hypnotists use at some time, and are included at the end of this chapter, will come in extremely useful during a progressive relaxation induction. Follow all that you've been taught, and the example induction as given in the earlier chapter and you will be able to carry out a progressive relaxation induction, both in the therapy room and upon the stage. As you will by now know, the basic techniques of what makes an induction work and of how rapport, observation, recognition and leadership dictate what you say to the subjects in a progressive relaxation induction, I will now give a few examples of additional distractions which can be offered to the subjects mind to promote the onset of trance more rapidly.

THE SIDNEY FLOWERS BLINK METHOD OF P.R.I.

This is in essence a progressive relaxation induction (P.R.I), which is also combined with a method to strain the subject's eyes. The subjects are seated as for other P.R.I.'s and are told to focus upon a spotlight, or a point on the ceiling, which they are not to take their eyes off (this also helps strain the eyes). You then explain that you will be counting, and on each number everyone will get more and more relaxed, and within a few short moments, everyone will find it so much easier to let their eyelids, which will become so heavy and tired, to shut, rather than trying to keep them open. You also explain that on each odd number as you count, they should close their eyes and on each even number, they should re open their eyes. For example:

On 1…….. eyes shut
On 2…….. eyes open
On 3…….. eyes shut
On 4…….. eyes open
On 5…….. eyes shut
On 6…….. eyes open
On 7…….. eyes shut (etc)

So that on each alternate number, from one they have to shut their eyes and then re-open them on the next even number count. Combine this with the fact they are staring at one point all the time and I'm sure, you can understand why their eyes become strained so quickly. And as the littler muscles in the corner of the eyes do become tired, they will find it much easier to allow their eyes to remain shut. You use your normal patter, which is formulated at the time through a combination of the standard phrases and the things that come to mind, due to rapport, observation, recognition and leadership. Obviously you will also keep suggesting that their eyes are becoming so tired and that their eyelids are becoming so heavy, so tired, so limp, loose and relaxed, as each second passes by. By the count of thirty, most, if not all people, will have had their eyes closed for a while already, however, if their should still be the odd one or two with eyes open, this is now the time to command everyone to close their eyes, and you then proceed directly into your trance deepening patter, to take them all to a deeper level of trance, in a very short space of time.

SPOTLIGHT EYESTRAIN P.R.I.

To cut a long story short, the principles used are identical to any other P.R.I., except, that here, it is very bright spotlights that strain their eyes and disorientate them, as you deliver your suggestions of relaxation as usual. The lights should be in the flies (the area above your head at front of stage) or front of house. For the consulting room, it can simply be a spotlight mounted on a wall. In either case, the lights should be above the subject's normal eye levels, so that they must strain their eyes in the first place in order to see the light. Add to this the intensity of the bright white spotlight itself and maybe now you can see why they become lethargic, their eyes glaze and then close and they do exactly as you say.

MUSCULAR RELAXATION P.R.I.

Very briefly, the principles are the same except here, they start with their eyes closed and you suggest that, as you mention different areas of their body, they are to imagine the muscles in that area of their body as ropes tied together in knots, and as they mentally undo the knots in their mind so that they become separate lengths of rope, so, in reality, all the muscles in that bodily area, will become so limp, so loose and so relaxed, as they also become so heavy and so tired. You start with their feet, and move around their body, getting them to imagine the same thing happening for their ankles, lower leg area, knees, upper leg area, hips and thighs, groin area, stomach, chest, back, spine, shoulders, shoulder blades, the whole arm area, wrist, hands, fingertips, neck, jaw, cheeks, brow muscles etc.

Each time getting them to visualise the relaxation and each time telling them that as the knots untie and the ropes become separate, so in reality all the muscles in that area, will instantly become so limp, so loose, so relaxed, so heavy and so tired, with each and every breath that they take.

You also, at various intervals along the way, insert some of the standard phrases, such as "The deeper you go, the better you feel and the better you feel, the deeper you will go." By the time you've gone round their entire body in this vein and have reached their heads, you will find that they are in a deep trance, and at this point, you would immediately deepen the trance further in the standard way. At the end, you would then say "Sleep" firmly and implant your post-hypnotic suggestions. This induction when done nice and slowly, which is why it's called a P.R.I., should take between six to ten minutes, dependent upon your speed of delivery. Remember that the techniques, which you have been taught in this course in other chapters, can also be combined into any basic induction outline, which I may give now or later.

THE COUNTING BACKWARDS INDUCTION

To do this induction upon the stage to best effect, you should have your voice recorded onto the background music, which you would use for any normal style of induction. Upon this voice on music tape, you must say something such as that in the example induction given in the verbal psychology chapter. For example:

"As you stand up straight upon the stage, or sit comfortably in your chair, you will retain perfect balance at all times. From this moment forward I'd like you to listen only to the sound of my voice, and you'll find that with every breath that you take, every noise you hear and every word I say, that you will go deeper and deeper to sleep.

Now, you don't know if you will go into a trance quickly, or if it will take some time. Really enjoy all those pleasant changes that are occurring in your consciousness."

YOU THEN CONTINUE, AS PER EXAMPLE IN VERBAL PSYCHOLOGY CHAPTER.

The whole induction, which should be changed by making the example of how to count backwards in their mind longer, so that you keep setting the pace of counting in their mind until you've gone back to 180 and then it's left to them to continue doing so in their minds, which distracts their conscious mind, so that all suggestions given go directly into the subconscious mind. Your pace of wording should be such that it suggests relaxation and then you end the induction as per the example in verbal psychology chapter. These are all dubbed over the induction music and reverbs is added to the voice, with an occasional "sleep" or "relax" added between each count backwards, to add an element of confusion too. This whole induction should last no more than five minutes in total, from start to finish and is "overdubbed" onto the induction music such as Jean Michelle Jarres "OXYGENE" or TRANQUILITY, which is a tape available from new age supply centres. This tape is set ready in the player and the moment the lights dim, as will be explained in a moment, is the exact moment when the tape is started.

Now imagine this, you have completed a few quick inductions and placed a couple of people into trance, but still have about 60 or more people upon the theatre stage, who have come up to have their hands separated. So why not try to hypnotise them all at once and then base your selection of the 12 best subjects, upon the 33 observable signs of trance and a few quick text routines?

To do this, you proceed as follows:

You ask everyone who is sitting down and not already in trance, to sit up straight in their chairs, feet together and flat upon the floor, with hands and arms rested upon their laps with palms facing upwards. Anyone who is standing up and not already in trance is told to stand with feet slightly apart, so that they stand firm and steady, hands down by their sides (unless still locked together) and then everyone in the audience is told to remain silent for the next few minutes whilst people enter the trance state or hypnosis, and then the fun will begin.

Everyone upon the stage is then told to close his or her eyes and listen to everything that you say and then imagine it as 100% total reality. You also say that should you touch them upon the shoulder at anytime they will pay special attention to what you say and ignore what you tell everyone else, whilst still counting backwards in their minds. At this moment, the stage lighting grows dim, so that the figures of people in chairs, or standing up can be seen, but only just, everything appears as a silhouette. This dim atmosphere in itself helps to promote the onset of trance. It also means, that for the next five minutes, whilst the recorded induction plays, you can go around the stage (with your radio mike switched off) pretending to talk into the microphone. The audience will assume what they hear coming out of the speakers at the time is what you are saying live, there and then. In actual fact, you are either just miming and know that the studio recorded induction sounds better than you could ever do it live, or you are saying other things to separate subjects whose shoulder you have got your hand upon.

I will leave you to work some of this out for yourself, but they've already been told, if you look back through what I've said at the start, that should I touch them upon the shoulder they will ignore what you say to everyone else and will know you are speaking to them and them only. As such, they will then take special notice of all you say. This means that you can touch people on the shoulder, talk to them and as the radio mike is switched off, the audience will be unable to hear you and will assume that what you are saying, is what they hear coming through the speakers. This means, everyone is being hypnotised, to a certain degree, just by the voice upon the tape and for dramatic effect, you can go up to those you feel are very susceptible, place your hand upon their shoulder and speak audibly into their ear to do a falling backwards induction on those standing up, or a body flop induction upon those who are sitting down.

As the audience will only be able to see an outline of each person, it will look most impressive to them as they listen to the induction, which they assume is you speaking live, to also see people falling backwards onto the stage or flopping forwards in their chairs like rag dolls, it will look most impressive indeed. And the moment the "subliminal" style induction recorded on the audio tape reaches the point where the lights on the stage go brighter, the tape will now be playing just relaxation music, the audience will be amazed to see people scattered all over the stage, and you now go into your group deepening immediately, this being done for real through the radio mike, which by this time will have been switched back on.

The post hypnotic suggestions are then given to everyone and lastly, in order to narrow down the onstage 60 people to the best 12 subjects, you go through a quick process of mind imagination screening, which is also quite entertaining to the audience, as well as serving it's required purpose. Those people who are obviously not in trance are dismissed immediately, and then simple suggestions are given, such as, it's a cold day, a hot day, you're milking a cow, you're a washing machine etc. You will be able to tell visually, by the subjects reactions to these simple, yet fairly amusing tests, who will make the best subjects, and of course these are the people who are kept on stage, the rest being slowly dismissed, once fully out of trance.

So, in other words, the show begins and continues, whilst the selection of good subjects and return of not so good subjects is still being made. This means that the fun, entertaining routines start a lot quicker and from the point of view of the audience, the show is much slicker and quicker than many I could mention.

If you ever get the chance to see Paul McKenna work live, in a large capacity venue, then you'll know exactly what I mean. You, at the end of all this will already have extracted many laughs from the audience, who will be thoroughly enjoying themselves and also will have selected your best subjects for use throughout the remainder of the evening.

So, here for your reference purposes, is the running order of events, which would make up a very professional and entertaining hypnotic stage show.

1   Intro music with voice over introduction recorded upon it.
2   Play on "Theme Music" as you walk upon the stage and take a bow.
3   Your opening comedy lines and talk about hypnosis.
4   The locked hands test, with suitable background music.
5   People have got to the stage area, whilst loud and exciting music plays.
6   Get to know the people etc. and establish rapport.
7   Do a quick induction, or two, such as falling back etc. to get about five people into trance very quickly and to establish total belief and expectancy.
8   Then go into the "subliminal" induction on tape procedure as detailed above, whilst you also do several more instant inductions on suitable subjects, whilst the tape with your voice upon it plays.

9   Group deepening of induction is done in normal way.
10   The major post hypnotic suggestions are implanted into everyone's mind.

11   Everyone is awoken and obviously unresponsive subjects returned to seats.
12   Everyone left is then put under again, at same time, by just saying sleep, and using the handsweep techniques below.
13   The mind/imagination screening begins and good subjects selected.

THE HANDSWEEP TECHNIQUE

This is a quick way to return everyone to the eyes closed hypnotic state once the major post hypnotic suggestion has been implanted in the subject's minds. It saves the time needed to go to each person in turn and snap you fingers prior to saying sleep, it also looks a little more dramatic than just facing everyone and saying "OK everyone, I'm talking to you all now, so just Sleep" (This is said as you snap your fingers in a downwards movement, facing the whole group, they then all go back under at the same time).

To do this, stand facing the audience and suddenly, you do a 360 degree turn on the spot, rather like a dancer would do and as you turn your hand is open, fingers outstretched and you say sleep (drawn out), so, that as you turn, each and very subject sees your outstretched palm pass by their point of vision as they hear command sleep and they all return to the eyes closed hypnotic state immediately. It's quick and very impressive.

Of course, anyone who does not react immediately is told to sleep and if they don't react this time they are, of course, dismissed as an unsuitable subject. This should not worry you however, as by this stage of the show, all the onstage subjects should be real diamonds and worth their weight in gold many times over. From a time length point of view the running order I've just mentioned would be as follows:

1   Intro music and voice over introduction to show (3 mins)
2   Play on music, enter stage and take a bow etc   (3 mins)
3   Opening comedy lines and talk on Hypnosis   (5 mins)
4   Locked hands test   (4 mins)
5   Getting people on stage as music plays   (3 mins)
6   Getting to know them/rapport/one liners   (3 mins)

7   About 6 instant inductions, with more one liners(5 mins)
8   Group subliminal induction of everyone at once   (5 mins)
9   Group deepening of trance   (1.5mins)
10   Group major post hypnotic suggestions   (1.5mins)
11   Return those not under to audience   (1 min)
12   Put all group under with handsweep and oneliners(1 min)
13   Start the first sketch/imaginations screening (30secs)

So, from the point when first piece of music begins for the start of show, up until the point where everyone is under and the first comedy routine begins takes:

A TOTAL TIME LENGTH ON THEATRE SHOWS OF THIRTY SIX MINUTES

Which, done in first half of the show, leaves about twenty four minutes for comedy routines, so that the interval comes one hour into the evenings' events. The interval in a theatre show realistically ends up being 20 to 30 minutes and then the second half of the show is done, which also keeps to the one hour each way format, this makes the complete theatre show, including intervals, two and a half hours inclusive, which for a stage hypnotism show is standard practice these days.

In the second half of the show you have, of course, only to come back on stage to do a few one liners (say 4 minutes) then you say "come and join the party" at which point all the subjects race back to the stage (2 minutes), you return them all to sleep after questioning them about the comedy routines they are still doing, which they did during the interval in and around the audience (4 minutes). This means 10 minutes into the second half, the show starts again properly, leaving 50 minutes in which to do comedy sketches. Of course, if you do the guaranteed handclasp text and the world record induction of over 12 people in 60 seconds, then this will take up about another eight minutes of the show. The end result being, however, that you have more volunteers to use if you wish. Obviously, the show would end by all suggestions being removed from the subject's minds and then them being awoken properly.

Please note, this is just an example running order, you are free to devise your own and indeed, I would advise you to do so. The point I am trying to make is this though. The hypnotic induction can be made as much a part of the show as the comedy routines you get the subjects to do. In fact, the general public is truly amazed watching people being placed under hypnosis rapidly, it does not bore them, so have no worries there. In a club or pub show you would have a smaller audience and you'd have less people to deal with, as result the whole procedure being much quicker. Ideally, in pubs and clubs, you want everyone under hypnosis with 20 minutes of your act starting, so that there is 40 minutes left for the actual comedy sketch routine section of your one hour spot, which incidentally seems to be the standard time required in pubs and clubs these days.

I hope this has not only given you an excellent idea for use of the verbal psychology induction, but also, I hope it has given you a better understanding in the way a hypnotic show is engineered and routined to make a "whole" that is both fascinating and entertaining whilst looking slick and professional.

THE LITTLE BOY INDUCTION

Yes, yet another different method of induction. However, I hope you have noticed that with all of the methods I've detailed, belief and expectancy in the subjects mind is the biggest factor which works in our favour.

This is a method which I would only use upon a very small in height subject, so that I could make a logical reason for what follows by delivering a few one liners aimed at how small the person is, and how they remind me of a little boy.

I would stand upon a chair, with the subject on the left hand side of me, with their right arm stretched up into the air, as high as they can get it. I would then take hold of their upstretched arm with both of my hands and tell them to stare forwards, preferably at a bright white spotlight, otherwise at a small point high up on the wall facing them. They are to stare at this point at all times, and you are now ready for the induction. You explain that you will count backwards from 3 to 1, and that, by the count of 1, when you say sleep, they will find it so much easier to just relax every muscle in their entire body, let their heavy eyelids shut and continue to breathe deeply and regularly.

"So on 3, as you stare intently at the bright white light, your eyes begin to strain and you just want to fall into a beautifully relaxed state. On 2, you can almost feel your legs becoming so weak beneath you, that you feel as though you will fall to the floor in a heap. But I won't let you fall and hurt yourself, instead I'll just let you fall into a beautifully relaxed state. And on 1, you can feel yourself falling to the floor, your legs are like jelly and cannot hold your weight as you sleep. (the word sleep is drawn out.)

As this is said, all the way through, in time with their breathing, you pull their arm upwards as much as you can on their in breath and then let it go slack again on their outbreath. This does two things, it acts as a disorientation method and a distraction for their conscious mind and also, for some strange reason, it blurs your vision. There is a pressure point in the armpit, which if hit hard, can make you pass out or vomit. Well, obviously, we are using nowhere near that kind of pressure and the pressure which we are using is indirect, as opposed to being directly on the pressure point. I believe it is possible however, that this indirect pressure to the point in question is responsible for the blurring of vision, combine this with the straining of the eyes caused by the bright white spot light and the power of suggestion and that's where the disorientation element comes in, it's also the reason why they end up collapsing in a heap to the floor when you command sleep, which, as you imagine, looks highly impressive to the audience.

What I have said may seem hard to believe, in this case I leave it to your experience to give you a true picture. But, I do know personally from use of this method that, if done correctly, it most definitely does work. This method although effective, is really just included for completeness; although I'm sure at some point in the future a performer will make a masterpiece of it.

100% CONFUSION INDUCTION

We have already established earlier in this course, that confusion and disorientation, play a large part in the success of all hypnotic inductions. Well, now to an induction which relies totally on confusion and disorientation, I will only explain how to do this induction briefly, because if you've already really studied the rest of this course, then you will be more than capable of working the rest out for yourself. Basically, you would proceed with saying things such as:

"Just notice how your left hand is hot and your right hand cold, whilst your left leg is light and your right leg heavy. Now experience the sensation of your hot, right hand becoming cold and your cold, left hand becoming hot, as your heavy, left leg becomes lighter and your light, right leg is becoming heavier all the time."

You would continue in this vein for a while and then suddenly inject your suggestions of relaxation and sleep amongst the illogical confusing statements, which confuse their conscious mind, as one moment a hand is meant to be hot then it's cold etc., all this becomes too much and within a short time the conscious mind shuts down and doesn't even bother to analyse the rubbish which you are presenting to it. It all goes directly into the subconscious mind of the subject and disguised suggestions of relaxation and sleep are then enacted upon. The rest, as I am sure you can work out for yourself, to finish however, here's an example of how to start adding sleep/relaxation suggestions to the confusion script.

"And notice now, how as your hot right arm tingles and your cold left leg feels heavy, that you relax more and more and your heavy eyelids start to shut."

SHOCK HYPNOSIS

This is just literally finding a most susceptible subject, whose hands have locked together well, observing their body language to check that they feel uneasy upon the stage, and then suddenly and most unexpectedly going up to them and both loudly and firmly, shouting sleep into their ear as your right arm pulls them back from a standing position to the floor, which disorientates them. Or you can literally just throw them back into a chair, as you make the command sleep, the end result will be the same.

I have seen a very well known adult stage hypnotist do this very successfully, on a regular basis, but believe me, it takes enormous confidence and works because you shock the person into hypnosis, you literally scare the person so much by your sudden actions, that they do everything you say and are in fact then scared to do otherwise.

I'll end this explanation of "shock hypnosis" by telling you how one well known stage hypnotist uses this method. To the audience it looks as though Mr? just walks up to the subject, who is staring at their shaking locked hands and knocks them on the back of the neck with the flat part of his right palm, as he commands in a loud authoritative voice "sleep". The subject's legs then fly up into the air and they literally fall in a backwards motion to the floor. Yes, your absolutely right, it looks very impressive, one moment they are standing up, the word sleep is said, and suddenly their legs fly up into the air and they fall down to the floor like a sack of potatoes, asleep.

Well, how? Firstly, let me say, that this is not a method which I condone or recommend any one to use, as it's very easy for someone to get hurt doing this. However, for information purposes only, here's what you do.

Your subject would be standing on the right hand side of you, staring at their hands, which are shaking (sign of good subject), you then simultaneously bring your right hand up, flat against the back of their neck and your right foot literally just knocks the back of their ankles very firmly, causing their legs to fly up into the air and, as such, they'd normally fall straight to the floor with a thud and hurt themselves. You however, have got your right hand on the back of their neck and can "cushion" their fall to the floor. To the audience however, all they will ever remember seeing is a person standing upright one moment, who, the next minute, goes flying in the air as you tap their neck and command them to go to sleep. It should go without saying that this is a very dangerous stunt to use and my advice would be not to use it, anyone doing so, does so at their own risk.

Obviously, as you knock their legs from beneath them is the moment when you shout sleep, which acts as misdirection so that people do not realise what you've done. As I am sure you can imagine the shock of hearing the word sleep shouted into your ear is very extreme to say the least, let alone the shock of flying up into the air and then down to the floor. This is a very extreme form of disorientation and the rest, once again, is down to belief and expectancy. Impressive as this looks, and despite the fact I have, in the early days of my career, used this technique, USE AT YOUR OWN RISK.

THE RUBBER LEGS INDUCTION

To the audience, this induction appears as follow:

The audience see 12 or more people standing on various parts of the stage and all are staring at their hands, which are locked together and shaking violently. As you verbally suggest that the people are relaxing etc., people start to fall to the floor "asleep" all over the stage, almost as if their legs had turned to rubber beneath them. Yes, just imagine that, you are standing nowhere near them at the time, but they all start to collapse to the floor "asleep" as if their legs have turned to jelly or rubber. As I'm sure you can imagine this looks a real showstopper and absolutely unbelievable from the audiences' point of view. So how is this miraculous induction done, I can hear you say? Well, you would proceed as follows:

You choose the 12 most susceptible subjects from those whose hands locked together and they are spread out around the stage, so that there is room surrounding each of them when they fall to the floor "asleep". They are all told to stand so that their right foot is on the left hand side of their left foot and both feet are flat on the floor. By that, I mean their feet are crossed over and are placed next to each other in this position, whilst flat upon the floor. They then have to stare directly at their locked hands, which by now are shaking violently. Once all of the people are in this position, you explain that this is one of the fastest and most powerful forms of Hypnosis known to mankind. Very loud and exciting music, such as the Bladerunner theme, or music from the Witches of Eastwick, begins to play at this point. As this music is loud and exciting and as we know excitement breeds excitement, the onstage volunteers will be getting more apprehensive all the time about what is to occur (belief/expectancy). As you will have, if you're sensible, already placed a couple of people under hypnosis with quick inductions, their belief and expectancy levels will be high and working in your favour. The lighting should also change to suggest that something dramatic is about to occur. Verbally, you now suggest to all the subjects who are standing in this strange position, something along the following lines:

"I'm going to count backwards from 3 to 1, and as I do, many of you will find that as you stare directly at your hands, which will continue to shake more violently, the harder you try to stop them, the more they will shake.

In fact, the more they shake, the more you will be going deeper to sleep with every breath you take, every noise you hear and with every word I say. Many of you will find your legs will turn to jelly and give way beneath you, when this happens you will not fall and hurt yourself; you'll just fall into a beautifully relaxed, deep, dreamy, sleep like state. You'll enjoy every minute of it, as the deeper you go, the better you will feel and the better you feel, the deeper you will go to sleep."

At this point you then turn to the audience and say. "Well, ladies and gentlemen, be prepared to be amazed, as this one of the most powerful and dramatic forms of Hypnosis know to mankind. Your attention please".

(Turn back to the subjects and say) "OK, now everyone, so on 3, already many of you will be experiencing that rather strange sensation as your whole body becomes so relaxed and as you stare intently at your hands, your legs are becoming like rubber, so weak they cannot hold your body up any longer and you just want to go to sleep. And on, 2, as you hands shake so violently now, you notice also that your whole body begins to sway. You cannot keep your balance, you can feel yourself falling, as your legs become more weak and rubbery with every breath you take, every noise you hear and every word that I say, so it is so much easier to relax and sleep. And on 1, your whole body so relaxed now, it's hard to keep your balance, now all you want to do is relax and enjoy that feeling of serenity as your legs turn to jelly, as your whole body begins to sway, as you feel yourself falling and you all go to sleep (say sleep in drawn out fashion).

At this point, anyone who may be standing up is approached from the rear, so that they don't see you coming and you hit the upper side area of their right leg sharply with the side of your hand, as if doing a karate chop. This is enough to knock them totally off balance, so that they do fall to the floor as you once again shout sleep and shock them into hypnosis. Most people will have gone under and fallen to the floor by then however and of course, this additional "push" can be given to those that you feel may be resisting a little, as you actually deliver the count back with patter from 3 to 1. If you are unsure that anyone would fall to the floor, then stand as I've detailed, place your hands as if locked together, and shake them around violently whilst staring at them as the onstage subjects will be doing, I'm sure you'll see that in less than a minute you will fall over too.

Then see what happens when someone knocks you on the side of the leg as detailed, whilst they also shout, sleep, firmly into your ear, this time I'm 100% certain you'll end up on the floor. Now do you believe me?

WHY WON'T THEY BE HURT?

Well, the reason is simple, any intelligent person will, as they start to fall to the floor, feel this is occurring and probably try to stop themselves. As they move towards the floor, their legs will naturally bend at the knee, which brings them nearer to the floor, before they "fall" properly, which means they will not freefall as far. When you combine this with the fact that they will probably fall sideways down onto their knees, and then sideways to the floor, this means that their journey to the floor will be far more gradual than it actually appears to the audience.

Try it yourself, and you'll see what I mean, it's almost an automatic thing to "fall" to the floor in this way, which is very similar to a sideways fall which some stuntmen use, so that they do not get hurt. Obviously, there is still a small element of danger and this can also be eliminated by softening the surface which they are to land upon.

To do this many hypnotists who work theatres regularly, have a nice soft carpet (size of an average stage) which they fix to the floor with gaffer tape, along all four edges, so that no one can trip up accidentally. This, then cushions that small final fall to the floor and the incident of people hurting themselves is practically non existent. However, as with all I describe in this course, proceed at your own risk.

THE ARM SPIN INDUCTION

For this one, the subject sits in a chair, feet together, whilst flat upon the floor, they interlock their fingers, as with the handclasp text, but leave them held loosely, so that when you wish to, you can immediately pull their hands apart and they will separate instantly.

They are then told to close their eyes and relax their arms, so that you are then holding the full weight of their arms and if you were to let go of them, they would fall down into their lap. Indeed you can do this suddenly to check that they have complied with your commands if you so wish.

All this should take but a few seconds to sort out and then you physically proceed by rotating their hands around in a circular motion, which in turn will move their arms in the same way also. This must be done in a steady circular motion, as you deliver your verbal suggestions of relaxation and sleep. The rotation must be done "rhythmically" and at the same speed throughout, so that it both distracts them consciously and also acts as a very low level disorientation method, whilst having a calming "rock a bye baby" affect.

You then deliver your usual kind of verbal suggestions having already "conditioned" them to believe that the moment you say sleep their eyes will remain closed at all times until you say otherwise and that they will enter trance at the moment in time. The moment you command sleep, you simultaneously pull the subjects hands apart and, as you will be holding each of their wrists in a separate hand, you not only pull their hands apart, but also in a smooth motion you pull their arms slightly towards yourself and downwards at the same time. The effect you want to achieve is to have them move forward in their chair, with their head moving down towards their lap, as in the body flop induction, except here we achieve it by jerking their body forward by use of their arms (again it disorientates).

The moment you have done this, you allow their arms to drop down by their sides so that they feel lots of physical movements of their body which act as non verbal suggestions of sleep, as they are downwards movements.

All this should be practiced upon a willing friend, so that at any performance, you are able to carry it all out so it just takes a matter of 2 or 3 seconds for all the end actions to be done with the result of them being flopped forward in their chair. In other words, you must be able to do it without any hesitation.

When done correctly the subject will start sitting up straight in their chair and the moment that you've said sleep and carried out the physical movements, their hands will be down by their sides and their head down in their lap with the upper area of their body slumped forwards, which, of course, looks most impressive to the audience.

Verbally, you would do the normal thing of, "I'll count from 3 to 1 and on 1, when I say sleep you'll instantly enter a beautifully relaxed state and your eyes will remain closed at all times, until I say otherwise". Then you'd count from 3 to 1, usually using the standard kind of phrases along the way and on 1 when you say sleep, all the actions are carried out quickly. I hope you have noticed, that besides belief and expectancy, another reason why this and most inductions work is because of the ritualistic actions you carry out and the importance which you attach to them, which in itself also heightens their belief and expectancy. Also your verbal suggestions begin by explaining in a disguised form what you expect to happen to them when you say sleep, they then know how to react and belief will do the rest for you. As we said earlier, co-operation is a key word in hypnosis.

WORLD RECORD HIGH SPEED HYPNOSIS TECHNIQUE

What I am about to explain to you, is presented to any audience as the fastest and most powerful form of hypnosis know to mankind. And, indeed, to them, that is exactly what it will appear to be. You, as a knowledgeable hypnotist, will know that there is a lot of "psychological" conditioning done in your lead up to demonstrating this method of hypnosis, which is usually done at the start of the second half of the show, by which time everyone has seen you place people into trance rapidly and, as such, their belief and expectancy is complete.

You do the "guaranteed hand clasp test" prior to getting people up to be instantly entranced for your world record attempt. The way you present this as a world record attempt, not only enables you to get free, large scale publicity at every large show you do, but also it makes everyone anxious to see you succeed and, as such, it puts them in the perfect frame of mind in which to do instant inductions upon them. The people whose hands are locked together, via the guaranteed hand clasp, are brought up to the stage and their hands are then separated, as detailed in the last chapter. You will no doubt, have many people who were upon the stage at the start of the show and wanted to be hypnotised but, as you sent them back, they missed their chance, or so they thought. So, when you ask for between 12 to 20 volunteers to remain on the stage and take part in the world record high speed hypnosis attempt, you will have many takers, as they will want to grab this second chance to be a star in any way that they possibly can.

The rest of the people are returned to the audience to a round of applause. The people are standing with a slight gap between each of them, in a straight row across the stage. They are standing so they are facing the audience and in a position ready for the falling backwards induction. You then use the I.I.C. principle to condition them that they might be an idiot if they don't enter the hypnotic state especially as this is the fastest and most powerful form of hypnosis known.

You then make sure they are standing feet together and hands down by their side, as in the falling backwards test. Next, you get each and every person to stare at the bright white floodlight which should be high up front of house and facing the stage. All front of house lights are switched off and the stage lighting is also made quite dim, so that the light which they are staring at intently literally "blinds" them and blurs their vision. (So don't look at it yourself!). In fact, if you have a modern image, a pair of dark sunglasses would not go amiss during this routine, so you can continue with no risk to your own vision.

Next everyone is told to stare directly at the bright white light at all times, and now the Bladerunner theme begins, which is a very loud and exciting tune, which will put a sense of fear into them. You then do your psychological conditioning of what will occur by saying something such as:

"Ladies and Gentlemen, in 1993, a famous television hypnotist, by the name of Jonathan Royle set a world record for high speed hypnosis. He placed over 12 people into a hypnotic trance in less than 60 seconds. Well, tonight, ladies and gentlemen, I don't intend to break that record, oh no, I intend to smash it.

In a few moments you will witness the fastest form of Hypnosis known. It is also the most powerful method of hypnosis. To this day, nobody has been able to resist its most powerful effects." (Now turn to your subjects).

"OK, now I'm talking to everyone, as you stare directly at the bright white spotlight, listen only to the sound of my voice. In a few moments I shall touch each of you upon the forehead, and the moment that I do, you'll instantly fall back into my arms and enter a deep, deep hypnotic state, as this is the fastest form of hypnosis known.

Now, I won't let you fall and hurt yourselves though, you'll just fall back into a beautifully relaxed state. (Turn to audience). OK, ladies and gentlemen, prepare to be amazed."

At this point the induction starts and everyone is placed under hypnosis as I will detail in a moment. (Once all under say) "Ladies and gentlemen, the fastest form of hypnosis known to man." (Here take a bow at your applause). At this point, you either awaken people and return them to the audience, or implant the major post hypnotic suggestion in their minds and use them in the second half of the show. Or, implant the post hypnotic suggestion that, when you say goodnight at the end of the show, they will all jump up out of their chairs and shout out loudly,

"WE LOVE THE WORLDS GREATEST HYPNOTIST JONATHAN ROYLE, OH YES WE DO!"

The moment they have done this and leave the building, all suggestions will, of course, then be completely cancelled out. Just imagine it, you say goodnight to end your show, and as you leave the stage 20 or more people jump up and shout out, "We love the worlds greatest hypnotist, Jonathan Royle, oh yes we do!" This is the kind of ending to a hypnotic show that guarantees a standing ovation.

OK, so what do you do physically? Well, quite simply, if the people saw you coming to touch their foreheads, then they would anticipate it occurring and could try to resist. That is exactly why we don't do that. Instead, we start at the left hand side of the stage, working along the row rapidly until we reach the right hand side. Always, when doing what follows, you must be standing on the right hand side of the subject as you stand behind them. Your right hand is then lifted up behind the subject's back and above their head. You then, suddenly, bring your hand down flat over their eyes, which they won't expect, and at exactly the same moment in time your left hand presses flat against the lower back area of your subjects. So as your right hand pushes your subject's head backwards, your left hand pushes their stomach area forwards, they then very quickly reach that point of no return and fall back to the floor, with you cushioning their fall slightly.

To cushion their fall, you lift your left hand up at the last moment to their upper back area and lower them slightly to lessen the impact. All this, in practice, should take one to two seconds to carry out, as detailed. One moment the subject is standing up, staring at a bright white light and the next moment, everything goes dark as your hand unexpectedly goes over their eyes and they fall back to the floor as you shout "sleep" firmly into their ear, if that's not enough to shock anyone into hypnosis, then I don't know what is. Add to all this, belief, expectancy and suggestions and you really do have a most powerful technique to add to your repertoire.

As the timing of the induction, from a world record point of view, only starts when you touch the first subject by placing your hand over their eyes, it is easily possible to place 40 or more people into trance in less than sixty seconds. This is a very impressive demonstration of hypnosis, which can also get you much free, large scale publicity to promote your theatre show in each town you go to. It really is the fastest form of hypnosis known and will make you a lightening speed hypnotist, use it and be careful.

HYPNOTISING THE AUDIENCE

The induction used for this would be a progressive relaxation induction of an eye straining nature. The techniques of rapport, observation, recognition and leadership would be used with the majority being catered for, so that the end result of many people going into trance whilst still sitting in their seats within the audience is achieved. The standard kind of phrases are used as suggestions along with the classic suggestions of "Your eyelids are so heavy and so tired, that they want to close, in fact the harder you try to keep them open the quicker they will close."

The focus point for the entire audience is a large Hypno-Disc, which is a large black and white spiral effect disc with a motor rotating at a steady speed and giving a black hole effect as if being "drawn" into the disc. The whole audience is told to stare directly at the spinning disc as your suggestions of relaxation are given in the usual way. The end result will be that as the disc both has the effect of straining your eyes and disorientating you, most of the people who do stare at it will fall to "sleep" in their seat and you will have to go out into the audience to awaken them and bring the subjects you want to use up onto the stage to take part.

THE EYE TO EYE FASCINATION INDUCTION

Watch the Jungle Book film and witness the snake staring at the young boy, as he says "look into my eyes", and you'll have an idea of how this eye to eye fascination induction works. I usually take hold of the person's left hand in my right, and this establishes an instant rapport and instant bond between you both. Then using the method explained earlier in the course, make them think that I am staring directly into their eyes and at no point do I blink or lose eye contact, this has a strong psychological effect upon them and, not only makes them feel slightly uncomfortable, but also makes their eyes become heavy and tired, via the eyestrain technique, already explained. I then start talking in a low tone of voice, at a steady monotonous speed, suggesting that they can feel themselves sinking into the chair, their eyes becoming heavy and they want to close them, as they feel warm, tingling sensations in various areas of their body, as they wish to go to sleep, etc.

Continue along these lines, only stopping for a second to take breath. The key with this induction being to keep their eyes fixed upon your gaze and bombard them with suggestion, after suggestion until their eyes close and they go under. At which point, you quickly deepen the trance, as usual, and they will then be your suggestible subject. The belief factor also comes in here very strongly, as people believe all you have to do is stare into their eyes, tell them to go to sleep and they will, well in this case, great, let them carry on believing, as it makes our job easier. The suggestion of sinking and a sensation of falling down a black hole creates powerful pictures in the imagination and, as we know, when the imagination and the will are in conflict, the imagination will always win.

This method can have a person in trance in less than 60 seconds, and is ideal for use in a social party situation. It's funny, but I've noticed that lots of women want to be around you when they find out you are a professional hypnotist. Oh well, I suppose there must be some perks to the job after all.

INDIRECT INDUCTION METHOD

Another powerful technique, which I have found always seems to work, is to say the following sentence at the start of your show.

"If you do not volunteer, it does not matter, you have already heard the sound of my voice and many of you will find that you go to sleep by yourselves whilst sitting in the audience, but don't worry I will wake you up, as the deeper you go, the better you will feel and the better you feel, the deeper you will go."

By implanting this suggestion into the whole audience's mind, it will go into some peoples subconscious and in a short time have the effect of making them react to the sleep suggestions you are giving to the onstage subjects. On more occasions than I care to remember, I have had people enter trance whilst sitting in the audience and I've had to go out amongst them to wake up the ones who have gone under. This, too, is the reason why the full hypnotic induction cannot be shown on TV or broadcast over the radio, as people would most certainly enter trance around the country. Now you should be starting to realise just how powerful suggestion really is.

Incidentally, Mr Peter Casson, The Chairman of the Federation of Ethical Stage Hypnotists, was on BBC 1 many years ago, with the end result of cameramen and the production crew entering the hypnotic trance during the live broadcast, yes, it looked amazing and caused a sensation, but, it also lead to a ruling that the full hypnotic induction could not be broadcast on TV or radio.

VARIATIONS ON INDUCTION

The point that I wish to make here, is that, as long as you follow all the guidelines, which I set out in the first part of this course, then your induction's will still work, however you should decide to alter them to suit your own style. This in itself is a most important point, you must be relaxed in all that you do, then you will appear more confident and professional and so ultimately, you will have more success. An example of a slight variation or an induction is as follows:

You tell the subject, that you'll count from 3 to 1 and say sleep etc. Instead, you suddenly just say one and sleep, and they will, if good, responsive subjects still fall back into your arms and enter trance. I suppose the shock element also comes into play here.

Another example is they stand as with the falling backwards induction, but with eyes open, you tell them to follow the microphone with their eyes and the moment you command sleep to close their eyes, enter trance and fall back into your arms. You then move the mike towards their head at an angle, then continue past their head, so that in order to follow the mike's path of travel, they must tilt their head back more and so on, until they reach that point of no return and start to fall back into your arms, which is of course the moment when you command them to sleep.

CREATING YOUR OWN INDUCTIONS

By using the tried, tested and proven to work principles which have detailed in this course and the example inductions which are in this chapter, you should be more than capable of creating your own new unique to induction. Perhaps you yourself will write a book detailing your creations in years yet to come. A good source of material is any literature/books/tapes etc. which you can get by a gentleman from the U.S.A., called Mr Gil Boyne. Mr Boyne, is an American therapist, who specialises in instantaneous inductions. He has literally hundreds of quickie inductions and any literature which you can obtain detailing his methods would be of immense use to you. Another book, which I recommend, is entitled Trance-Formations, the book is by Richard Bandler and is very interesting reading on Hypnosis.

Another subject, which I would recommend you to learn, in order to become an expert at rapid induction, is anything on the subject of Neuro Linguistic Programming (N.L.P.) which is an extremely quick way to change perceptions of the mind and the way in which people think. It is also a very useful subject to have knowledge of for use in the hypnotherapist's consulting room, should you wish to pursue that avenue of financial gain. Remember, that old saying "Knowledge is Power", well, that is very true.

You are advised by me to study several other people's viewpoints on hypnosis and to then make your own decisions, then, and only then, will you be happy and confident in all that you do. The hypnotism industry is one of the most cut-throat and competitive area of show business, and it's also one of the most lucrative. Integrity is a key word in this business, which, unfortunately, many hypnotist don't seem to have. You must never talk about people behind their backs, you must never spread nasty rumours and certainly you should never try to stop a fellow hypnotist from getting work.

STANDARD PHRASES WHICH HYPNOTISTS USE

To end this chapter on induction methods, I will give you some examples on the kind of "Standard Phrases" which would be used by a hypnotist during the induction process. The rules I explained in the verbal psychology chapter, would of course be followed when giving these suggestions to the on stage subjects. Firstly though, allow me to recap a little. Hypnotism becomes possible through five essentials:

1   The fixation of the gaze of the hypnotist.
2   The execution of certain passes that the hypnotist must know.
3   The delivery of commands of suggestions must be in a voice filled with conviction.
4   The ability of the hypnotist to concentrate on the suggestion which he wishes to impart.
5   The ability of the subject to assume a passive state, to concentrate on the suggestions given and their willingness to accept same.

The last subject I feel that must recap is something, which even some very experienced hypnotists seem to forget, and that is to cancel out all the commands which you have given to the subjects after they have been carried out. In other words, all commands must be cancelled out completely before a person leaves the building unless they are beneficial. This is a most important point and one which you forget at your own risk. In fact, I usually mention it in my opening patter and awakening speech in a similar way as follows:

"Whenever you leave this room/building/theatre/area etc., all my commands will be completely cancelled out."

Or

"When I awake you in a few moments, you will feel on top of the world, full of energy and optimism and in fact, you will feel better than you have ever felt in your entire life. You will not have any headaches or side effects of any kind. You will, in fact, feel really great. When you leave here tonight, all my commands and suggestions to you will be completely cancelled out, in other words, you will be as you were when you first came in here tonight."

Obviously, this only applies when on stage. During therapy sessions you should reinforce all suggestions as much as possible and encourage your client to REMEMBER the messages for the rest of their life. [Please see the hypnotherapy course for in depth knowledge of this process].

Notice, the strong emphasis on "You", this tells the subject, that you are speaking to them and them alone. This kind of emphasis must continue all the way through, it is you, the hypnotist that they must relate to all the time. If they start to notice what the audience is doing you will have lost them, unless it was you who brought the audience to their attention. Anyway, back to the original subject in hand, that of standard phrases which you can use during your hypnotic induction.

STANDARD PHRASES FOR HYPNOTIC INDUCTIONS

"The deeper you go the better you will feel, and the better you feel, the deeper you will go to sleep."

"With every breath you take, every noise you hear, every word I say and every thought that you think, you'll go deeper and deeper to sleep."

"Every muscle in your body from the tips of your toes to the tips of your fingers, now becoming so limp, so loose and so relaxed."

"Each and every muscle in your body, now becoming so heavy and so tired."

"Your eyelids are feeling so heavy and so tired, in fact, the harder you try to keep them open, the more they want to close tightly, as you relax completely."

"As you sit (or lie) there in the comfortable chair, it almost feels as though every movement would be a great effort, as though you are sinking down deeply into the chair and into calm, satisfying, relaxation."

"This feeling of warmth and relaxation is now travelling around your entire body and as you continue to breathe deeply and regularly, you are drifting deeper and deeper to sleep."

"All the worries, stresses and tensions of days gone by, are leaving your mind and leaving your body now, allowing you to relax completely."

"In a few moments, when I awake you, you'll have an overwhelming desire to do almost everything I say, you'll find that you'll enjoy living your part in tonight's show to the full, and will carry out all that I suggest, as an automatic reflex action."

"Something that you thought would be difficult to achieve will turn out to be ridiculously easy to do."

"Each morning when you awake, from this moment forward, you will awaken with an inner warm glow of confidence, a renewed optimism to life and a more positive attitude to get things done."

NOTE: I hope these above examples will give you a much better idea of how on stage suggestions should be worded for maximum, positive effect.

Common sense and a little thought is all you require to word your own suggestions to give your own on stage subjects, just remember the golden rule, that there must never be any doubt in their mind of what you want them to do. Good luck with your induction's and enjoy "entrancing" people, but don't let the feeling of great power go to your head or else you'll end up like far too many other hypnotists in the profession, who have a Messiah complex and treat others like dirt, as they believe they truly are the best thing since sex was invented. This is OK on stage, but if it is carried over into your personal life, then you'll end up with no friends and your family will turn against you. To end this chapter, below are two little techniques, which can make life easy for you.

HANDSHAKE TECHNIQUE

This is basically just a way to tell, in the time it takes to shake a subject's hand, whether or not they will make a good subject. When you shake their hand press your fingers against the palm of their hand and feel how much moisture is there. The drier their hand is, the more relaxed the person is already and, as such, the easier it will usually be to hypnotise them. On the other hand, the more the subjects hand is perspiring, the more nervous they are and the harder it will be to get the subject relaxed for a normal style induction. These people, with waterlogged palms, are either not used to, or are shocked into hypnosis, as they are already too tense for the slow P.R.I.

TWO ARE BAD SUBJECTS PLOY

This is just a psychological ploy, which can be used to increase the chances of people wanting to be hypnotised and also the number of people who end up under hypnosis. At the start of your act, once the subjects are on stage ready to be hypnotised, you say:

"Well, I must say ladies and gentlemen, that there are two people on this stage who cannot be hypnotised, or at least I think they can't. The reason being, they don't have the correct powers of I.I.C. and we will not be able to use them. I won't point them out however, as they might surprise us and start concentrating a bit more." This, which you have just said to the audience, is pure waffle however, as each person on the stage starts worrying if it's them they'll all put 100% effort in to being hypnotised. Now your chances of success are considerably increased. Just imagine how daft people will feel, returning to the audience, having not gone under, when you have said something like that. My experience shows me they are more likely to remain on stage and act hypnotized, and take part in the show before looking a complete fool and returning to audience.

See you in the next chapter.

<u>**PART TEN**</u>

<u>**"BITZ 'N' BOBS"**</u>

A CHAPTER OF GENERALLY VERY USEFUL KNOWLEDGE

"Each man and woman will, in their lifetime stumble over opportunity. Unfortunately, most will simply pick themselves up and go through life as if nothing ever happened."

"You have, with this course, been offered a complete business plan, on how to earn big money from stage hypnotism. I hope you have the vision to see the bright future, which can now be yours, if you so desire."

This chapter has no particular format at all, that's the way I intended it to be. By having no format, you will have to put your own mind to work more to see the truth of what I'm saying and teaching to you, so here goes.

Always remember, that positive thoughts breed positive actions, as they are contagious, and positive actions bring positive success. To be a successful hypnotist, you must have a "magnetic" or attractive personality. This personality is a sum total of your health, appearance, habits and attitude. This type of personality is a plus personality, and a plus means that something is added. Negative, is an away sign and you cannot possess negative qualities and be successful. Therefore, any negative qualities you possess must be removed.

Keep healthy, reasonable hours, eat good wholesome food, keep clear of colds, no over indulgence and treat others as you would sincerely expect to be treated yourself.   Then you will develop for yourself a magnetic personality. Also remember, that it is vital to master self control, as you will never successfully control others if you cannot control yourself. This point is often overlooked, except by the successful few. Strive always to be healthy in mind, body and soul. You may have some negative attitudes or nervous habits, which must be eliminated, if so strive to get rid of them rapidly. Cut pride and any desire to be important, this is not easy when you know that you have the secret for success, which by the end of this course you will have.

Keep this secret to yourself, but ensure that you carry out the formula. You must master your negative desires, before you can possibly hope to master others. Listen with respect, to the views of others, and always find the good in what is expressed. Do not try to show that you know more about the subject, even if this is the case. People who do this have very poor self control. Never interrupt with objections, better that you spend time saying what is good about the discussion. You will always gain more influence over others by giving credit for what is good and very intelligent. Agreement, more often expressed makes and keeps friends, you just forget the rest, it is better to do so than disagreeing, the latter is negative and to you a loss. So in future, observe the things that you do wrong. Unconsciously these are bad habits, done with little or no conscious thought, they are your disabilities now and they have to be corrected.

Nervous activity is the responsible source for most bad habits. This activity is power, so it is much better to put it to a positive use, learn to control all of your bodily actions and mental actions.

The most important qualities, which a good subject should possess, are confidence, belief and faith, with expectation in the power of hypnotism. The qualities just mentioned alone, will lead the subject to co-operate with you, as a result they will be very susceptible to your suggestions. Make certain that your publicity ensures a good attendance on every appearance. A good audience is what makes a successful hypnotist, a good write up in the local paper is a must. If you can manage it, get a good publicity man at the very start, it will cost a lot, but will enable you to get free, large scale national publicity right from day one.

Remember, the bigger the audience, the better chance you have to get some good subjects, who will go under quickly, you will, in fact, have the law of averages on your side. Always live by this saying and think positively. "Best, better, best, may I never rest, until my best is better than my betters best". Another very important phrase to believe in and live by is "Every day, in every way, I am getting better and better".

You may not know, but it is not legal to show the full Hypnotic induction process on TV. The reason for this being, that, in 1946, a hypnotist called Mr Peter Casson, inadvertently hypnotised the engineers on the control panel whilst doing a broadcast for the BBC. This alone should prove that hypnosis is a genuine phenomenon. But still, many so called learned men, argue about its reality. In fact, a man, by the name of Theodore Barber, believed that you could get the same effects without going through the hypnotic induction process. Well, if that were true, I'd like to see him go up to someone and get them to imagine that they are a washing machine.

The way that your personality comes across on stage is a most important part or heart of any hypnotist. Confidence, directness, assertiveness, being totally positive in everything that you do, are all very vital qualities that you need to develop for your career to be a success. You must be able to confidently force your personality, in a non aggressive way, onto the volunteers or your clients, as this is an important part of the induction process. Observe Paul Daniels, Bruce Forsyth and Michael Barrymore in action, they are all masters of forcing their personality upon the audience, each of them is able to get people to do the most ridiculous things, and yet they use no hypnotism at all. So, if you can come across to an audience as they do, then it goes without saying, when you add the power of hypnotism, then you have a very strong hand of cards to play with.

Now, also believe this. Everyone on stage at the start of your show, will be hypnotised, they may not know it and albeit it will be in varying degrees, but everyone will be hypnotised to some extent. This is the point where I will now mention the subject of stooges. Some hypnotists, including myself, on occasions of importance, do have a friend or two, who they enjoy working with. Now, by occasions of importance, I mean when members of the media are to be present and the success of your show is vital for your future publicity. In these cases it may be as well to employ the services of someone you know who is guaranteed to co-operate and react in the manner you wish. Also remember, that one stooge is useful to bring the "sheep" effect into play, as once the subjects have seen one person go under quickly, then they will follow the leader so to speak, and follow suit themselves. Stooges come in two forms:

A. Those people who are good actors and you pay to play along to your stage suggestions.

B. Those people who really have been hypnotised by you before, and allow you to place them under hypnosis again prior to the show to implant a post hypnotic suggestion that, when they come up onto the stage that night they will go back into trance instantly. This kind of stooge is genuinely under hypnosis, but you have paid them to be there, as you know they will react well to your suggestions.

It should go without saying, that in either case, should you ever actually use stooges, the audience must never know, in fact, the only people who should ever know are you and the stooge. Don't ever tell your agent/manager, as it could ruin you reputation. I will end the subject of stooges by saying, they are not required if you do as outlined in this course, then you will have a most successful and 100% genuine show. However, it is worth bearing in mind stooges should you ever have to do a TV show performance, or you know that the media in general will be present at one of your shows.

During the early days of your career, it is advisable to proceed with a fairly standardised induction, such as the falling backwards or P.R.I. Then, when you have a few hundred or so inductions under your belt you can become more daring and start to use instant inductions, as by then, you will have the enormous self confidence levels required to make instantaneous inductions work for you.

When talking to the onstage subjects, you must have a forceful tone in your voice, yet, at the same time talk in an assertive manner. By forceful tone, I mean a tone of voice that suggests that you mean business. Remember your aim is to hypnotise them not scare them to death. Should you touch the subjects when you say the word relax in your induction, and later when you say sleep, then always touch them in the same place for whatever you are suggesting to them. Never confuse them by altering things.

When you command sleep or relax, if you should move your arm, always ensure that it is a downwards movement. Then later when you say wide awake, let them observe an upwards arm movement, this conditions them psychologically to react in a certain way to each type of arm movement, even if you later were not to speak to them.

When counting for relaxation or sleep, count downwards, ie. 5,4,3,2,1, and when terminating the state count upwards, 1,2,3,4,5, etc., so that you are doing the opposite thing, it has the opposite result. Whenever you should click your fingers, make sure that it is the same number of clicks for whatever suggestion you are giving. By that I mean, use the same suggestion for the same number of finger clicks, so that once again it becomes a conditioned reflex.

When you've got the subjects upon the stage and are suggesting their hands are getting tighter and tighter, walk amongst them and suggest that the more they stare at their hands the more relaxed they will become. You then get hold of the subjects to be tested by holding their arms, which you then push in towards their own chest, at the same time you push their head down towards their clenched hands. You do not require much physical force when doing this, but your voice must sound direct and positive, as you suggest hands getting tighter and tighter. You then let go of the subject's head and arms, as a general rule of thumb, if they spring back into their original positions, then you can safely say, that there will be more responsive subjects. However, if they stay exactly where you positioned them, then you know they have obeyed your non verbal command, and as such are good people to place into the hypnotic trance.

Another clever technique to use within your act, when performing the induction process, is this, you say to subject, "OK, just take a nice deep breath in (the word in being drawn out), hold it and then out (the word out being drawn out)". The words in and out are drawn out to coincide with the subject's inwards and outwards breathing rhythm. This has the effect of verbally "mirroring" their breathing rhythm and helps to establish a stronger rapport. This then allows the subject to relax more and as such the trance state sets in.

Another general rule of thumb, I have found, is this; when the subject breathes out (in other words, on the out breath), it is the best time to suggest things such as, sleep, deeper, relax etc. Psychologically, subjects associate breathing outwards with letting go and relaxation, and this is the best time to suggest such things.

There are several different states of hypnosis which it is possible for everyone to enter. However, when a volunteer is in trance, the depth will fluctuate, just so long as they don't drift into the somnambulistic state, then you will be OK. If they do, then awaken them, stand them at the side of the stage and a few minutes later, and when you are sure they are fully alert you can return them to the audience. If in this somnambulistic state, they will be so deeply relaxed, that they will not react to your commands and will not be of use to you and your show. There are five states of hypnosis, and these are:

THE WAKING STATE (HYPNOIDAL STATE)

This is the initial stage of hypnosis that begins the moment you ask them to clasp their hands together. It is a lovely lazy state that we all drift into prior to sleep or, although fully conscious, just before we wake up. Many volunteers in your show will be in the hypnoidal state, but that's OK, as they will be relaxed enough to react to your suggestions, to let the ego be subdued and to throw themselves into the routines you suggest.

THE LIGHT TRANCE (LETHARGIC)

This is the next level of hypnosis, and in this light trance, as the title suggests, the subjects feel quite lethargic. A flickering of the eyelids is often noticed or a movement of the eyeballs under the lids (known as R.E.M.'s, Rapid Eye Movements). This merely shows that the subject is entering a deeper level of trance. When the subject is in a light trance, it is easy to work with them for the same reasons as when they are in the waking state.

THE MEDIUM STATE (CATALEPTIC TRANCE)

In this state, the person feels detached from their surroundings and very often has a hazy recollection of events when the hypnotic state is ended. This state will cause you no problems, as the subject will still respond to your suggestions. In fact, for information purposes, this is the state of trance you'd want a subject in to make their body rigid and support them like a plank of wood across the back of two chairs. Or to move a blow torch across their arm with no pain as will soon be described.

THE DEEP STATE (SOMNAMBULSTIC)

This state is an absolute nightmare for you in your role as a hypnotist. The reason for this being, in this state, they will be enjoying hypnosis so much, that they will want to be left alone and will not want to participate. If any subject should enter this state, then awaken them, stand them at the side of the stage for a few minutes and then return them to the audience, when you are sure they are fully conscious.

THE POST HYPNOTIC STATE

This is the state they are in when you say, wide awake, they are apparently removed from trance and then react to your suggestions. I prefer to call this an eye open trance state, as even with their eyes open, in this state you can suggest more things to them and they will immediately react. You can also tell them that when you snap you fingers in front of their face they will realise what they are doing and be really surprised.

SPECIAL NOTE

The only other state after somnambulism is the COMOTOSE state, which as the name suggests resembles the state of coma. To get someone into this state takes a lot of trance deepening and will not even bother you upon the stage. However, as in this state the body mechanisms are slowed down, it is the state of trance that would be required for such a genuine stunt, as the sleep for a week in a shop window, which Peter Powers did in 1993, upon a man in Liverpool. A much greater understanding of the body, the mind and hypnosis should be gained before ever even contemplating to place someone into this state. In the meantime, you can always engineer a fake version of the stunt if wished.

IDENTIFYING THE TRANCE SUBJECTS ARE IN

The oldest known, and most mentioned scale of hypnotic susceptibility, or scale for measuring the trance state depth, is the Davis/Hubard scale of hypnotic susceptibility. Another scale, is that of Leoron/Bordeaux, and both of these can be obtained from any good book store, contained within the pages of various hypnotherapy literature. I will not mention them here, as to be honest, 95% of the population are most likely to go into a light (lethargic) trance, which is ideal for us. Of the population as a whole, only 55% are likely to enter the medium trance, which again will still be of use to us. As for the somnambulistic trance, which will cause us problems, only about 20% of the population can enter it, and on stage this is highly unlikely, as it would usually occur in the consulting room. Should this occur during your therapy session, you will be able to verbally guide your client back into the state required. As a general rule of thumb, the better they react, the deeper in trance they are, with the exception of somnambulists, when the opposite applies.

HYPNOTISABILITY OF THE ENTIRE POPULATION

5% Unable to be hypnotised
95% Light trance, the majority of people can participate in your show.
55% Medium trance, Cataleptic.
20% Deep trance, Somnambulistic

A few indications that a person is in hypnosis I will briefly mention. A full list however has been given in the previous chapter. These listed here are the ones I most commonly find however. Once you've done a few shows it will become second nature almost to spot these things which indicate the hypnotic state. For now, here are the main ones to spot.

THE FACIAL FLUSH

The skin tone colour changes as the hypnotic relaxation sets in.

EYELIDS FLICKERING

Eyelid flickering indicates the onset of trance, or a deeper level of trance.

WHITES OF THE EYES

You will notice with some subjects, that their eyes have floated upwards behind their lids. There is no cause for concern, if you observe the whites of their eyes through their slightly parted lids, in fact, it just means they are certainly in a trance.

EYES REMAIN OPEN

If this occurs, but the person is actually in trance, then there will be a kind of glazed look upon them. In this case just close their eyelids gently with your fingertips.

THE SCRATCH

Some subjects may begin repeatedly scratching themselves on various parts of their anatomy. Don't worry, carry on, they do not consciously realise they are doing it.

QUASIMODO RESPONSE

Some subjects, as they relax, will distort their features into the most laughable of unpleasant shapes. This is an involuntary action and they are unaware of it occurring.

OBVIOUS RELAXATION

If their heads fall forwards, or to one side, their jaws sag open, facial and bodily features relax etc., then the suggestions of relaxation, which you have been giving, are influencing the motor actions of their body.

CATATONIC STATE

Sometimes this occurs without suggestion. Some or all of the subjects' muscles become rigid or stiff. If this occurs of its own accord, try to reverse it with suggestions of muscular relaxation.

SLEEEEEP

With somnambulists they demonstrate all the signs of actual, genuine sleep. However, they are just in a very deep trance. They will not react to you and their speech will be slurred and lazy. You must awaken these people, make sure they are full conscious and return them to the audience.

TIME DISTORTION

When a person is in hypnosis, time distortion is experienced to a factor of two to two and half times. A two hour stage show will, to the subject, seem like about 20 to 30 minutes, and they will be sincerely amazed when they realise the truth. In a rare case or two, it can be the reverse and the odd subject thinks it was twice the length of the time it actually took.

ABREACTION'S

Abreaction's, as the name suggests, are abnormal reactions, which are sometimes experienced by a subject in trance and you should certainly be aware of this. You may never experience a person on stage have an abreaction, although if you enter the field of therapy, then they will become a regular occurrence to you. On stage abreaction's occur so rarely, that should it occur you will be knocked completely of guard and it will come as of much of a shock to you as to the audience.

When under hypnosis, a person relaxes the critical (analytical) area of the mind. The ego switches off, so this can enhance a subject's long term memory. If an abreaction did occur, it would just mean that the subject had drifted back through their thoughts, back in time to an earlier period in their development. Back into their childhood, the subconscious mind retains within its memory banks, past experiences of traumatic natures, as well as numerous other incidents/events which have long been forgotten. The reason these things are "blocked out" or "repressed", is because as a youngster, they were far too traumatic to deal with, but now, from an adult viewpoint, it would be easier to come to terms with them.

These repressions are often the cause of fears and phobias that the person has. (The phobias become an outward expression of an inward problem). The moment an abreaction occurs and the traumatic event (repression) is released, so the cause of the problem will be removed and as such all the symptoms will disappear. You see the mind is like an electric kettle, when the water becomes too hot and has boiled, the thermostat in the kettle causes it to switch off, so that it does not boil dry. So it is with the mind, that if a young mind experiences an event of a traumatic nature, then it may be too "hot" for that young mind to handle, so their emotions repress that memory and lock it into the subconscious mind. But the person believes they have forgotten it and even, in some cases believes the traumatic event never took place. In fact when they release the repression, people are usually unaware it was there, or that the repressed event ever took place. So, just as it takes emotion for the event to be repressed, it also takes a lot of emotion to release it and that's all an abreaction is, an emotional release of a repressed memory.

The fears or phobias which that person may have been experiencing then stop, as they were created by the hidden problem in order that the subject be consciously drawn to finally sort out those fears/phobias, which in turn also ensures that the repressed problem is eventually dealt with.

Although it's very dramatic to witness, the end result for the person it's happening to, is that their life will improve no end, and fears/phobias they once had will now no longer trouble them. So the result of an abreaction is strong, emotional and/or bodily reactions. Now as a therapist, we'd just let them continue experiencing the state, until they came out of trance naturally, as it would in a therapeutic sense, do them tremendous benefit. [See the hypnotherapy course for more details]. On stage, however, we are there to entertain, so stop this state of emotion spreading amongst the subjects (remember the sheep effect), if one person cries, another will. So if this occurs, we on stage must say to the group as a whole:

"I am talking now to everyone upon the stage, just relax, feel good, I am talking to everyone now. Just imagine that you have got that nice Sunday morning lazy feeling and you will carry on experiencing this until I touch you on the shoulder, until then, nothing can, or will disturb you."

Then release the abreacting subject from trance by saying:

"I want you to bring your feelings out now, up to this moment in time, forget about the past, feel relaxed, feel good, feel like you did before you came on the stage tonight." (This is said with hand on their shoulder). Continue in this manner until their feelings return to normal. If necessary, explain to the audience what has happened and that no harm can be caused with hypnosis, then return the abreacting subject back to the audience in a fully conscious state and continue with your show. The audience will respect you for putting your subject's feelings first. Now just go and tap the others upon the shoulder and they will once more start reacting to whatever you say.

HARD TO AWAKEN SUBJECTS

If they don't awaken when you give them the commands, don't worry, they are probably just more relaxed than they've ever been. Blow in their ear, lift their arm, shake them. These may awaken them. If not, ask them why they will not wake up and rephrase their response back to them in order to awaken them. If unsuccessful with that, then suggest that when you count to 3, you'll prick their arm with a sharp pin and they will immediately be wide awake. Then count to three and just touch their arm with the tip of a pencil, they should believe it to be a pin and as such, will awaken. If not, don't worry, they'd just slip into a normal sleep state and awaken in an hour or two. However, on stage, you may not be able to wait that long, so, as a last resort only, lean over them, whisper the word DANGER in their ear and get out of the way quickly. When in hypnosis and you mention the word danger, they will react in a primitive fashion, but it will release them immediately from trance.

PACING AND LEADING

Pacing and leading, is where you match your speech rhythm to the volunteers rate of breathing. When you are in sync with their breathing, slow the pace and rhythm of your speech even more and the subjects breathing will deepen. Ask the volunteer to close his eyes and concentrate on the sound of your voice, and then ask the subject to pay attention to his breathing. As the depth of breathing gets deeper, match your "relaxing," "letting goes" etc. with the ebb and flow of his breath. Then, when you are ready, lead the subject into trance by acting the way that you want them to and they will react in turn.

MY SECRET OF HYPNOSIS

When I go on stage, I think this phrase in my mind, and I follow it to the letter, knowing that if I follow it, then success is GUARANTEED.

"I want them to believe I can do it. They will then believe I can do it and as such, I am able to do it."

Once again we are back to belief and expectancy, which are the two main keys to anything connected with hypnosis.

PART ELEVEN

THE LAWS, REGULATIONS AND RED TAPE OF THE HYPNOTIC INDUSTRY.

This chapter deals with all the hassles you are likely to encounter in your quest to become a top professional stage hypnotist. It also gives you all the solutions, so you don't have to spend two years finding all this information. As such, this chapter is worth the price of the course alone, many times over.

I always say that if something is man made, then it is there to be man broken, in much the same way, if you search long enough, there is a loophole which can be legally exploited in every law of the land. Some of these loopholes are detailed in this chapter.

BRITISH ACTORS EQUITY MEMBERSHIP

British Equity is open to all professional show business performers, be they circus or variety artistes, actors/actresses, stunt men or even one of us poor misunderstood comedy stage hypnotists. Once you are a professional stage hypnotist you could join this independent trade union, if you so desire (Personally, I would recommend it). I, myself, am a member, but in the end, it's your choice to join or not.

At the time of writing, to join equity, all applicants have to supply contractual evidence, detailing their professional engagements. The requirement is a minimum of eight one off contracts at professional fees, these are the ones which should be submitted when wishing to join. Of these, two should be for shows within the last month, two should be for forthcoming shows and the other four should be for shows that you have done within the last year.

When you have got a few shows under your belt and a few bookings in advance, I am confident that your membership will then be processed without any problems. I will, of course, as your tutor, sponsor you for membership. Equity are our representatives in important matters, and here I quote Eddie Saville, the Assistant Secretary of Variety for Equity, in a recent letter.

"Clearly, Equity monitors all aspects of the industry, and we are aware of the current publicity which stage hypnotism is getting. We will watch very carefully the developments in this area of our business, and will react accordingly to defend our members interests, should this be considered appropriate."

This statement is clearly an expression of the Trade Unions support for stage hypnotists, a much misunderstood area of the show business industry. For more information on joining criteria etc., send a S.A.E. to:

Equity, Guild House, Upper Street, Martins Lane, London WC2H 9EG.
Tel: 0171 379 6000

Equity, 65 Bath Street, Glasgow, G2 2BX.
Tel: 0141 332 1669.

Equity, Conavon Court, 12 Blackfriars Street, Manchester. M3 5BQ.
Tel: 0161 832 3183

Equity, Transport House, 1 Cathedral Street, Cardiff.
Tel: 01222 397971

As a note on the side, once you have got your equity card, if you get a photograph and CV done and sent off to several Theatrical Casting Agencies, (see Stage and TV Paper), then you may be able to earn some extra money doing television and film extra work or small parts. Not to mention the possibilities of TV Commercials etc. When you are a member of Equity, they will gladly advise you on how to go about entering this field of work, also give you any advice on the show business industry in general, which you feel you may need to ask.

PUBLIC LIABILITY INSURANCE.

Hypnosis is, I've already state several times, a totally harmless state. However, because the effects of it are all in the mind it would be very hard to prove that the ex-subjects are not a result of our hypnosis. We know it's just not the case, they know it's not the case, but if someone did decide to sue you, in a way like this, for psychological damage or making them feel ill, it would then be your problem to defend yourself in court and prove that it was not hypnosis that did it. So unless you are very rich, an incident such as this example, which by the way, is highly unlikely to occur anyway, (but better safe that sorry), would make you bankrupt trying to defend yourself in court. Unless you had taken out suitable public liability insurance which would then cover you for the costs of legal cases etc.

Another reason for getting public liability insurance, is that it also covers you if someone falls over you equipment, or your speaker drops onto their head. Once again, the compensation, or the legal costs, would be paid for you by the insurance company.

Lastly, and probably, most importantly, another reason you must have public liability insurance is to be able to get your licenses for the shows you do granted in most UK towns. Although it's not part of the 1952 hypnotism act, most UK towns will now only give permission for a hypnotic show to take place if you have got one million pounds worth of public liability insurance cover. This cover must also cover members of the audience, who are actually going to be hypnotised. So all in all, as a working professional, it's a necessary expense, which of course is tax deductible.

If you intend to practice in therapy only [after doing the therapy course], the insurance premiums are more easily obtainable and carry far less premiums – around £50 per annum- and an application form is supplied.

By joining a Professional Organisation such as P.O.S.H (The Professional Organisation of Stage Hypnotists), the insurance companies, know then for certain, that you have signed a legal document to agree that whilst a member of the society you will:

A   Abide by the 1952 Hypnotism Act and Amendments of 1972.

B   Abide by the 1989 Government guidelines for hypnotists.
C   Will only work in a venue with permission by the council.
D   Are a working professional Stage Hypnotist who knows their
       craft.
E   Will, in general, do a clean, safe, ethical show, which cannot harm
       anyone.

In other words, they then know that you are an extremely low risk and as such, it's highly unlikely that they will ever have to pay out.

To join one of these societies, I'd advise that you send them a S.A.E. for membership details. In general, however, you need to show several contracts from past and future shows, as with joining Equity. You usually have to already be an Equity member and you also send them a copy of your publicity materials and agree to abide by all the points that I've just mentioned. All the societies have a membership fee, some cost more than others. Some give value for money and some don't. So it's it up to you which you join. Once a member, you can then approach the insurance companies and get your one million pounds cover for a modest fee. Most of the societies will send you details and application forms for the insurance upon you joining them, you then just pay your fee, and they do the rest for you on your behalf.

To become a full member of P.O.S.H. the only requirement, after studying this course is to study the SAFETY FOR STAGE-HYPNOTISTS video course which we can supply entitled "The Transparency Template".

INSURANCE, CATCH 22 SOLVED

To get insurance for stage work, you are placed into a catch 22 situation, as to join certain societies which can get you the insurance, you need several contracts from past shows to give them. And to do many shows these days you need the public liability insurance, which is where the catch 22 situation is created. The obvious way around this would be to make up some fake contracts, which could then be used to gain membership to both Equity and your chosen hypnotic society. However, although you may get away with this, I don't recommend it, as its fraud.

What I do recommend is this, contact Bartlett & co. insurer in Leeds (address elsewhere) and ask them to send you the application form for one million pound cover for a hypnotherapist. When the form arrives, you fill it in and send it back along with a copy of your hypnotherapy diploma. This copy of diploma and the completed form are returned along with a cheque to the company. Then your cover note of insurance is sent back, and you are covered as a hypnotherapist for 12 months, for any claim up to one million pounds, this will include all people who you will hypnotise. This is worth every penny, as:

A. It means you can open up a therapy clinic and treat people with hypnotherapy for their emotional problems [see hypnotherapy course] and:
B. You will also be able to get your licenses for shows granted by the local councils, but how, I hear you cry.

Well, quite easy really, the proof of insurance certificate will say on it Hypnotherapist Public Liability cover, which includes hypnotised people and also have on it your name and contact details etc. You must send this along with your application for permission to be granted. On your covering letter, which should be sent typed upon your letterhead, it says you are a hypnotherapist, not a stage hypnotist and you want permission for a light hearted demonstration of how hypnosis can be used for entertainment and for therapy. As you will be agreeing to the 1952 hypnotism act, and as far as they are concerned you have your insurance cover, which says Hypnotherapist, and as it says the same on your letterhead, they have no reason at all not to grant you permission. Even from a legal point of view it's not fraud, as you will be a qualified hypnotherapist, that's why you got the insurance cover. And hypnotherapists sometimes do public demonstrations for research purposes, so if ever a claim was made against you to the insurers, you'd say the demonstration was for research purposes, which a hypnotherapist is entitled to do without even being granted permission from the local council. So, because of loopholes in the 1952 hypnotism act, technically speaking, if you say the show is for research purposes every step of the way, then you'll be covered by the insurance and not have to apply for permission to be granted by the councils before your shows go ahead.

If you do operate things in this way, then there is one more thing which I would do. That is to inform the audience right at the start of your act, that anyone who comes up onto the stage is volunteering to take part, and as such, takes full responsibility for their actions. Here, the line, "You came of your own free will, and remain at your own risk," comes in useful. Before you place the people who come onto the stage, under hypnosis, you ask them for their permission, now, if they agree and they were to hurt themselves or tried to sue you for side effects, then they would not have a leg to stand on. The reason for this being, English law states that if a person willingly places themselves in a position of possible danger, then they are the only ones who can be held responsible for any consequences as a direct result. So you always warn them, that, if they partake they have volunteered and also gain their permission to hypnotise them. Then as long as you don't break the 1952 hypnotism act, all the risk then becomes theirs, as they have willingly placed themselves into a potentially dangerous position of possible danger. We will now move on to the subject of how to get permission for your shows granted by the councils legitimately.

THE 1952 HYPNOTISM ACT

In order to perform as a stage hypnotist at public venues, by that, I mean pubs, theatres, civic halls etc., you need to apply by law for permission from the relevant local councils licensing department for your show to go ahead. Failure to do this can result in a fine for you, a fine for the venues licensee and the venue can lose its entertainment licence. As a professional and ethical stage hypnotist, who agrees to abide by the 1952 hypnotism act and 1989 government guidelines, being a hypnotist who's got public liability insurance and is a member of both a professional hypnotic society such as P.O.S.H., and also in Equity, your permission will usually be granted without any problems whatsoever.

If, however, the permission is not granted, then you can make an appeal through the Magistrates Court. If this ever needs to be done, just phone up the clerk of the court and explain that you want to make an immediate appeal against the decision, he will advise you of how to go about it, as would your professional hypnotic society. This court appeal can also be used in towns who say they have "banned" hypnotists, and it is possible to have the "ban" lifted in court so that your performance can go ahead. So never think that anyone can stop you from performing. The only snag with this, is that the council themselves have seven days to appeal. So from the date of your appeal, until the date the permission is granted by the court will be about 10 days, so if your show fell within those 10 days it could not go ahead. If you give the council their 28 days to process your application and allow extra time for court appeals, then there should never be a problem and your shows should always go ahead as planned. It has to my knowledge, never happened yet, but if your appeal in court also proved to be unsuccessful, then you could always go ahead with the show anyway by doing it in the way that I will explain later and your show would still be operating 100% legally.

By the way, doing it this way, you would not be in a position where they could sue you. Now there are a few important points to remember, the first is that you are only responsible for getting the permission if you are promoting the show yourself, ie. when hiring a theatre etc. However, when you are booked to perform at a venue with your show, then it is the person who has booked you and given you the contract for the show who is responsible for seeking this permission from the council. If neither of these is the case then the venue itself is responsible for applying for the permission. For example, if booked for a pub, through an agent, it would be the pub licensees problem. You would be well advised, however, to inform all venues and booking agents, that they have to apply for permission from the local authority for your act to go ahead. Should you then be booked and no application has been made, as will usually be the case, then the show would go ahead with no problems. But if a police constable did enter the premises to check if permission had been granted then as you'd warned them, legally you would not be in the wrong, this could be stipulated in your show booking contract.

To apply for permission, when promoting your own shows, I would advise that you follow the following procedures:

1. If possible, go to the relevant councils licensing department (or phone) and obtain the appropriate application from them for permission for a hypnotic show to be granted.

2. When the form arrives, fill in all the details and send it back by

registered mail, or recorded delivery, so you have proof of it's postage, along with the following items:

A. Your Equity membership number.

B. Copy of your public liability insurance certificate.

C. Copy of your professional stage hypnotists society diploma.

D. A copy of your hypnotherapy diploma.

E. A copy of your first aid at work diploma if you have one.

F. A brief outline of the shows contents, so that they know it's not obscene.

G. A couple of complimentary tickets for the show, with the request that, if they are not satisfied with the enclosed, they are welcome to send anyone to attend the show to view it and check that it is as you've detailed to them.

H. The names, addresses and contact details of six venues, at which you have performed within the past six months and who will, if the council ask for it, supply them with a reference that your show was conducted safely etc.

I. Also, if you have one or two references from venues/agents etc., already, which state that they felt your show was conducted safely, ethically and also professionally, then send these as well.

This whole package should be sent at least 28 days prior to the performance date so that they can consider it. If you want to allow time for a possible court appeal, then the package should be sent at least 35 days prior to the show.

1. Call them the next day, after sending the package, to confirm that it has arrived and is in the hands of the correct people.

2. If you have heard nothing by the end of the second week, then call up

again and pin them down to a definite time and date upon which the decision will be made. If need be you have also here another chance to send copies of everything to them if they have "misplaced" it.

3. You will, by the time of the show, either hear that permission has been granted, or not. If not, continue with the court appeal and I'm sure the show will go ahead. If you should hear nothing, which sometimes happens, then as you've made every possible effort to help the council come to a decision and can prove this, I would just go ahead with the show anyway. As if they did try taking you to court, they would be laughed at when you told the judge you had carried out the above mentioned procedures to the letter.

If you follow this procedure to the letter, then there is no reason at all why they can possibly not grant you permission for your show.

Oh yes, and one last point, some councils charge a fee for processing the permission, in Trafford it's £16.50, and in Blackpool, I was quoted £110. But they are allowed to add any extra conditions they desire, unfortunately. Also some councils, such as Bury, Bolton and Preston, have a complete ban on hypnotists at public shows, however, this can usually be remedied in court. The councils which do impose a ban cannot, however, stop any shows which are run in private members clubs, or at private parties. Also they cannot stop any which are for research purposes. So don't worry too much, as there are so many loopholes in the hypnotism laws that there's a way around them all. Remember to check though, as each council has different bye laws and can also add different conditions to your permission to perform if they so wish.

LEGALLY BREAKING THE 1952 HYPNOTISM ACT

This next section will explain how to completely break the 1952 hypnotism act legally. This means, you will be able to perform at places where hypnotism is usually banned, or where they will not grant you permission to perform. The best thing is, you won't be breaking the law, you will, in fact, just be exploiting the loopholes within it. This of course is very useful information to know, however, I accept no responsibility for anyone using this information and anyone doing so, does so at their own risk. If you wish to check the validity of what I say, then please consult your solicitor for more details and show them what I am about to reveal to you.

BREAKING THE GOVERNMENT GUIDELINES 1989

A. Read section A, and you will see this is down to commonsense only.

B. Section B states, "no person shall be caused, while under the influence of hypnotism, to do, or say anything offensive to the audience which are there." Well this one is a matter of personal taste and censorship. So, for example, if you were doing a family show it would need to be very clean and non racist or sexist etc. However, if you were doing an adults only show, and the posters and advertising stated "stay away if easily offended", then there would be no comeback to be made, as you would have warned people that they were to see a show for broad minded adults only. Also, as it's down to personal taste and censorship, the only problem could be if several people complained who had not been warned what they were about to see.

C. Section C, part 1 says: "any experiment involving the age regression of the subject". Well, it's only age regression, if they really regress in their minds back to that age. However, if you tell them, that when they awaken they will "imagine" they are 8 years of age, then they will only imagine it and as such, from a legal view point it is only role play and not genuine age regression.

Section C, part 2 states: "the giving of hypnotherapy, or any other treatment". Well, look at section D of the 1952 hypnotism act and you'll notice that nothing in the act shall prevent the demonstration of hypnosis for scientific or research purposes, or for the treatment of mental or physical disease and as such, there is not anything in the act which can stop you. As such, you can carry out hypnosis to stop people smoking etc. which lets be honest, is caused by habit (in the mind), and can cause physical disease, so you are in effect treating both things at once. Therefore you can do hypnotherapy and if you were to stop a couple of people smoking and helped a couple of people loose weight within your show, then essentially your demonstration could be classed as being for the treatment of mental and physical disease. As such, no licence would be needed to do the show, as the act does not stop demonstrations of this kind.

PART THREE: "Any experiment in which the subject is suspended between two supports as in Catalepsy". Well, as I said earlier, if you inform them of what they are to do, and they then agree to take part, they have willingly placed themselves into a position of possible harm. As such, English law states you could not be prosecuted if they are hurt by accident, as they volunteered to take part, in full knowledge of what they were to be made to do. Also it does not stop you "hypnotising" the female partner of your act, then performing the "Catalepsy" upon her, as she too, would have volunteered and as such, it is her responsibility. Or you could get your female assistant to present it and you could self-hypnotise yourself and be the one who is supported across the backs of two chairs, here it was your own personal choice and as such, nothing can be done.

PART FOUR: "The giving of suggestions to the subject that they should perform any act or behave in any manner which is likely to be interpreted as indecent, offensive or harmful, nor that they shall consume any substance which is either noxious or harmful". Well, once again, it comes down to taste and censorship. So if anything some class as "rude" is to be done, then make sure that these types of people are not at the show, by warning them of the shows nature in your advertising, then it will not be considered "rude" by the people at the event. Also, as for the consumption of harmful or noxious stuff is concerned, an onion is part of many peoples every day diet, so it is not noxious or harmful, in fact it is healthy to eat. So making people eat an onion believing it to be an apple is OK. Also, if someone was given a tin of catfood to eat believing it to be jelly, well catfood has to be fit for human consumption, as such, it cannot be noxious. You could, of course, just empty out the tin, wash it and then fill it with meat pate to act as a cat food substitute. So here, it is down to using your own common sense.

PART FIVE: "no persons under 18 shall be placed into trance". Well if both parents are present and it is witnessed by the full audience, and the child is also willing to take part, then as long as the parents agree that their child can partake, it technically is legal and the responsibility then lies with child's parents. However, I would never hypnotise anyone on stage under the age of 16, even with the consent of their parents and to be honest, I wouldn't consider it wise to use under 18 at all. In fact, you'll have so many people wishing to take part that you'll never need to even consider doing this. If someone under 18 does take part in your show, without parental consent, then your only defence is that you honestly did not know and believed that they were old enough to participate.

SECTION D: Obviously its common sense to cancel out all suggestions you give the subjects before they leave the building. However, you can give them suggestions to carry out in the interval, even when you are not around, just so long as they are in the building in which the show is taking place at all times. And, of course, if they have been commanded that, should they leave the building for any reason, all suggestions will immediately be cancelled out, then there aren't any problems which can occur.

SECTION E: Have in small letters on the description that you submit to council, "subject to change without notice", then once the permission is granted, you can with the law, do as you so desire.

SECTION F: This speaks for itself, but you can pay people to play along as if hypnotised because they aren't in a real trance.

SECTION G: Once again, use your common sense here, but it's down to censorship, personal taste and obviously where the advertising is to be displayed.

SECTION H: Do exactly as it says, there is no need to ever break this rule.

SECTION I: You can't break this, but there again, if the subjects have volunteered, then they have no legal comeback on you.

SECTION J: There is no need to ever break this rule.

SECTION K: No need to ever break this, but if you're a qualified first aider up to health and safety at work standards, then you could get away with playing that angle. Otherwise, send free tickets to your doctor and get him/her to come along, you will then have given them a free night out and you've kept to the conditions.

SECTION L: No need to ever break this, but as you'll see the 1952 act has more loopholes than may have first thought.

SECTION M: As these are actual law and I don't know the loopholes in them, you had best abide by them 100%.

BREAKING THE 1952 ACT

A. This does not stop shows in private members clubs, or shows of a private nature where the audience are invited guests only.

B. Again, it does not stop shows of a private nature, or shows held in private members clubs, such as social working mens clubs etc.

C. Once again, it may be possible to use under 18's if they consent and consent has been given by both parents. As the act says, a police constable may enter the premises if they feel the act has been broken, however, note these very important points. As you cannot be prosecuted for a crime until it's been carried out, in much the same way, even if you were illegally breaking the act which you don't need to, the police cannot stop it until you've finished, unless the show is pornographic and breaks standard laws of England and Wales. They can enter and stay there until the end of the show, then arrest you for breaking the law, but they cannot stop the show whilst it's occurring, or proof to commencement. As what right have they got to stop a legal show before it starts, as they don't know for certain what you will be doing and whether it will break the law. You can only be prosecuted for a crime, if you have committed that crime, you are innocent until proven guilty, remember that.

Another point here is, they can't exactly stop the show anyway when the subjects are in trance, as then they would be placing the subjects into a position of potential harm. Because the act only says that police constables may enter the premises, this means that council officials have, in fact, no legal right whatsoever, to come in. In actual fact, as it's up to each venue owner who they allow to enter their premises or not (when you're booked) and when you've hired a venue, it's at your discretion who is admitted to the venue. So if they tried to enter the venue without permission, they would in fact then be breaking the law themselves and would be trespassing. It is only the police who have a legal right to enter when they wish, and even then they must have a justifiable reason to believe that something is being done to break the law.

D. As mentioned earlier, this means you can do hypnotherapy whenever you wish, as long as it's for "research purposes" or purposes of a scientific nature.

E. This means, that if the subjects upon the stage hypnotised themselves and then you just conducted or directed the show, then it could go ahead without permission and would not be breaking the law. So in order that the subjects have legally hypnotised themselves you must not touch them during the process of induction. If you touch them, then you have induced the trance, however, if you don't touch them and say things such as, "I'd like you to allow yourself to relax and allow yourself to go deeper", then when they react they are allowing themselves to do it. As such, it's self hypnosis and as a consequence, the 1952 act has no validity whatsoever. Your show can then go ahead without permission, and also you can perform catalepsy etc., as it does not fall under the act of 1952, as they've hypnotised themselves and volunteered.

Lets take this one step further, you could even call yourself a "persuasionist" or "relaxationist", instead of a hypnotist, you could then say you are just going to guide them into a deep relaxation not a trance, not a sleep state and certainly not hypnosis. This then completely blows the 1952 act apart, but you would of course have to be careful to never mention the words sleep or trance within your act. Instead you would just have to use the word relax all the time. This means you're then 100% in the clear to do as you wish, as the act does not stop self induced hypnosis and it certainly does not stop you helping people to relax a little more.

F. This section is irrelevant, with what we are dealing with here.

Well I hope you now see just how badly worded the 1952 hypnotism act and 1989 guidelines are, and just how easy it is to exploit the massive loopholes to our own advantage.

So you are booked to do a show, or are promoting a show yourself and either they will not grant you permission to perform, or the council has banned hypnotism shows in that area. What do you do? Well, here are five ways in which you can legally go ahead with your show, even if the council has not, or will not grant any form of permission.

1. If the venue that has booked you and is a private members club then permission need not ever be applied for. The reason for this being, it's not then classed as a public show. Private members clubs usually include places such as, Labour and Conservative clubs, special interest clubs, working men's clubs etc. So here alone there are more than enough venues at which to earn a living from and they are exempt from the 1952 act.

2. Any show at which the audience are specially invited guests and it's not open to the general public at large. For example, wedding receptions, birthday parties etc.
3. If your show is one open to the public and is to be held in a public venue, such as a pub or theatre etc., then the way round it is this;

You advertise that only members of your private fan club are allowed to enter on the night, this makes the show a private members club performance, as such no permission is needed. You, however, point out that temporary one night memberships to you fan club are available for just £10, or whatever the intended ticket price was to be. So as they are paying for a one night membership to a private members club, and not purchasing a ticket to a public show, then it's legal to perform without permission being granted by the council. As of course full members of your fan club, which may or may not exist, are admitted free of charge.

4. As we have already discussed, no permission is needed if the show is for research or scientific purposes. So if you were to advertise that the show is for research purposes, this is the loophole. If asked what you are researching, you can say, "I am researching the effects of Hypnosis and Hypnotic suggestions, and who these things affect most." i.e., what age group responds best, are men better subjects than women, can people be hypnotised easily in public etc. I'm sure by now you've got the general idea, by saying this it's up to them to prove you were not researching these things and that's practically impossible.

5. The 1952 act does not include hypnotism, mesmerism etc., which is self induced. As such, if you require to perform without a permission then just word your suggestions carefully as earlier detailed and have the people

place themselves into the hypnotic state.

So there we have it, you now know how to completely break both the 1952 act and Government guidelines. You are also in a position to perform when you so desire, without applying for a permission to perform. Use this knowledge, like all other knowledge in this course, wisely, also keep it to yourself at all times. If someone else wants to know the details within this course don't tell them, or lend it, you paid hard earned money to find all this out, it's only right that other people should do the same.

To end the subject of laws relating hypnosis, allow me to say this, at the time of going to press, you don't need any qualifications to become a hypnotist or hypnotherapist, as such, there is nothing to stop you setting up a show or consulting room. This, however, I feel is a ridiculous situation, as it means there are so many cowboys getting away with giving our misunderstood business a bad name. I will end this chapter, by giving you the criteria which mush be met in order to join the Professional Organisation of Stage Hypnotists.

THE ASSOCIATION (P.O.S.H.)

Membership to P.O.S.H. means that you will comply with a code of ethics of the very highest order. All venues and booking agents and councils will know that as a member, you will always present a safe, legal and ethical performance. This means that permissions to perform, which are applied for, will be granted without any problems. As a member, you will receive a certificate of membership, which is signed. This can be copied and then sent out to councils to prove that you are indeed, a member when applying for permission to perform.

P.O.S.H. members are encouraged to help each other out in anyway that they can and we promote an equal opportunities scheme. We are neither racist nor sexist. As a member you can obtain professional help and back-up support and advice. Special seminars at discounted rates are organised for members on all areas of the hypnotism industry and related subjects.

Our aim is to professionalise the art of hypnosis on stage with our standards. People will always know that when booking a member they are booking a safe, legal and ethical professional performer, who knows their craft 100%.

PART TWELVE

MAKING MONEY FROM STAGE HYPNOSIS

This chapter contains stacks of knowledge, which has been obtained from real life practical experience and can help you make up to £36,000 or more in your first year of trading. If you follow my step by step plan to hypnotic success, then financial freedom can be yours.

This part of the course is a collection of advice on how to get to the top, quickly and with as little effort or expense as possible. You see I live by an old saying of millionaires, "why work hard, when you can work smart". In order to do this, you must grab every opportunity that comes your way, now don't say you never have opportunities and that you are unlucky, because I will suggest that this is not true. In this life you create your own "luck" and "opportunities". In fact, I truly believe and my own personal life experience shows me, that the only limitations which we have in life, are those that we psychologically impose upon ourselves. So never forget that positive thinking is a most positive force, as it breeds positive actions and from positive actions come positive success, as it brings you one step closer to your ultimate goals, whatever they may be.

I'll give you another two sayings here, which contain within them the secrets of success. A. "As man thinketh, so he becomes" and B. "How do you eat a big elephant?" Answer: "One spoonful at a time and very slowly, but you'll get there in the end if you don't give up."

Remember, inch by inch, piece by piece, it is possible. You may be thinking that this is all starting to sound like an American Motivational Training Seminar, on how to run your life and the reason for that is, because it is. In the days of Music Hall and like, the motto would have been, "it's 99% show and 1% business" which will open the door of success. Now I'd say, in this modern day, it's "99% business and 1% show", which will give you the income and lifestyle that others only ever dream of.

What I'm saying is, learn your hypnotism, yes. In fact, learn it off by heart, but once it's second nature to you, spend 99% of your time on sales, marketing and publicity. Remember, it doesn't matter what product you are selling, but the way that you sell it is all important. If you are an unknown act, then you want to get famous quickly, as then you'll be in great demand and as the economic laws of supply and demand state, you will then be able to charge more for your shows. And charge even more if you are unique in the style of act you do, as then you have a competitive edge.

If you can afford it, get a good Public Relations Agency working for you right from the start. This will cost you a few thousand pounds per year, but they really can make you a star "overnight", and turn you into the countries most publicised and talked about hypnotist. Once you're a household name, you will automatically be earning telephone number style fees for your theatre shows. A public relations company will create a huge nationwide or worldwide demand for you right from day one for your career, if you have the money to invest into your future. After a while, the media, radio and TV will all come and ask you for stories, by which time you'll just be referring them to your personal manager.

Another way to make it, probably the cheapest, is through personal contacts that you know, as, remember the old saying, "it's not what you know, but who you know," is indeed very true.

I will now, also make what some will consider to be a very controversial statement, but I speak here from personal experience. The casting room couch syndrome still exists. Oh yes it does. If you're male and you can hang out in the bars, where the people to meet go. Then if you've got the charm to chat up the females (or males if so inclined) and you are successful, you will also get many perks as a result. For example, I frequented a place called "Stringfellows" in London during March/April 1993, whilst working two shows a night, three nights a week on a weekly basis at the London Bus Emporium Night club, in High Wycombe. Although I only went in once or twice weekly, for four to six weeks, I made several contacts, who are indirectly, or in some cases directly responsible for the position I hold within the Hypnotic industry today. I'm just making the point that, if you want peanuts you associate with monkeys, if you want gold, see the organ grinder.

Remember, each person you establish as a close contact on first name terms should be treated with the very best respect, in return they will ensure you get that TV appearance instead of someone else. I know it sounds horrible, but that's the way this business really is at the top. For example, I once dated a female, who works for a certain television company, and during our relationship I got a lot of TV interviews and offers, it's a case of you scratch my back and I'll scratch yours. It's not that hard, despite what people say, to make it to the top business level (the top of the tree financially). The hard thing, however, is stopping yourself from getting knocked down again, once you're there, or at least, if you do get knocked down, being in a position where you never have to worry about money again before it occurs. Money can make you a sight happier than being on the dole. With money, you can live in the poshest area of town/city, drive a brand new sports car every year, wear suits that cost what an average person earns in a month. In fact, you can do whatever you want when you are financially secure. Setting goals is all important in life and business.

Remember, it must be in the mind first, before it becomes action or reality. It also helps to get mental images of what life will be like when you are in that successful position, act as though it's guaranteed to happen.

Another way, which I use to get work, is to have top quality publicity packs printed on the best quality paper. Then have them distributed to every single agent, venue, manager, show booker/promoter, holiday camp, theatre, in fact, every possible place you could work and could afford to send to. The more people who know of your services and know your name, the more likely you are to get lots of work. It's the law of averages. Have good, in fact, excellent materials for publicity made up first, and if monies are short, send out good quality photocopies from these professional laser copy quality masters.

As soon as you can afford to have a promotional video of your act done, then do so and duplicate many copies of the tape. This tape, with colour laser copy cover, should be sent to all the top people in the business, who can afford to pay the kind of fee which you wish to be earning. So don't start from the bottom, like most people. Keep going, contact all the top people and you yourself should take control, act rich, dress rich, live beyond your means for a few months, go thousands into debt on your plastic cards, lease a flashy sports car and guess what? Yes, you'll owe a whole stack of money, but also you'll start earning huge sums of money, as people always like to give money for anything in life, to those who don't seem to need it. (Don't ask me why, but they do).

Another way is to hire shows and self promote shows yourself, not forgetting, of course, to send free tickets to agents, media and TV etc., so that they come and see you working live. Theatres can usually be hired on a straight fee basis or a percentage split of the door take, which means no risk to you except advertising costs etc.

Keep plodding along in this vein, keep phoning the agents you mailed your publicity to and then you'll get given some poor gigs by them to shut you up. Do an excellent show, even if it means on this one occasion, using loads of stooges, as you can bet your life that a representative from the agency will be in to watch you, so be world class and then you'll get classy work as a result. From there, you may be lucky and get a personal manager, which then means, they do all the marketing, telephone calls etc. You can concentrate on what you do best, which is showing up early at the venues and doing world class shows every night you are booked to perform. Success is then near.

A weekly publication which you should subscribe to, which runs adverts from venues and agents requiring acts for immediate work, is the Stage and Television Today, you can subscribe to it by contacting them directly at:

The Stage and Television Today Newspaper
47 Bermondsey Street

London
E1 3XT
Tel: 020 7403 1818
Fax: 020 7378 0400

A yearly publication called Showcall, which is sent to all agents, venues and bookers, is well worth running a full page advert in, at a cost of under £100 for the year, it's a bargain at that small cost. The advert just bears your photo, contact details and notable achievements to date upon it, but please remember, the KISS principle of sales and marketing. Keep It Short and Simple. To place your own personal advert in next year's edition of this vital book, contact them directly by sending a S.A.E. for full details to them at:

Showcall Publication
47 Bermondsey Street
London
SE1 3XT

Another place in which it is worth running an advert and, believe it or not, the adverts are free of charge. They do produce results, as I have found out.

The White Book International Production Directory
P.O. Box 55
Staines
Middlesex
Tel: 01784 464441
Fax: 01784 464655

Incidentally, it's also financially worthwhile to fund a box advert in the "artists" section of the Stage and TV paper. A decent sized advert, the size of a matchbox, costs as little as £10 per week to run and does produce profitable results.

From a marketing and sales point of view, I'd recommend three audio cassette training programmes, which really will help you onto the ladder of success. These are:

1	Unlimited Power by Anthony Robbins (6 cassettes).
2	Unlimited Power. 30 day guide to success (24 tapes and written textbook).
3	Lead the Field by Earl Nightingale (6 cassette programme).

All three of these highly recommended audio training programmes contain the tried, tested and proven to work secrets of success and, I would say, have changed my life. I know it sounds corny, but it's also very true.

Also a book, which I'd consider essential reading, is The Magic of Show Business by Simon Lovell. This is available from: www.magicalguru.co.uk

This company also supply numerous other titles which would be of use to the trainee hypnotists.

The Simon Lovell book is one that I value highly, as it reveals in detail the secrets of getting TV, Radio and Media publicity on a national scale and on a regular basis. How to get work, get an agent and then a personal manager.

To continue, business cards should be carried at all times, and state that you do both stage shows and private hypnotherapy consultations, if this be the case. Hand these out to everyone you meet, people are fascinated by hypnosis, the card will be kept and may result in a show, or therapy session being booked at a later date. It happens more often than you'd think. Remember, that Word of Mouth advertising is, by far, the best on earth, so get in the media as much as possible and do some regular shows of a high standard and very quickly, you'll get a good reputation, both within and outside of the business. Remember the old show business adage that all publicity is good publicity, just so long as they spell your name correctly. I whole heartedly believe this to be true. As Barnum and Bailey, the American Circus Proprietors, once said, if you have something to sell them, then advertise it, even if it's with your last dollar. But make sure you have a product worth selling first.

Another avenue of work available, is to work the forces bases, this itself, is good in two respects, A., Its good money, and B., the people who will see you are more than used to taking orders and as such, will go under very easily.

Below are several contact details for publications and agencies, with regard to establishing yourself in this lucrative area of the hypnotism industry:

N.A.A.F.I. Entertainments,
Imperial Court
Kennington Lane
London
SE11 5QX
Tel: 020 7725 1200 ext. 2270 or 2800 and ask for the forces entertainment magazine.

Germany N Entertainment
Rheindalen
Tel: 010 49 02163 or 47178

N.A.F.F.I. Entertainment
BFPO 40
Tel: 010 49 02163 4031

Combined Services Entertainments
Tel: 0171 828 5646

ECHO (Forces weekly Echo)
Gutenberg Strasse 1
4700 Hamm 1
(0 23 81) 2 98 29

Advertising representative for the UK
Combined Services Publications Ltd
P O Box 4
Farnborough
Hants
GU14 7LR
Tel: 01252 515891

So with these contact details, I leave you to find and explore that field of work, which for many hypnotists has proven to be very successful and financially rewarding.

You may still ask how do I get work? Well simple answer, go out there and find it. Where did you see a hypnotist work? Start there and try to book yourself in at that venue, as they are obviously open to the idea of a stage hypnotist. To convince a venue that has never had a hypnotist on before, say things, such as, "hypnotists are now so popular, I've had to turn people away at recent shows, due to the great public demand. You see, it's a very funny show, it's very popular and of course, your overall profits will be increased." The words, "your profits will be increased," do the trick and bring the greed factor into play. In fact it paints a mental picture in their mind of the financial gain they will make, that's what everyone in business wants, so you stand a damn good chance of closing the sale and getting the contract.

Now a few more important points to cover, firstly agents. Your agent, or venue agent? Do not mix up the two breeds. Yours, theoretically, works for you, in practice, they work for themselves. They often represent a club or forces base, hotel or pub, and as such, you can only get work at that venue through them. They are the agent for that establishment, not for you. Remember, that they will charge you from 10% to 20% of your fee in commission for getting you the show. He/she will book in any hypnotist that they can get at the right price and will not actively seek work for you and you alone.

A personal manger, well, they look after you, arrange where you work, when, for how much and in fact, all that's necessary to arrange, they do it and actively seek you work. His or her fee is an arrangement made between you both. It will most certainly be a higher percentage of commission than the agent takes, but then again, you'll be getting more and higher paid work as a result. You work for him on the same basis if you get a job yourself, you will still pay him his normal fee, or he can forbid you to do it because of the contract that you will have signed between you. He may, if you have the money, arrange for a public relations company to sell you to the public in various ways, which is well worth while, and can turn you into a star very quickly. If you get a good reliable manager, or even agent, then they are well worth sticking with, as you can then concentrate on what your best at doing, which is doing shows before audiences who wish to be entertained.

CONTRACTS

Your work as a hypnotist, will be controlled by contracts, written or not. They stipulate all that both parties must do, by that I mean you and the show's booker. So read them carefully, including all small print and ensure that they are Equity approved. Make sure also, that you understand all that it says fully, as they are binding in law. You will often think the contract is with the venue, when in fact you may find it is with the agent. You see, by law, usually the person who signs the contract is your employer and, as such, is legally the person bound to the agreement by law. So I can only repeat, read them very carefully and if it's for work abroad, then ensure also that it's an Equity approved overseas contract. In fact, as an Equity member, ensure all your contracts are all Equity approved and if in doubt check with a solicitor before signing, better safe than sorry.

I have at the end of this chapter included a copy of an example contract which is Equity approved and which is fairly self explanatory. Two copies are done, one signed by the booker is given to you, one signed by you is given to the booker. The legal agreement has then been made. You of course, can have your own contracts designed and extra clauses added. When you have a good reputation within the business, then you can have a clause in the contract which states that you get paid whether or not anyone ends up being placed under hypnosis. In other words, you get paid if you show up to perform and attempt a show whatever the actual outcome may be.

Always photocopy the contract you're given by the booker, leave the original at home and take the copy to the venue with you on the night as proof, should you have any difficulties in getting paid. The reason for the copy is simple, if it gets damaged or torn, then you will still have the original copy at home should you need it for later use in court to claim your money.

VIDEOS

If people want to video your act, unless it's TV etc., then amateur or not, the short answer should be **no.** Otherwise you charge them twice your normal fee for the show and restrict it's showing to no more than 10 persons at one time, for personal viewing only, not for commercial use. As such, it is never to be shown in a place of public or private entertainment. Put all this in writing, signed legally prior to the show and on your contract add a note that videos will not be allowed at the show and send a copy to the venue. Place a notice at the entrance doors to the theatre etc., stating that recording by any means mechanical or electronic is strictly forbidden unless prior written permission has been applied for and granted. If anyone then videos your show without consent, you can sue them and obtain substantial damages, but only if this procedure has been followed to the letter. Remember it's your lively hood which they are trying to steal from you.

CHASING YOUR FEE

If you have not been paid within a reasonable time, you have written asking for your money and you have a legal contract, then do this:

First write to the agent or venue, whoever is paying you and give them seven clear days to send you the money. Date the letter and keep a copy for yourself. This letter, incidentally, is sent by registered post. If after 10 days have elapsed, you have not got the cash from them, then write again. This time stating that if you have not got the money in full by (give date 7 days later) then you will immediately issue a courts summons upon them in you local small claims court. If the money arrives even a day late, it will be too late, and the court costs will also be added and they will have to pay them once you have placed the matter into the hands of the court, which you will do seven days from date of letter. Again date this letter, take a copy and send by registered mail to them. Then if you do need to go to a small claims court don't worry, as the clerks will help you fill out all the forms to take out a summons. This is fairly cheap to do and you get it all back after the hearing from the agent or shows booker. It is heard by a local judge or registrar, they are most helpful, especially when you have the copy of all letters sent and original contract to show them. A free booklet is available from the court which will tell you in full the details which must be followed when making a claim. If you are and Equity member however, you can get them to do this for you on your behalf and at their expense, just so long as the contract issued was an Equity approved one.

PLACES TO WORK

Hire a theatre, a hall in the summer, either or both in a seaside town. Anywhere large numbers of people go for a holiday. Discount your tickets to the selling agent, tobacco kiosk, newsagents, corner shops, landladies and anywhere that will sell them for you and where the public go on a regular basis, this includes the pubs and hotels. Sometimes, give a very big discount if they buy a set number of tickets at once. Remember that it is much easier and more enjoyable to give a show in a large theatre than in a working mens club or public house. You can hire most theatres, especially on a Sunday night. If you want to hire for the summer season, then apply very early, as demand for the venue will be high. Apply to the local council for your license long before you give the show, it can take them a long time to agree permission and of course if they don't, you can arrange another plan of action based on this course contents. It is also preferable to get your solicitor to apply for the license on your behalf.

Telephone and send all your particulars to working men's clubs and similar venues. Most districts have their own club magazine, advertise in this and work will result. Find out all the addresses of forces bases that you can, and mailshot them, marking the letters for the attention of the Entertainment's Officer of the Officers Mess, the Sergeants Mess and the Corporals Mess. Find out the addresses of all the Holiday Camps that are privately run and send them your details also.

Also send your promotion pack to the entertainments officer at Head Office for Butlins, Warner and Haven Holidays etc., as they employ their own agents to supply them with acts. Also go to the travel agent and get loads of cruise brochures and send to the Head Office of each of the cruise companies your details, as this is a most lucrative and pleasurable field of work to be in. In other words, spend money sending your publicity pack everywhere that you could possibly imagine and from whom you might possibly get some work. You must always speculate in order to accumulate.

COMMERCIAL VIDEOS

Make certain that you know the terms of contract, as the video may be sold to anyone. Your show is personal to you and once it's on tape you could be losing money. It is better to forbid all videoing unless it involves substantial financial income to yourself. It's your livelihood they want to sell to others.

NO SOLE AGENT

This means you work for yourself, find your own jobs and do all your own publicity etc., whilst accepting shows off all and any agents who may wish to pass them your way. If you have good sales and marketing skills, then this may be the option for you.

SHOW LENGTH

Most Hypnotists give a club show of around 45 to 60 minutes of duration. A theatre show would be at least two hours, including the interval time and two hours thirty minutes is closer to the norm. Universities and college shows are usually 60 to 90 minutes long, forces bases are from one to two hours long. TV shows as long as they want it, will usually be timed in minutes. Your show length is of course up to you at all times and what the venue wish you to provide for them.

TV SHOWS

On TV you cannot do adult routines prior to 9pm, due to the threshold set down by the I.B.C. Family style hypnotic routines, can be aired at all times, but the full hypnotic induction cannot be shown or heard. Edited highlights, as in the Paul McKenna TV show, can however, be transmitted. On TV interviews always look directly at the interviewer, unless told otherwise.

When it's a live performance that's just being filmed, work as if no cameras are actually there, when being filmed think of the camera as your audience at home who are watching and these would be who you play your act to.

When you put the subject under prior to a TV show or break when live on air, then remember always to use a code word or phrase to control them when you are not around. This code word will also put them back under rapidly in the second half of the show. TV exposure is worth its weight in gold, whether you are paid for the appearance or not it can ultimately lead to increased popularity in your act and as such, an increase in your performing fee.

INTERPRETERS

When working abroad, you will usually find that it's an English speaking audience you've been booked for, in which case no problem. If you are booked to appear abroad for the natives and you speak their language, then do the act in the foreign tongue. However, there may come a time when you need to work with an interpreter, don't let this scare you one tiny bit. It will work perfectly well if you follow these guidelines. Have a new voice over intro done for your act, which introduces you in the foreign language, by your interpreter, so think carefully what you are to say. For example, I'd take the trouble to learn the foreign pronunciation of the two words sleep and wide awake. You can then, via the interpreter, hypnotise them so that when you say sleep they will go back under and when you say awake they will awaken and do as they have been told by you via the interpreter. They will know you are speaking to them, as you'll place your hand upon their shoulder. Explain that your hand commands must be obeyed (make these up as needed.) At the start of the act appear to hypnotise the interpreter and place them under your control, now this may sound corny, but it must be done, so that you appear to be controlling them in order for the belief and expectancy factor to come into play. When hypnotising them use a method in which you are touching them, such as the falling backwards test, this means that you still get some kind of instant rapport with your subject. Apart from that, proceed as normal, just allowing for the fact that it has to be interpreted before it is acted upon. Oh yes, although you may be working through an interpreter, it's very handy to know enough of the local lingo in order to be able to order food and drink etc.

An excellent way to learn most foreign languages within a week, is with the Paul Daniels language courses that uses a memory system, which is so effective that even I managed to learn French in just a few hours. You can get full details of these by sending a S.A.E. to Mr Trevor Daniels, Magic Marketing Ltd (Courses), 39 Alston Drive, Blackwell Abbey, Milton

Keynes, MK13 9HA. I believe that the courses still cost £125 per language to be learnt. This itself is excellent value for money and of course it's tax deductible.

PUBLICITY MATERIALS

Off course, if you are to send out top quality publicity materials to as many potential bookers as possible, then you will need to know from where to purchase them, so here's some leads for you.

STICKY BACK PHOTOS

These are photos of you, which are reproduced in different sizes and have a self adhesive back, making them ideal to stick to envelopes, letterheads and small posters etc. For details contact: Sticky Back Photos (Colab Ltd), Herald Way, Coventry, CV3 1BB. Tel: Coventry 440404

BUSINESS CARDS AND LETTERHEADS

Both are essential, as you'll come into contact with people everyday who potentially could offer you work and in any business you will always need to write letters. Local suppliers of both items can be found in your Yellow Pages. But as a general rule of thumb, for that successful image, always use Conqueror top quality paper for the letterheads and have the cards printed on finest quality cardstock. The place where I personally have all these kind of things printed is: Mr Stuart Ferguson, Speedy Printing, 9 Lupton Street, Denton, Manchester. Tel: 0161 336 8357 or send a S.A.E. for full details.

BROCHURES AND POSTERS

Your brochure can of course be printed in black and white upon good quality paper, in which case Speedy Printing can help you. I however prefer full colour photographic brochures, as they look far more impressive and successful, that's the image that you need to create in order to demand big fees. The cheapest colour printers, I've found in the UK, are Interprint, they do top quality work at incredibly low prices, for a catalogue and samples contact: Interprint Colour Printers, 81 Washway Road, Sale, Cheshire. M33 1TQ. Tel: 0161 905 1805. Fax: 0161 905 1531. Although based in Cheshire, they have offices all over the UK and do operate a mail order service, as do all the contacts that I shall be passing your way.

PHOTOGRAPHS AND LARGE SHOW POSTERS

You will also require 10 x 8 colour repro photos to send to all potential bookers and agents etc. Also, possibly, postcard size colour photos for autographs etc. These items along with full colour cassette covers are available from the below address: Cresment Printing Services, Freepost, 30 Church Lane, Mansfield, Nottinghamshire. NG18 TBR. Tel: 01623 21192. S.A.E. for list. At the time of writing, 10 x 8 colour photos with super gloss finish cost £175 per thousand, including caption, post and VAT. Delivery being free of charge. 1,000 A3 full colour show posters are just £360 including delivery and VAT etc. If you order both the photos and posters at the same time, they will give you a £50 discount off the total cost of order.

GENERAL PUBLICITY MATERIALS

Invoices, receipts, compliment slips, letterheads and in fact almost all printed matter are available, again by mail, order from Delaney and Smith, (Printers and Stationers) 331 Squires Gate Lane, Blackpool. FY4 3RG. Tel: 01253 48612 Fax: 01253 485963. also for samples etc.

GOLD, SILVER FOIL BUSINESS CARDS ETC.

For gold and silver metalic foil finish business cards and promotional merchandise, such as key rings, badges, mugs, cards, T-Shirts etc., which you can sell for profit at gigs contact. Ron and Brenda Anyon, The Name Machine, 57A Chapel Street, Blackpool. FY1 5HF Tel: 01253 20245.

PHOTO MASTER COPIES

To have photographic reproductions done by Crescent, you will of course need a professional shot done in a studio first of all. To find a photographer who has experience of doing sessions for show business acts, look within the pages of The Stage and TV Newspaper. You may have to travel quite a distance, but the expense is well worth it. I can however recommend:

a. Michael on 0161 792 5291
b. 0161 860 4235 for The Contact Studio
c. Derek Parsons on 01706 39069

All three have experience in this field, for example Derek Parsons did my shots and Michael, I believe, did some shots for Peter Powers (Hypnotist). You should look immaculate on the photo, make up can go a long way to helping achieve this desired effect. A straight 10 x 8 head and shoulders shot is all that you require to send out to agents etc. A full length postcard shot will do for autographs to give your fans after shows. For some reason, all stage hypnotists seem to do weird things with their hands on photo and on posters. Well on posters I think it looks OK and sets the scene, but on photos I think it looks crap and really all the agent wants to know is what you look like. A mirror held up in front of you can help you get the pose you wish the man behind the camera to see through his lens. As a general rule of thumb, I would say never look directly into a camera, unless a last resort.

SOLICITORS

At some time you'll need the services of a good solicitor and it helps to use one that has a sound knowledge of the show business industry and how it works. As an Equity member, you will be put in touch with a suitable solicitor, but one that I personally have found to be excellent is: Flacks Ross Solicitors, 35 Peter Street, Manchester. M2 5GD. Tel: 0161 834 7368.

PROM VIDEO MASTER

A promo video is a most valuable tool in getting work. As these days many agents and venues wish to see you perform before booking you and by having a video to show them it saves the need for an audition etc. You can have a cheap publicity video made for around £500 with a local company that you can find in Yellow Pages. However a broadcast quality video, shot by professional cameramen, on several cameras and professionally edited etc. will cost between £2000 to £3000, for everything that needs to be done to produce you master tape for you. From this master tape, numerous copies can then be made and sent to potential bookers, agents etc., and clips can even be used by TV companies, should they interview you, that's why you need your video to be of broadcast quality standard. Usually shot with two or three cameras, professionals will know how to make you look like a star. The expense is a once in a lifetime investment. It's tax deductable and if the tape is of broadcast quality you will usually be the first hypnotist chosen to go onto chat shows etc., as they can save both time and money by just paying you some extra money and transmitting material from your tape, instead of filming a hypnotist live at work. So in time, you can actually make a profit on your investment. Many production companies are around that can help you, they advertise in the pages of the Stage and TV Newspapers. However, for information the company which do all my promotional tapes and teaching tapes etc. is: ICE International Productions, 50 Fearndale Avenue, Whitefield, Greater Manchester. M45 7QP. Tel: 0850 730171. Contact Mr Anthony Sharman. Their head office is in sunny Malta and believe me, they are real professional, having shot feature films for the European and worldwide market, so you will end up with a video which you can be proud of.

EFFECTIVE ADVERTS

One of the best places to advertise, as it is sent to the licensees of pubs, clubs, night clubs, theatres, holiday camps and in fact, most places you could wish to work in, is a monthly publication called, Night Life Journal Magazine. Ads in this magazine produce big results as the ads are seen and the magazine is read by people who do book acts such as yours. Contact them at: Nightlife Journal Magazine, 21 Devonshire Road, Wirral, Merseyside. L43 4UP Tel: 0151 651 2216.

PUBLIC RELATIONS COMPANIES

As I said earlier, these can make you a star, see your local Yellow Pages for details, although to be honest the best companies to use are those that specialise in show business acts and you can find details of these in the White Book International Production Directory. One company which I can recommend personally is: Celebrity Marketing, Star House, 39 Star Street, London. W2 1QB. Tel: 0171724 4343. Fax: 0171723 5463.

A company which I can personally recommend that will, for a price, work hard to get you national scale publicity on radio, TV and in the media is

Saatchi & Saatchi Direct, they can be contacted at 80 Charlotte Street, London. W1A 1AQ. Tel: 0171 636 5060. Telex: 261580. Fax: 0171 637 8489.

A personal pet reporter can also be invaluable, as they will, whenever they think of a story connected with hypnosis, contact you and feature you in it. A personal reporter is very hard to find and of course an element of trust must exist between you, which can only be created after a long working relationship of a harmonious nature. You will have to hang out where reporters go and buy them drinks, get friendly and then they'll do you favours. One important point I must mention here, is that most feature stories in newspapers only contain 10% or less of actual truth, the rest is untrue. However, the paper itself does not usually know this and only you and the freelance reporter will ever know. My pet freelance reporter has got me a feature spread in a leading ladies magazine, several features in the Sun and much more.

MAKE UP AND GROOMING

You must always look like a film star, both on and off stage, when you are in the show business industry. Every aspect of your personal grooming should be immaculate, but I'll cover this subject only briefly as it is dealt with in depth in, The Magic of Show business by Simon Lovell, available from Repro Magic. For a quick sun tanned image, use a sun bed for short time each day, use fast tan tanning tablets in conjunction with this.

For stage make up ask in Boots Chemist, available manufactured by Leichner of London at various prices. I, however, personally prefer to use a ladies all day pancake base make up by Max Factor and powder off with a colour toning powder by Yardley or Max Factor. A black eye pencil is used to blacken my eyebrows and to underline my eyes for that sinister and mysterious look. Lastly, some very subtle and lightly coloured lipstick/grease paint is used to pick out my lips slightly. Now let me assure you on stage you do not look effeminate, you just look like a person with a suntan, who appears successful and don't forget, without the make up, under the stage lights, you'd look white like a ghost. To apply the make up is something which you must learn, through practice, until you get it right, advice, however, will be freely given to you by the sales assistant in your local Boots make up department.

To conclude briefly, you must always be clean, remember deodorant and subtle after shave, your hair must be washed and combed and in other words, you should have made every possible effort to look your best in every way. I always wear "Pheromones" on stage, which is a liquid spray "musk" after shave, which contains within it powerful "pheromones." These "pheromones" cannot consciously be smelt by women, but they do have the psychological effect of attracting women towards you. It can also make them more willing to do as you say and they can be purchased for £10 a bottle from any of the companies which advertise in national papers and adult magazines.

COSTUMERS

Here it is just a case of finding a good tailor who can do what you want and have the best hand made clothing that your money can buy. These days, however, it is becoming more and more acceptable to wear off the peg, high class clothing, which although of a similar style to that worn by the general public, is one million times better. For example, theirs is a black shirt and yours is a black shirt encrusted with imitation diamonds upon pure silk material with a designer label. It is most obviously a fashion designers creation, direct from a Paris catwalk show.

PONTINS SEASON/SEASONS ABROAD

For a season on the Pontins Holiday Camps or abroad on cruise work etc., the agent to contact is: Kennedy Leisure and Management, Sagar House, The Green, Eccleston, Chorley, Lancashire. PR7 5QQ.

FEMALE/MALE ASSISTANT

For a male performer, a female assistant can be of use and for a female stage hypnotist a male assistant can be of use. She/he can escort people from out of the audience up to the stage, she/he can set props upon the stage ready for the next routine and of course, he/she could be used to participate in the onstage routines with the hypnotised subjects. For example, he/she could be the lovely model that the entranced members of the opposite sex turn down for a blind date and then wish they hadn't when you snap your fingers and they return to reality and see the stunning model before them. So with a little imagination, I am sure you can easily see how a male/female assistant can add much sparkle, polish and professionalism to your on stage show.

MIDNIGHT HYPNOTISM SHOWS

Mr Robert Halphern was the first stage hypnotist to present a show at midnight, the witching hour, this he did at an Edinburgh Festival Show many years ago. Since the Peter Powers and myself have both presented shows at midnight and there are certain advantages to doing this. For example, as a hypnotist show has very little in the way of props etc., to set you can quite easily go into a theatre after the standard evening performance has finished and be set up ready for a show at midnight. As such you can book up a tour of theatres quicker than usual, as they will already be open that night and to stay open a few extra hours will not cost them much more, as such, unlike usual, when you have to book the venue many months in advance, a few months notice can often be given for a midnight show.

The midnight hypnotism show is also a gimmick, which you can use to obtain much free publicity for your shows and it sets as eerie atmosphere for the show. The best nights for such shows are Fridays or Saturdays, as you will then attract the night club style crowd to the show, who are out anyway at that time of night. Incidentally, as Peter Powers has done many times in the past, as you are aiming for the night club clientel, you can do a midnight show and then a 2.30am show. The second show catches all the people as they come out of the night clubs and as strange as it sounds, these shows can be very well attended indeed. The only drawback with such shows, is that the venue usually demands that extra security staff are employed and you must then pay for this cost from your own pocket.

COMBINING MAGIC WITH HYPNOSIS

Magic tricks and illusions can, as I have found with my own stage show, be used within the hypnotic show to make your show different than those the audience may have seen before. Without giving away too many of my ideas, let me just say that it looks better to magically be produced from "nowhere" than just walk on stage at the start of the show. Also it can amaze and shock the audience to see an entranced subject be by hung on a gallows or in an electric chair.

Also, why chance hurting someone by piercing their skin with a real needle, when there is a magical way to achieve such things? Now that I've set your mind thinking on this subject, I will leave you to come to your own conclusions, however many excellent magical props, illusions and effects, which can be combined within your show, are available along with books of plans for illusions etc. from these companies: www.magicweek.co.uk

COMBINING SINGING AND MUSIC WITH HYPNOSIS

In much the same way as magic can be combined with hypnosis, it is also possible to combine vocal songs sung by yourself and the playing of musical instruments into your act. My colleague, The Astounding Anthony "S", has already done this with great success and has established himself as the original "Song and Trance Man." He has the volunteers react to key words within a song he sings by reacting in hilarious and relevant to the song ways. When singing such songs, he also plays the music to accompany himself upon his guitar or other instruments. With a little thought you could adapt this idea to suit your own manner and style.

SOUNDMAN/DRIVER

You will most definitely need to employ someone to operate your music and change the tapes etc. As you will have to pay them for this, I always make sure that I employ a soundman who drives, so that I can just pay the petrol/diesel money and he then also takes me to and from the show as well as acting as my soundman. This means that after the show I can have a drink or two if I desire, I can also go to sleep on the way to and from shows. If your soundman also happens to be on the very muscular side then he can also act as your body guard and intervene should any nasty situations occur. This means that you will then not get hurt during the time it takes from any agro starting to the moment the establishment's bouncers get to you and sort out the situation. This in itself is worth its weight in gold. So how do you find a soundman? Well, simple answer, I just found a well built (bouncer style) guy on the dole, who had a car and wants to earn some money on the quiet. You agree to pay all petrol costs and all they have to do is drive you to and from the venue, help you get your gear in and set up, act as your bodyguard and control the music tapes during your act. For one nights work you will pay them £50.

As for the music cues, it's quite easy. Each piece of music is recorded onto a separate audio tape of the highest quality that you can afford. The name of the routine it's to be used for is then written both onto the cassette and onto the cover. This way, if they get separated you will always know which goes with which. The reason each track of music is recorded onto a separate tape, is because sometimes you might let a routine run three minutes and sometimes only for a minute, dependant upon the audiences response to it.

As a general rule of thumb, I have the track of music recorded five times in a row onto the tape. This usually gives me 5 minutes of continuous music upon each tape, this way you can be 100% sure that the music will never run out during a routine which you are milking for laughs. I have the music recorded onto the tapes, so that it's always on side A, so that the moment it is place into the tape deck and started the music starts to play. You must always have the tapes set in their covers prior to a show so that the right tape is in the right cover, also so that the music will instantly start to play when placed in the tape machine. The tapes, of which I carry around two sets of 45 tapes a case, are transported inside one of those executive style cassette tape holders and are in the order you require. The routines name is written on the edge of the cover so it's visible with the case lid open. For example, the music might be the Bladerunner theme, but upon the cover it say 60 second fast induction music. The Birdie song is used when making them believe they are chickens laying square eggs, so on the cover it just says chicken, on Jailhouse Rock it just says Elvis and on Like A Virgin, it just says Madonna.

Hopefully by now you will have got the general idea of just how easy the music cues will be, as your cue is given automatically within the commands that you give to the onstage volunteers. For example, if you said "in a few moments, when I awake you and the music begins to play, you will be Elvis". Then the soundman just looks for the tape which says

Elvis upon it, places it into the tape deck and presses play when you give him a nod, it really is as simple as that. You could of course invest a lot of money and have all your music recorded onto a couple of Digital Audio Tapes (D.A.T.S.), these give CD quality sound and full shows music will fit upon one DAT tape, which can be in the DAT player at all times. You can then, by infra red remote control, start whichever track of music you want from the tape at any time, in just the same way as you can select any track from a CD player.

P.A. SYSTEM

At the start of your hypnotic career you'll need a P.A. system consisting of a 200 watt amplifier, two speakers, two speaker stands, a double dolby system tape deck, radio microphone and all the connecting leads. As you'll be working mainly in pubs and clubs to start with, a 200 watt mixer amplifier with four channels minimum, will suffice along with two speakers, which must be capable of handling 200 watts per channel each.

You can buy all your new equipment from local suppliers, who can be found in your Yellow Pages directory, they may even be able to supply you with some good quality second hand equipment. Your local Free Adverts paper is also a good source for second hand equipment, of high quality at cheap prices. You should expect to pay between £500 and £1500 for second hand and from £1000 up to £3000, for a high quality brand new set up with guarantees etc.

You could, of course, hire a P.A. from a local music shop on a nightly basis until you have earned enough to buy your own. However, when you are working a lot, it's much more profitable to own your own, as it can cost from £20 to £40 a night to hire a suitable P.A. system. Anywhere which needs amplification of more than 200 watts will have their own P.A. in house system, which you can just connect your radio mike to. You can of course, eventually have in the rider to your contract, a condition stating that the venue is responsible at all times for providing a suitable P.A. at their own cost. This then saves you the aggravation of transporting and setting up your own P.A.

Incidentally, by law, all places which have been granted an Entertainment's Licence, are meant to have their own in house P.A. system, although obviously, this is not always reality. The systems are easy to connect up and whoever sells you one will be pleased to demonstrate which leads connects to what socket etc. The speaker stands are used to raise the speakers up into the air to avoid "feedback" as you walk around, I'd advise you to purchase a top of the range sure radio mike so that you don't get interference from taxi cabs etc.

FEMALE STAGE HYPNOTISTS

There is already one by the name of Saphire and one by the name of Lo Reid and lovely people they are too. So there is definitely an opening in the industry for female stage hypnotists. I feel that it's harder for women to become stage hypnotists because of the stereo typed view that the public at large have of all hypnotists being men, as such, this can affect the belief and expectancy factor. However, I do feel that more females should take up the art and I for one, would give them all the help I possibly can.

DUAL HYPNOTIST ACTS

I believe that I was the first person, certainly in the UK, to do half of a dual hypnotism show, entitled "Battle of The Hypnotists." In its most basic format, there were two separate halves to the show and two very different hypnotists. One hypnotist did the first half of the show and then the influence was changed from hypnotist A to hypnotist B, so the subjects would react to the new performer in the second half. To transfer the influence from one hypnotist to another, you would just say, "I'm now talking to each and every person upon the stage. For the rest of this evening, whenever you hear this voice, (hypnotist B then says, sleep and relax). Yes the moment he says (hypnotist B says sleep and relax), you'll instantly react to whatever he says for the rest of tonight's show and carry it out as an automatic reflex action. So you will now only react to this new voice (at this point hypnotist B says sleep and relax and then takes over the act, with the people on stage now reacting to his commands.)

It is very easy to transfer the influence in this way from one hypnotist to another and it looks very impressive to all audiences, whilst also being a good ploy to use in order to obtain much free publicity for all the shows you do.

If one of you was male and the other female, you'd also have the battle of
the sex's element coming in play and once again, much free publicity
could be obtained. Another advantage with dual hypnotism acts, is that
you can apparently hypnotise you partner and then perform such banned
stunts as catalepsy across two chairs on them without ever breaking the
law. With a little thought on your part, much comedy banter could be
devised along the lines that you keep trying to place each other under
hypnosis and get one another to do stupid things.

Look in the Stage and TV classifieds for comedy script writers, they would
be able to devise original routines and scenarios for you dual hypnotism
act.

PROPS

As we have covered in depth already, you can't see hypnosis, but you can
see the effects of it upon people. The use of props makes a lot of routines
much funnier than they would have been otherwise. The reason being, the
audience have more of a visual element to observe and enjoy when props
are combined into your shows. Judicious use of props will enhance any
show, look around, you will be very surprised what you can use as a prop
and with a little thought many ideas will present themselves to you.

Words of advice though, a blow up penis may seem funny, a blow up
rubber doll also, but both carry implications of pornography, so please, for
your own sake, do not use such items in your show. They may be funny at
private parties, or among friends, but never at a public show. No, the
audience are not narrow minded, they just laugh at different things in
different situations of life. In a club or theatre, that is not the place they
will find it funny, obscene yes, funny, no.

COMEDY TECHNIQUE

To learn the art of comedy timing is something which only comes with
experience of doing live shows. So the more shows you do and get under
your belt, the better you will become. A good book, which I thoroughly
recommend on the principles of presenting comedy and the psychology of

comedy is, Comedy Techniques for Magicians which is available from www.magicalguru.co.uk

YOUR GUIDE TO £36,000 INCOME IN YEAR ONE

Firstly let me point out, the research and development of this course started in 1994, and prices as mentioned were correct at time of writing. Should you be reading this in years to come, the principles will remain the same, but just bring the amounts up to a more realistic figure for your time of reading. So let me start this chunk of the money making chapter by stating that it's much better at the start of your career to do 10 shows at £125 each, instead of 5 shows at £250 each. Now the reason for this is simply that although you'll end up doing double the shows for the same money, you will have gained twice as much practical performing experience with your act. No amount of money can buy you this experience, which will teach you more than any course or book ever could. Once you have polished your act to perfection and have created a demand for your act then you can raise your fee and demand your own price. Even if you only worked pubs, you can have an excellent income and lifestyle. I well remember, that when I did work, then I was rebooked at the same venue every 6 to 8 weeks, that means, that one pub can have you on up to 6 or 7 times a year. Now if you get 16 venues who'll book you every eight weeks then if you book them in staggered and charged just £250 a show you'' have 16 venues providing eight shows a year, each which is a total of 144 shows you be doing year. And 144 shows by £250 per show equals and income of £36,000 each year and as all the pubs would be in your local area, most of this would be profit. This itself is a good income by anyone's standards, you'd still have loads of time left to promote your own theatre shows, which could earn you up to £15,000 or more profit a night on each 2,000 seat theatre that you fill at £10 a ticket. So hopefully you can now see that if your act is well planned and presented you really can earn an income and live a lifestyle that others only ever dream of getting. All you need to be in business is, yourself, costume, make-up, small case of props, music tapes, P.A. system and radio mike and your advertising materials.

Even if you're not very good at sales and marketing, you must be able to find 16 venues that will book you every eight weeks in your local area for £250 a night. If this is hard, drop your price to £125 and find 32 venues that will book you each eight weeks, you will then still be on an income of £36,000 a year, you'll just be performing more regularly for it. In your first year of trading this would be a good idea, to perfect your act before taking your show on a theatre tour of England. Charging £250 a show as stated above, you would be working on average three nights a week, at £125 a show you'd be working on average six nights a week, which not many people in show business are doing. You can earn an additional income by doing private hypnotherapy sessions [See the hypnotherapy course] in the daytime at a charge of around £40 an hour, also by selling home hypnotherapy tapes by mail order.

After 12 to 18 months of doing this and saving most of the money, you'll then be in a position to promote your own theatre tour of the UK and start earning up to £15,000 or more profit on a nightly basis. As you have been doing so many shows all over the area, you will have built up a following and your first theatre show should, as a result, be sold out many weeks in advance. So, let's just say only 40 people from each of the 16 regular venues came to your theatre show, that's 640 tickets at £10 each, which would have been sold almost instantly. £10 by 640 people is a total of £6400 cash, which would have been pulled in almost instantly and this alone would bring you into profit on the cost of hiring the theatre and publicity. You'd still have about 1360 seats to sell at £10 each, which when sold, would be another £13.000 cash profit for you after all expenses. So you see in the long term, the really big profits are to be made in promoting your own theatre shows, which can realistically, within a couple of years, turn you into a millionaire, even without having had your own TV series. When you are up to this level and people want to book you for show, you should then be charging an absolute minimum of £500 a night and in fact, I'd say £800 to £1500 is closer to the mark.

Also, remember, that in the hypnotism industry, there are so many avenues of income to be made, some of which include, shows, TV series, hypnotherapy, and corporate stress management hypnosis sessions, sale of audio tapes, books and videos of various natures. Training courses, personal appearances, advisor to magazines, TV and films on hypnosis and many, many more avenues, including article writer on hypnosis for magazines etc. etc. In fact, the ways in which hypnosis can be put to use to earn money, are only limited by your own imagination and skills in sales and marketing.

Now I may have made all this sound so easy. But if you have a good act, good sales and marketing skills and can "win friends and influence people" which, incidentally, is the title of a book I highly recommend by Dale Carnegi. Then you truly will be able to "think and grow rich" which is the title of another book I recommend by Napoleon Hill. So you see that the income and life style that you have always really dreamed of is now realistically in your grasp. And the plan I have just outlined will start you earning money from day one and set you on a three to five year plan to financial freedom of the very highest standard.

2017 UPDATE = In England during 2017 even Stage Hypnotists who are just starting out are charging between £250 to £350 for shows even in small venues and thus on that basis the Marketing Plan just explained could actually help you to earn £72,000 or more in your first year.

You would be wise to grab a copy of out Free Book on Marketing for Stage Hypnotists which can be obtained from: **www.elitehypnosisbootcamp.com/freebook/**

<u>**PART THIRTEEN**</u>

COMEDY SKETCH IDEAS

The appeal of a stage hypnotist's show to an audience is two fold.

A. They like to witness or experience what they believe to be a great power, and:

B. There is nothing funnier on this planet than seeing your friends make complete fools of themselves and not be able to stop their own actions, which become automatic.

To conclude the area of stage hypnotism there follows a comprehensive compilation of routines to ensure a successful show. This chapter contains numerous ideas for sketches which you can use. With a little bit of thought you can adapt the examples I give or come up with brand new ideas, which will then give you your own unique show. How you word the suggestions you give and how you present these scenarios to on stage subjects I will leave you to work out for yourself, as your should by now be armed with more than enough knowledge to do this. I will however, point out that where possible, there must be continuity in your suggestions, so that one routine leads into the next one logically. This will make the whole show look that much more organised and professional and as a result will make it more entertaining for your future audiences.

For example, at the end of a routine where the subjects have been freezing cold and snuggling up to each other in bed, you will be able to logically link it to the next routine by just saying. "It's no longer 7am in the morning and it's no longer freezing cold. In fact, we are in a new time altogether, it's 4pm in the afternoon, it's now lovely and warm and we're all on a sunny Spanish beach."

Another example of how routines can be linked together is that they are cold and told to hug themselves. The moment they do this, their arms are now in the correct position to tell them that they are stuck inside a straight jacket and there is a ferret running around inside it. Music then starts and they become the Saturday Night Fever dancers, extending one arm out into the air whilst one arm remains against their chest.

Can you see how cleanly this makes the routines link together? I hope so, as this is the kind of thing you should be aiming for in your own comedy hypnotism stage show. Another example, they are riding their horses along at a canter, they are John Wayne, out to catch Billy the Kid. Then the music changes and it's now a new time altogether as they are now all jockeys at the grand national races. Can you see now, how the routines can be linked logically, either by words, continuity or an overall underlying theme, which links them?

Enough said on the subject, this is something which you must do for yourself, so that your show becomes unique and personal to you. Another technique to get maximum comedy exposure is a running gag, which carries on for a while and gets funnier in the audience's eyes each time you refer to it. An example of this being that a subject is told to stand at the side of the stage and start counting from one up to three million. At intervals throughout the show you go to the subject, hold the radio mike to his lips and the audience hear that he has indeed gone much higher with his counting. Now this may not sound at all funny, but believe me, in reality, each time you return to him, it becomes funnier. Obviously you must be careful not to milk the gag for too long, as always remember, the old adage, "always leave them wanting more". A final example is that one subject is told they are Madonna and one is to be Elvis. Just as the Madonna girl sits down, the Elvis music starts, so it's instantly into that. This is then done in reverse and repeated a few times, the resulting mania of people diving out of their chairs and being a famous star one minute, then acting as if they have done nothing the next, becomes hilarious to the audience. The comedy hypnotism show is situation comedy at its best. Obviously you must suit the style of routines that you use each night to the venue, audience, age ranges and tastes. Family shows are 100% clean, adult shows a little naughty, but not over the top. Stag and Hen night shows are as blue as you like and you can, as long as it's legal, do whatever you so desire.

Also remember to check if people are allergic to onions before getting them to eat as apples, or check that they are not allergic to feathers before giving them a feather boa to wear and turning them into Shirley Bassey. You must always put the Health and Safety of your on stage subjects first, foremost and last. Also ensure you know clearly what kind of show the person booking you wishes you to present, that way you won't offend anyone and will always get paid. Basically, it's all down to thinking on your feet and using your common sense, so if in doubt about a routine, leave it out. Remember too, that for someone to try to put their hands up a woman's skirt but being stopped in time is funny. To allow them to do so for real is rude, vulgar and in bad taste and could well get you a smack on the nose from the girl's boyfriend or husband. Things can actually be funnier by letting the subjects only go so far and then leaving the rest to audience's imaginations who will then draw their own conclusions on what would have occurred if you hadn't stopped them.

Also always ensure that the subject has understood the commands which have just given them, a good phrase to use for this is: "Just nod your head if you understand."

Also ensure that if giving several suggestions to different people one after the other in succession, that each subject knows for sure which one they are meant to act upon, a good phrase to use here is: "I'm only talking to you if my hand's upon your shoulder."

Obviously if you want everyone to react to the same suggestion at the same time you would just say something like: "I'm now talking to each and every person upon the stage."

Another way in which to increase the comedy element of the act is to say: "As soon as the music stops you'll wonder what the hell you're doing." This means, that they awaken, the music plays and they then do as you have commanded. Then, when the music is stopped unexpectedly you will find that the sincerely puzzled look upon the subject's faces is hilarious in itself. Another very useful phrase to use is: "In a few moments when I awake you." This makes sure that they know when to carry out the suggestion and also, ensures that they do not awaken whilst the suggestion is being given to them.

ADAPTABILITY

Being versatile and adaptable is the key to success in the show business industry. When working a stag night with an all men audience, the show must be planned to suit the occasion. By far the best way to make regular money until you've made it big is to do squeaky clean family style show that will offend no-one and will entertain all. If you are engaged for a cruise, generally the audiences will be made up of the older generation. Ideally try and get any younger ones up to participate, but if required to use the elderly people, then do not give any controversial type commands, only use middle of the road ones. Also bear in mind that running around trying to catch invisible grasshoppers may be funny, but it's not very nice to expect an old person to do this (they may have heart trouble). Use your common sense and judgement at all times, with an older audience. The guaranteed handclasp test should be used at the start of your act, so that your credentials are immediately established and belief and expectancy sets in to make life easier. Also always flatter the older ones, (don't patronise) as flattery, correctly used, will get you everywhere in life.

In smaller social situations act reluctant to give a demonstration for free, then when everyone keeps asking you to, they will then be in the correct state of mind to be placed into hypnosis easily and rapidly. Lastly, before we consider the subject of routine and sketch ideas to get the hypnotised subjects to carry out, let's now discuss the subjects of stage lighting and how it can be used to best effect in our hypnotic show.

Lighting can in itself create different psychological moods and atmospheres. It can also add to the comedy effect of a sketch within your show. For example, you make someone believe they are Elvis and they start dancing to Jail House Rock, here the coloured spotlights on stage should flash on and off in time to the music to create a rock concert effect. Another example, you make a number of men dress up in tights and become the worlds greatest ballerinas, the lights should dim to just blues and reds and then two follow spots should follow the "star" ballet dancers around the stage as they do their stuff.

A quick word here on the subject of costumes for the onstage subjects, a person becoming Madonna can be very funny, it can however be even funnier if it's a man and he is dressed in a wig, bra and Madonna style outfit for the sketch. The subject can be sent offstage to be dressed by the stage crew and is then brought back on at the correct time to do the routine. So give the subject of costumes a thought as well.

Obviously, the use of props and background music helps to enhance any comedy sketch that you do, so use these most effective tools also. Large comedy items of use are available from all novelty supply stores.

Back to lighting; For intro and opening patter use stage lights on reds and blues and you work under a white follow spot. As subjects come up to stage, stage lights full up (white) and house lights on too. Once all subjects are upon the stage turn out all the house lights, but leave the stage lights full up and start induction's etc. From then onwards I suggest lights of reds and blues for each test, with a single subject with a spotlight directed upon him/her and stage lights full up for all group routines involving all subjects. NOTE: You must be followed by a follow spot at all times during the opening patter etc.

When the subjects are made to perform sketches within the show they are then the real stars, not you and as such, either the spotlights are upon them or the stage lights are full up.

ADDITIONAL LIGHTING EFFECT IDEAS

A. Have a baby spotlight mounted overhead in the flys. Have amber gels upon it and focus it vertically downwards at your special "hypnotic" chair. Or have a few over the chairs or different relaxing colours to aid the induction process. Incidentally the idea of a special chair is just pure showmanship and you use it for the best subject to sit in.

B. A baby spotlight in the wings, focused at the performers face, with stage lights dimmed, can be very effective when doing an induction and staring at a subject in the eyes. (Try a green gel here).

C. A floor lamp behind the subject's chair directed over his shoulder gives an interesting aura effect.

D. A double faced mirror on a revolving turntable with a spotlight focused upon it where it is in the wings. As it revolves, it gives (reflects) out flashes of light around the stage and makes a really weird atmospheres, ideal for induction's.

E. A revolving mirror globe, fixed over the stage in the flys, with a light focused upon it will send flashing lights throughout the entire theatre. A good effect for when they are entering the theatre at the start of the evening.

EFFECT OF COLOURS

Yellow seems to increase suggestibility, whilst purple, blue and green, all help to induce the hypnotic sleep state. As such, if you have lights in the flys pointing at the subjects, so that the light shines into their eyes as they look up for the P.R.I. eyestrain induction, then the following colour effects can be used to enhance the induction.

1   When commencing the induction (yellow on).

2   (As eyes close) off yellow and into purples.
3   (When sleep and cold day) blues for effect.
4   (When sleep and hot day) reds for effect.

I hope all this has given you an idea of how much effect a few lighting changes can have upon your entire show. Your onstage backdrop, ideally if left blank should be a dark deep colour, such as black, blue or rich wine, so that the subjects clothes make a good contrast and do not blend in. Paul McKenna has a black backdrop with little fibre optic lights all over it, with an opening in the centre shaped like a human eye which he steps through at the start of the show.

Peter Powers uses large cut out caricatures of himself, which are then scattered one on each side of the stage, with a large evil looking head caricature set centre stage which he steps out from behind of, to make his appearance at the start of the show. I use a sign of one man making another fall back to the floor with the name "Hypnotic Party Time" on for family shows. This is then fixed to the centre area of the backdrop and I make my entrance from the wings.

For entrance, I have the curtains set so I can come on from centre stage out towards the audience, or on big shows I am magically produced from an illusion. Well that should have set your mind thinking on some more important elements, which can make your show that much more professional, now to some ideas for sketches which can be used within your hypnotic show. A good comedy script writer, like the ones who advertise in the Stage and TV, could no doubt come up with some new ideas for you.

ADULT AND FAMILY SHOW COMEDY SKETCH IDEAS

Very cold morning and shivering, snuggle up to the person next to them. In love with the person next to them, getting more and more intimate with the one they love. All relax again and when awoken, one has a sore bum, one man has a funny taste in their mouth and wonder what they've been doing. A women has a smile on her face, doesn't know what she was doing, but knows whatever it was, she enjoyed it a lot. Two are awoken and are paralysed from the neck downwards until you cough they cannot move and two men are awoken, one with his hand on the knee of another he cannot move it for thirty seconds.

Very hot day on the beach and they're sun bathing, so hot they need to rub invisible suntan lotion into their body and the hotter it gets, the quicker it has to be rubbed in. 100 degrees, 150 degrees etc., etc. Now it's so hot all the men's feet are burning and so are all the women's arms, as they rub in the suntan lotion as quickly as possible. Now relax it's cooled down and you'd like nothing more than a lovely delicious ice cream. The moment I give you your ice cream you will start sucking and licking it as quickly as you can. (OK, all relax now, when you awaken sir your hand is covered in dog dirt and you really stink of it and you madam will find your hand is stuck around the ice cream and you cannot remove it from your mouth until I say bananas, bananas. Wide awake. Stare at me again "bananas, bananas". OK now, just put it down please. Go to dog dirt subject. Have you had a bath recently sir? (Then put all others under and awaken after saying). In a few moments when I awaken you, everyone will realise that the man, (here you describe relevant person) really smells and the more I snap my fingers, the worse the smell is going to become, in fact, it's the most horrible thing you've ever smelt. Wide awake. (Snap fingers several times) OK, now everyone, you've just realised it's not that man, it's actually you who smells because you've s… yourself and it's starting to run down your leg and when I awaken you in a moment, you'll make up crazy excuses for why you smell.

Sleep. When you awaken this time you really need a drink of water to take that horrible taste away from your throat. When I give you the glass of water, you sir will find that the water is 100% proof alcohol and you'll get drunk on just a few sips of it. You sir, will find that you cannot get it to yours lips, in fact, your arm will get stuck 4 inches from your mouth and you'll spill it all over yourself. You sir, will find that the moment the glass touches your lips and you take a mouthful, that the liquid will taste like cat pee and everyone else will just get inebriated, as the water becomes 100% proof alcohol. (They are then given a plastic cup each with water in.) Here a couple of people can be told to stand up and walk around in their drunken state which gets laughs. You've all had a wonderful night out on the beer and you've got to get home, now so we'll all drive home in our cars, but we're so drunk, we'll all pretend we are high speed racing drivers, (milk it). Then, OK now, we're no longer high speed racing drivers, we are now all horrible greasy bikers and we're on our Harley Davidsons, rev the bike, make rude signs at the person behind you.

We're now in the Apollo space rocket and preparing for take off, belt yourself in, check the meters, hold on tight, take off, wave at people below. Now we've arrived in space and when I awaken you, upon the moon you will be, there is no gravity, you are lighter than air and you will leap and float around the stage. This time when I awaken you, we are all still in space, the hypnotist is invisible, you cannot see him, but you can see everything which he moves around. To avoid the things, you'll still have to float and bounce around the stage. Then into invisible hypnotist routine, carry objects around, tap them on shoulder etc., then the top half of you is visible and the bottom half invisible, then the bottom half visible and top half is invisible.

Sleep. In a few moments when I awaken you sir, you'll be a Martian from outer space and you speak fluent Martian and can see only through your finger tip. You sir, will also be a Martian, speak fluent Martian and see only through your fingertip and you madam will be a Martian interpreter and you can speak both English and Martian and will interpret for us. Everyone else will have returned back to earth and just be witnessing a live interview with the Martians we have brought back from space. Then ask the Martians various questions via the interpreter. Sleep. You've all been such wonderful volunteers in this the first half of the show, that I'm going to reward you with an apple, it will taste, smell, look and feel like a juicy delicious apple. (They then eat onions as apples), when I awaken you in a minute you'll be eating an apple, you'll just think everyone else is eating an onion, you'll try to stop them (they have argument etc). OK, this time when awoken, you'll realise it's you who's eating the horrible bitter sour onion, you will not be violent and will not hit the hypnotist, but will dispose of apples as quickly as possible. Sleep. All awaken, give invisible water, mouth will taste better. Sleep.

You sir, when awoken will be five years of age, it's your birthday party and you'll be eating your jelly and ice cream. (He's given tin of catfood and spoon to eat,) everyone else will imagine you are five years of age, but you are all being badly behaved, as five year olds would be. (Awaken). Sleep, when awoken, if you lie you will get a red hot tongue and feet. Who did what to who? Everyone just sleep (use half face masks of famous stars here, like politicians, royal family etc.) When awoken and the more outrageous lies you make up the more relaxed you'll be, you are John Major, You're the Queen. Then milk it, asking about the famous people's lives etc. Sleep.

At this point, implant the suggestions that they are to react to during the interval and then to give them a taste of the second half. Make a women fall in love with the hypnotist, the more you ignore her, the more she falls in love and wants to marry you. Then awaken everyone, send them back to audience and take a bow because it's time for the 20 to 30 minute interval section.

During the interval the 12 or more hypnotised subjects will be walking around the theatre carrying out the things you have commanded, so a show within a show will be occurring. For example:

One man will believe that the moment he goes to the toilets, which he will have to do every five minutes because he will be caught short, that a large gorilla will come in after him. He'll run out screaming, look out in the loos fellows, there's a big gorilla. Another man is told that he is a Casanova and will be trying his skills during the interval. A women is told she has lost her pet kitten and will be trying to find it, a man is told he has lost his money and must try to find it.

A woman is told she is a member of that strange cult religion, who worship Harry Corbett and she will walk round trying to convert people to the Harry Corbett religion, who all pray to their God Sooty. (A Sooty hand puppet is placed onto her hand.)

A man will find out that every person in the audience is a long lost relative or friend and he hasn't seen them all for years, so will be greeting them all happily. A woman believes that in the interval, she is the world's most outrageous gossip and will go around telling stories about audience members to other audience members. A man is given an empty video case and told it's a mercury bomb, which he has to look after, should the case get tipped then the bomb blows up.

Another man is told he has lost their pet duck, Webster, and is given a duck call to try and find it during the interval. The audience is warned not to tell him that it's in the video case, otherwise he'll end up chasing the guy who's got the mercury bomb. Another man is told they will be looking after an invisible lion, that is very visible to him. It's escaped from the zoo and it's a very vicious and ferocious lion, it will be dragging him all over the place and he must stop it from attacking people. One woman is told that every time someone asks her who is the best hypnotist? she will instantly shout out "Jonathan Royle is the greatest hypnotist of them all, Hallelujah."

The final person of the twelve on stage is told that when they hear this noise (Music plays) that they will instantly become the world's greatest bouncer, they will not be violent and will not hurt people or touch them. But they believe it's their job to get everyone back into the theatre in time for the second half of the show.

Each and every person upon the stage will instantly race back up onto the stage the moment you say, "Come and join the party". They will still be doing the jobs that you give them to do.

When the second half begins you come on, do your opening introduction patter and then say, "come and join the party," at which point everyone rushes back up to the stage to a round of applause. You then spend a few minutes questioning them on the events of the interval. Have they found their money and kitten etc? Then return them to sleep. In a few moments when I awaken you sir, you'll find that the man in the front row has got your money, you'll be furious and you want it back. Wide awake………… Sleep. When you awaken this time sir, you'll find that your money is back in its rightful place, in your pocket. Wide awake. Sleep.

Madam, when I awaken you, you'll find not only has your pet kitten returned, but every time I snap my fingers like this, your kitten will become more adorable. Wide awake. (Click fingers a lot for comedy reaction). Sleep. OK, now everyone, when I awaken you, your hands will be rigid, stuck in the position that I place them and only I will be able to move them around. Wide awake. You then place all their hands above their heads, gags such as, now I'll nick all the stuff out of your pockets and do you trust me lady? Well you shouldn't, are used here. One woman is made to place a finger in her ear and twist it around, being unable to remove it to the line, you understand that I'm not picking on you of course.

Well ladies and gentlemen, now that we've proved that their imagination would put the headline writers of the Sunday Sport to shame, I'd like to try an experiment with you all. Her the guaranteed handclasp routine is done, prior to getting people up and doing the world record high speed hypnosis induction and implanting the suggestion that, when you say goodnight, they will all jump up and shout out, "we all love Jonathan Royle, Hallelujah."

Each and everyone of you, has now got ants all over your body, they are itching, so give them a scratch, in fact guys, you've got ants in your pants and women, you've got fleas on you knees, so scratch them hard. Fellows put your hands down your pants and scratch, then sleep. When all the guys awaken, their hands will be stuck down their trousers. Wide awake……………Sleep.

When all the men awaken this time, you'll all have 48 inch boobs, you'll be really happy and show them off. Wide awake. When I cough your left boob falls off fellows, then the right boob. When awoken all the men will find they are giving birth to babies. What's it's name, sex etc? Sleep.

You sir, will use this megaphone and each time the audience laugh, you will think you are the theatre manager and will tell every one to stop laughing, as it's banned in this theatre. You sir will go back to the audience and the moment you sit down, you'll rush back to the stage and ask for some food, because you're hungry. The moment I give you a pie it will go plop, straight into your face, then you'll sit down and each and every time your bum touches the seat, you'll instantly return to the stage and ask for another pie and each time it will go plop, into your face. (Here you use custard pies for comedy.)

You madam, will find that I send you back to the audience and the moment you get down the stairs you will see a hole in the stage and water is flooding in through it, you'll put your finger in the hole to stop the water and save us, each time I ignore you as you shout out Mr Royle, help or we will drown, the more I ignore your cries, the more angry you will become.

You sir, will find that when you hear this music, (Rocky Theme) you are the worlds greatest shadow boxer and you'll dive out of your chair and be boxing an invisible opponent. The moment the music stops, you'll knock yourself out, fall to the floor and stay there until the music starts again. At this point, you milk the routines, switching from one to another in quick succession for maximum comedy impact. This will kill about 10 easy minutes of the show. At this point, if running short of time, continue as follows, if there is plenty of time left then add a few fills in here. Sleep. OK, now I'm talking to each and every person upon the stage, when you are awoken you will be the worlds greatest ballet dancers, its Swan Lake and you are all swans. Here the music starts, they are awoken and react, then say, ladies and gentlemen, please welcome the stars, Rudolph Nurev and his female partner. The two guys who were sent off earlier are now returned, in tights and short ballerina skirts with big cod pieces and wigs, they prance around the stage. We are now all dying swans, dying, as we fall to the floor to sleep.

When awoken, the legs are made of rubber and will try to drag yourself back to the chairs. Wide awake. OK, back to your chairs please. Can't move? What a shame because every time I cough your hands give way under you. Then sleep and all returned to seats. (During this routine a guy has been sent off stage and dressed leather bondage gear, like Madonna.) In a few moments when I awaken you sir, you'll enjoy putting your hand on the guys knee next to you, the more you do it the more you enjoy it. You sir, will enjoy the man next to you placing his hand on your knee and will positively encourage it, you sir, will be upset because you think it should be your knee that is getting rubbed. Wide awake. Milk for a few minutes, then sleep.

In a few moments when I awaken you, it's the last routine of the show and after it all commands will be cancelled out. When awoken, you all are the worlds greatest male and female strippers, the more noise the audience makes, the more clothing you will remove. Now we need some music for this, so invite my very special guest, Madonna, who will interact with all the strippers to prove how erotic she really is. Like a Virgin, begins to play, on comes the man in bondage gear, they all go through a simulated strip routine and interact then. Sleep.

IMPORTANT – When giving suggestions that they will become strippers, ensure you include a phrase such as "……you will become the worlds greatest strippers. You will not remove any articles of clothing past your shirt, jumper etc". If you do not include a safety clause, you may find yourself in trouble with a number of naked subjects on stage.

Gag, if enjoyed me I'm Jonathan Royle, if not Andrew Newton and say goodnight, at which point, loads of people in audience jump up and shout out, we all love Jonathan Royle, Hallelujah.

(POSSIBLE STANDBY ROUTINE FOR EXTRA TIME)

Dogs and rubber bone, fetch bone, heel etc. Both male dogs start to make love to each other.

Shops, dummy and voodoo doll routine, where what happens to the dummy they feel the pain. Dummy is then hit, arm twisted etc and subjects react.

Audience seen in the nude through special glasses, then they are in the nude and have only got very small willies, now six inches bigger than they thought they were.

Invisible razor blade with a bit of cardboard. They believe the cardboard is a razor blade, they can see the blood, feel the pain. You then mutilate yourself.

Two people in a dingy, rowing it, one gets lazy and the other gets fed up. Water starts coming in and they have to empty out with their hands. Sharks start to attack, helicopter flies over and they shout for help, dive out and swim to shore, at which point shark comes back, chases them and then all back to sleep.

ADDITIONAL COMEDY ROUTINES.

When awoken you can't count, think or say the number seven, it no longer exists for you. Then ask how many dwarfs Snow White had? How many wonders of the world were there? How many brides for how many brothers? Then get them to count fingers, they will count, 1,2,3,4,5,6,8.9.10,11 etc.

Your noses are made of rubber, bend stretch them and rub them, and it's very pleasurable. Then stretch all their noses out and let them go twang back into their face.

(You place a clean bra in a man's mouth, knickers in another man's mouth and a pair of men's briefs in a woman's hand) When you three awaken, you won't know what you have done, but you know whatever it was, you really enjoyed it.

At end of show, we will all join hands and take a bow, but when we do, a 10,000 volt electric shock will travel through the line and get more powerful and then through the person at the end of the line to the floor.

When you awake, you're the world's most bad tempered sergeant major and you will believe the audience are your recruits and you'll order them around.

(Do this with a stooge) give a man real scissors, tell hem he's Vidal Sassoon and get him to really cut another mans long hair short.

You can have a card on double sided tape and an empty staple gun and appear to staple gun something to someone's back.

Whenever this music plays, (James Bond theme) you will all become James Bond types, with guns in your hand and rolling around the stage to hide from the enemy.

Woman in house watching TV. Audience are people in her house having party, drinking beer from her fridge, being sick, spilling beer and stubbing cigarettes on her new carpet. She can say and do whatever she wants, but cannot hit anyone. Possibly can always only speak Japanese and no one understands her.

You sir, will have a terrible pronounced stutter. You will speak fluent Chinese and you fluent Japanese when I awaken you.

Two people can become ice cream/popcorn sellers, trying to sell their wares to the audience in the interval.

Everyone is in a band playing invisible instruments. One is standing limp wristed, hand on hip bending his knees in time to the music.

All are now teapots and lean over to pour out the tea.

All toothpaste tubes, being squeezed tighter and tighter.

All top female glamour models, pout and blow kisses to the camera.

All goldfish in bowls, swimming around.

All actors, taking part in screen test for comedy / horror / dramatic / sex / erotic / war and science fiction films.

All now mad professors in their laboratories.

When the music plays, you are the world's greatest band conductors, here you can give someone a feather duster to use as a baton.

Whenever I awaken you sir and a woman shouts out Tarzan, you will instantly jump out of your chair and do a Tarzan call three times and then realise what you are doing. When you wake up madam, whenever I say there is a man who swings through the jungle and his name is…… you will then instantly jump up into the air and shout Tarzan. All the rest of you, when you hear a man do the Tarzan call three times you will jump out of your chairs and shout, the Russians are coming to kill us. IE There's a man who swings through the jungle and his name is (woman gets up and shouts Tarzan). Then bloke gets up and does Tarzan call three times, then others get up and shout, the Russians are coming to kill us.

Floor is moving like a ship, you keep falling down every time you get up.

Big dog coming down the beach, stopped at you, has urinated on your leg, all over your shorts. Oh get them off now, now it's all over your hands. Oh dear, take your shirt off and use it to clear all the wee off yourself.

It's Monday morning, do what you would be doing at 10.30am.

It's Friday afternoon, do what you'd be doing at 4.30pm.

You are a bull (foam horns on head) you are a matador (give cloak and foam sword). They then have a bull fight simulation.

The world's greatest musical pianist.

Playing Starwars with the 3D screen images trying to kill you.

Play 3D cowboys and indians with the film image.

Two of your fingers are now totally missing.

When asked their name they shout out a rude word instead.

Invisible fairies routine. Feed them sugar puffs, tickle them under the chin, say hello, what colour are they? What's their name? They are running away, sad and cry for them. Then hypnotist jumps on them and kills them.

High wire circus tightrope walker and proceeds to lay string on floor and do it.

The worlds greatest comedian, or worlds greatest hypnotist and when they tell you to go to sleep they fall to the floor to sleep instead.

When you close your fist the audience disappear, then open your fist and they reappear.

Turn white guy into a black and black guy into a white.

Turn a man into woman and woman into man.

You are deaf, dumb, blind, limp etc.

You've just found £1000 and no-one saw you, now here comes a harassed man asking if you've seen it.

Woman next to you has a see through dress and no bra on underneath. Man next to you has fly undone and has no underwear on.

(Give guy a spanner) During interval, you are a plumber, trying to get odd jobs from the audience, in the toilets etc.

(Give guy a cap)In interval you are Steven Speilberg and all the audience are in your next movie, you need them back in the theatre now to start filming.

Stick all the subjects together in a weird chain hands on peoples bottoms, on their head and generally in strange positions.

When music plays you are Elvis Presley (use an inflatable guitar here, or a broom.)

All on your horses at the grand national races and trying to win the race.

Each time you return to your seat in the audience you will realise that you have forgotten your tie and will return and I'll give you your tie. Every time you return to your seat you immediately come back to get the tie which you have forgotten.

When awoken, you will have an invisible bucket and spade and be building a sandcastle on the steps of the stage, some idiot will keep stepping through it and if they do you will be really angry.

World's worst behaved class of six year olds. Ring a ring a roses etc. A velcro rip apart teddy, which they have a fight with.

When woken man/woman in front of you is person of your dreams.

Man made to believe he's a frigid woman wearing a dress and everyone can see up the dress. He's embarrassed about it and gets upset. Has no knickers on.

Two men made to think one is the mother and other is baby that she's breast feeding, changing nappy etc.

Man has invisible basketball, world's greatest player. Hypnotist and him play with invisible ball, bounces it around, does the fancy tricks, spins it on finger etc. Then you burst the ball and he's upset, then you re-inflate it with an invisible pump.

Bought new sports car, pride and joy. Go for a fast ride, miss trees by inches, tell police to get lost, park up, get pay and display ticket turn around and watch your car explode in front of you.

Two men, one made into woman and they both have a camp conversation.

Are all chickens jumping around, flapping wings and trying to lay square eggs.

M.C. Hammer dancing live at Wembley. Michael Jackson with bendy body and all the flashy dance moves.

Forgotten their name, where they live, how old they are.

When looking through glasses, when you cough they see the people with long giraffes necks, elephants ears and clowns noses.

Women become Mr Muscles and do body building routines to the music. Men become the world's sexiest female catwalk model.

When I say, bananas, bananas, you will jump out of your chair and shout I believe in fairies and give a big wet kiss to the man nearest to you. (Do with man.)

When hear a certain noise, they all run to bar, shout can we buy you a drink Jonathan and then argue over who's paying, before kissing and making up etc.

One is given (any object) and told its worlds most precious antique and must look after it and must not let anyone have it. Another is told that they want the object and will try to get it but each time they touch it they will receive a mild electric shock.

All are now farmyard animals, milk the cow etc.

There are mice on the floor and bees buzzing around you in the air.

You're in your house, it's on fire and you must try to blow it out.

Think you have inherited a million pounds then find out its wrong.

Get into bath of beans and wash hair with ketchup, thinking its clear water and shampoo.

They are worlds leading authority on parrots. (Use stuffed parrot.)

They are bad tempered traffic warden/football referee.

I cough and the person next to you has pinched your bum and angry about it.

They get up to tell you something, as they get to you they forget it. You speak and they say get lost.

On a ship, sun bathe, eat, drink, be sick, relax etc.

On sleigh with reindeers helping Santa to deliver the presents, avoid the trees, do Ho, Ho, Ho, etc. and tickle reindeer under chin, give food etc.

Given a brush and told its Miss Broom, woman of his dreams, he then proceeds to chat her up before trying to cement the romance.

When awoken will think the guy next to you has just molested you.

You're a man of wisdom, saying wise sayings to the audience, like don't drop a brick on your foot, it hurts, etc.

You're a gospel preacher, trying to convert everyone and the more people ignore you, the more you will try to solve their sins and convert them.

Aerobics teacher with whistle around their neck and they are demonstrating the keep fit moves and trying to get the audience to join in with them.

Guy thinks he's the lounge lizard and every woman in the room wants him very badly.

The glove puppet upon your hand will keep insulting you and you shout at it, hit it etc, but still it insults you and the more angry you become.

Tell them you will touch their skin with a cigarette then touch them with pen top and the burn will still appear.

Find out what their sexual fantasies are and make them live it out in their imagination.

Cigarettes become joints, they stop smoking when you cough, they become reformed non smokers and go around the room putting out everyone cigarettes. They cannot get it to their lips, then smoke it through their elbow and another roars like a dragon as he exhales.

You're Mick Jagger with the handclaps and sticking out bum.

Slow motion football player, miming the game and then playing for real with a balloon as a football.

When awoken all men have got women's names and when asked their name they say it seriously and everyone else's because it's a female name etc. and then it happens to them.

You are washing machines, tumble driers, cheeky little monkeys, pop up toasters, milking a cow etc.

Have now got a big wart on nose, your eyebrows have been shaved off, etc.

Being a strong man, lifting two balloons upon a cane and then another person can't do it.

Deaf traffic warden, just gave you a ticket in your own driveway.

They are typewriters, grandfather clocks etc.

Shoe is now a puppy, tell everyone whilst stroking it.

When hear the ringing noise, the shoe of the person next to you has become your mobile phone and you must answer it.

(To E.T. music). Watching E.T. crying because E.T. is dying, hands on the handlebars and feet on pedals, pedal bike to save him. Ring your bell to let him know you're coming, almost there, wave to let him know you care. Now grab hold of him and place him into the basket at the front of your bike, now pedal faster so we can take him back to his home high in the sky. We're there now, give E.T. one big goodbye kiss and put him back on his planet and wave goodbye. Now chain up your bike, lock the padlock, throw the keys away and sleep.

Scottish dancers in time to music.

Are all contestants of different nationalities in the Eurovision song contest.

(With invisible dog leads from joke shop) Are all exhibiting their dogs at

Crufts and getting them to do tricks etc.

They have lost their belly button and the person next to them has got it.

All become tap dancers in a chorus line.

Two become Flamenco dancers, one with dish mop in mouth as rose and one using a tennis racket as guitar.

FINAL NOTE ON COMEDY ROUTINES

I have given you more than enough ideas now to set you thinking on some original ideas of your own, you really are only limited here by your own imagination and with a little adaptability, many adult routines can be cleaned up for family shows and vice versa. For additional ideas go and see several hypnotists performing live and see what they do. Purchase the Paul McKenna and other tapes and you'll see many more routines in action. You will then have far more routines than you will ever need to use. A comedy script writer can also be employed to devise routines, so there will never be a shortage of new ideas.

I will now end this chapter by explaining how to perform several dramatic stunts, some of which are quite rightly banned as they are potentially harmful to the subjects and are included for information purposes only.

THE BRIDGE (HUMAN CATALEPSY)

This is the routine which gave hypnotism a bad name and is on of the reasons why the 1952 hypnotism act was implemented. This stunt is banned by the 1952 act. I would advise any reader not to break the law and not to use this stunt.

For this you need two straight backed chairs, or two small flat top step ladders. Two cushions are also required, as the shoulders and feet rest on the back of the chair.

To perform this in practice, normally a suitable young male subject would have been used. Then having entered the hypnotic state whilst standing up by saying, "sleep, you can stand and you have perfect balance at all times." Then the subject was instructed to place their feet together, hands down by their side, which should then take a firm grip of the side of their trousers and pull outwards from the side of their body at all times. Also their head should be tilted well back, they were told to imagine that they are now stiff, rigid as an iron bar and their whole body is stuck in this position. At this point the subject is lifted up by one audience member by placing their hands under the armpits and by another man placing his hands under the mans ankles. The hypnotised subject was then positioned such that his ankles were resting across the back of one chair, whilst the other chair is positioned in line with his shoulder blades on his back. In this position, as his head will be tilted well back and he is pulling outwards on his trousers, his body will be arched upwards in the centre slightly, like a cantilever bridge and just like a cantilever bridge, this means he is able to now support more weight.

An audience member could now be stood upon the subjects chest, positioned so that one foot is flat upon the chest area and the other foot is flat upon the area above the guys knee, (side towards groin). This means that the weight is distributed across the whole surface and in actual fact, most of the weight is taken by the backs of the two chairs and not by the hypnotised subject. If wishing to stand two people upon the subject, one is placed so that they are standing upon the chest area and the other so that they are supported by the upper leg area. This looked very impressive.

THE BED OF NAILS

Another dramatic looking stunt is to make a subject feel no pain, then have them lay upon a bed of six inch nails before a person stands upon their chest in this position. Now believe it or not, this is very safe and is an old circus performers trick. The secret being, that as all the nails are so close together the persons weight is evenly distributed over them and as such they feel no pain.

Full details of how this works and how to make your own bed of nails can be obtained by reading Derek Lever's excellent book, "Stranger Than Fiction", which is available from the Supreme Magic Company. Once upon the bed of nails a person can be made to stand upon the hypnotised subject in much the same way as in the catalepsy stunt.

PAINLESS SURGERY

Painless surgery is an old stunt where you place needles through various areas of a subject's body whilst they are in trance and they feel no pain. The secret of this is also in the Derek Lever book.

THE 24 HOUR WINDOW SLEEP STUNT

This stunt, in effect, gives the impression that you place a subject under hypnosis and then leave them resting in a bed in a shop window for 24 hours. Which in turn generates much free publicity for both the shop and your show. Now this is a stunt, which can be easily faked by having identical twins and switching them over in the early hours of the morning when no-one is around on the street outside the shop window which the bed is in. It can however also be done genuinely by placing the hypnotised subject into a comatose state and slowing down their bodily systems slightly. But I do not recommend you try this until you have much more knowledge and experience about the subject of hypnosis.

Several trance deepenings would have to be done and very strong post hypnotic suggestions would have to be used to get the subject deep enough into the deepest level of hypnosis. They are then placed into the bed and left for 24 hours being awoken the next day. This is a very old stunt, which old time hypnotists used to gain publicity for their shows. However more recently in 1993, Mr Peter Powers used the stunt with a slight change, he placed a man under hypnosis and left them in this state for a full eight days without food, water etc., or at least that's how it looked. A wet sponge was upon the subject's head and water cress was grown upon this, to prove that the subject had not moved. In actual fact, the truth was, yes, the person was in the bed for a week. Yes, they were under the hypnotic influence. And yes, they were there for eight days. But they were awoken at intervals of several hours, so that they could go to the loo, have water etc. and of course an experienced medical team was on hand at all times.

I'm sure you can think of many ways in which this stunt can be faked, but I have enough knowledge of hypnosis to know that this can be done genuinely and enough respect for Peter Powers to tell you he did this for real. Obviously the post hypnotic used is such, that each time you say sleep they will re-enter trance except this time they will go 100 times deeper. And of course they are awoken and made to re-enter the trance until they are very deep. Then usual trance deepening techniques are used to take them into the comatose state required to perform this stunt genuinely. A good bit of publicity hype (but also serious) used by Peter Powers, was that an audio tape had been given to the medical team containing his voice. This would remove the person from the hypnotic trance, should Peter himself be killed in an accident, or not be present for any unknown reason. This is the kind of stunt, which done correctly, can make you an overnight star, but you must have a far greater experience of hypnosis than you currently have to do this.

OTHER PUBLICITY STUNTS

Other stunts which can be done along the lines of the window sleep, are to place a subject in trance, have them then dress in a garden gnome outfit and they are then placed, fishing rod in hand, upon a toadstool in a large shop window for 24 hours, which also contains a poster for your show. The incentive to the shop being that as the stunt will attract much free publicity, their business will improve as people will flock to the shop to see the person under hypnosis. You could even get them to pay a fee for getting publicity for their shop and of course, posters for your show are displayed throughout the store. Which in an establishment such as Debenhams, would practically guarantee that with the people who would see it your future shows would be sold out in advance of the event. Always remember, you must gain the written permission of the subject and observe proper medical and back-up requirements for stunts such as these.

HYPNOSIS VIA SATELLITE LINK/LETTER/TELEPHONE ETC

As long as a person wishes to be hypnotised and can hear what you say at all times, then they can be hypnotised even if you are not present in person. I was asked to hypnotise someone by satellite for Channel Four's "The Word" show and basically all I would have done, if their plans had not changed at the last moment, to make my spot a studio item, would have been that some subjects in the studio would have been sitting on chairs facing spotlights and the video screen would have been to the side of them. I, via the satellite link, would then have performed a P.R.I., such as the spotlight eyestrain method and people would have entered trance and reacted to all my post hypnotic suggestions, even though I wasn't present. The same goes for over the phone, if a speaker phone is used at the subject's end, so they have nothing to hold onto, then being able to hear your voice, they can be made to enter trance and react to your suggestions.

As for hypnosis by letter, the secret of this is to have secretly hypnotised the person in advance of the publicity stunt and leave within their mind that, when your letter arrives, on a certain date, in a certain coloured envelope, the moment they open it and read the word "sleep" they will instantly re-enter the state of trance until you say otherwise in person. In all three above cases, co-operation is required and the people must want to be hypnotised, but with hypnosis far more is possible than you could possibly imagine. It's all down to belief and expectancy once again.

Part 14

Conclusion

You now have an extremely good knowledge of hypnosis and in particular stage hypnosis. Read and absorb the material contained in this course and you will realize you have the tools to become a professional stage hypnotist. I hope you have enjoyed reading the course.

Hypnotherapy and Psychotherapy form an ideal partnership and combined with the stage side of things, can provide an excellent business. For this reason I urge you to read and absorb the contents of the hypnotherapy course (if you have not done so already). It will not only open up more earning potential for you, but will also set you a few steps above most hypnotists in the business. So good luck and happy studying!

PLEASE REMEMBER = The contents of this book were originally written in 1994, hence is any money mentioned or dates seems out of date that is why!

You would be wise to Grab The Free Book on Marketing, Advertising, Publicity & Promotion which can be downloaded for Free along with PDF copies of two of my other Hypnosis Training Manuals from the site of:

www.elitehypnosisbootcamp.com/freebook/

You will also find that there are 47 Step by Step Training Videos that when studied will help to make you a far better Comedy Stage Hypnotist included for your further education on my website at:

www.HypnosisWeek.com

 And in terms of Learning **STAGE HYPNOSIS SAFETY** you would be wise to get a copy of the video training package "The Transparency Template" which is available for Instant Download from:

https://sellfy.com/p/ckff/   or from **www.magicalguru.co.uk**